Elections as Instruments of Democracy

G. BINGHAM POWELL, JR.

Elections as Instruments of Democracy

MAJORITARIAN AND
PROPORTIONAL VISIONS

Yale University Press
New Haven &
London

Printed in the United States of America.

Library of Congress Cataloging-in-Publication Data
Powell, G. Bingham.
    Elections as instruments of democracy : majoritarian and proportional visions/ G. Bingham Powell, Jr.
        p.   cm.
    Includes bibliographical references and index.
    ISBN 0-300-08015-8 (cloth : alk. paper) —
ISBN 0-300-08016-6 (paper : alk. paper)
        1. Elections.   2. Democracy.   3. Representative government and representation.   4. Majorities.   5. Proportional representation.   I. Title.
    JF1001   .P674   2000
    321.8 — dc21   99-059159

A catalogue record for this book is available from the British Library.

The paper in this book meets the guidelines for permanence and durability of the Committee on Production Guidelines for Book Longevity of the Council on Library Resources.

10   9   8   7   6   5   4   3   2   1

Contents

Tables

Figures

Acknowledgments

Lynda Powell was my first collaborator on issues of representation, in an article on representation in Austrian communities (Powell with Powell 1977), which contains some important conceptualizations now reflected in this book, particularly in chapter 6. Since then, she has provided invaluable advice on many issues of substance, method, and presentation, as well as unfailing support and encouragement, for which I am deeply grateful. This work also owes a great deal to the contributions of four talented graduate students who worked with me on various parts of this project, including development of ideas and analysis as well as data collection, during the past ten years: John Huber, Guy Whitten, Georg Vanberg, and Gail McElroy. John Huber was not only the first to assist with collection and analysis of the data, but also played an essential role in critical issues of conceptualization and measurement, both early on as a student (as reflected in Huber and Powell 1994) and later as an "external" commentator and advisor.

The Rochester political science department has provided an unparalleled research environment that influenced the development of this work in many ways, beginning with formative exchanges and arguments with Bill Riker in the 1980s. Undergraduate students in a freshman seminar called "Issues in Democracy" and later in my introductory "European Political Systems" course encouraged and required me to apply theoretical ideas to comparing and explaining specific elections in particular countries. Various faculty colleagues were willing to offer valuable critiques at several presentations in department seminar series. My comparative politics colleagues John Carey and Melanie Manion at various points gave valuable suggestions and support in an area empirically, although not theoretically, distant from their own.

Continuing encouragement as commentators at various stages, as well as inspiration provided by their own work, came from Arend Lijphart and Kaare Strom. Specific debts to their work will be obvious in the notes; broader ones are harder adequately to express because so numerous and incurred over a long span of time. Less directly, I want to acknowledge Gabriel Almond for his steadfast demand to consider the big picture and for letting me work some of these ideas into relevant chapters of our introductory text, thus fitting them into the broadest framework of comparative research and analysis.

I have also received numerous helpful suggestions from commentators at conferences and from reviewers for the various journals that have considered, and sometimes published, various articles generated by this project and for the academic presses that considered the final book manuscript. Ray Duch, Matt Gabel, John Huber, Arend Lijphart, Melanie Manion, Lynda Powell, Matt Shugart, Randy Stevenson, and Georg Vanberg provided valuable suggestions on all or part of the (nearly) final manuscript.

My gratitude to all these scholars for their advice does not diminish my acceptance of final responsibility for the errors and misconceptions contained herein.

PART I

Citizens, Elections, and Policy Making

I

Elections as Instruments of Democracy

When the War of Independence was terminated and the foundations of the new government were to be laid down, the nation was divided between two opinions — two opinions which are as old as the world and which are perpetually to be met with, under different forms and various names, in all free communities, the one tending to limit, the other to extend indefinitely, the power of the people.

— *Alexis de Tocqueville,* Democracy in America *[1835]*

This book is an empirical study of elections. It examines elections in twenty democracies over the past twenty-five years — about 155 elections in all. Unlike most election studies, it is not concerned with explaining who won. It is a study of the roles that competitive elections can play in giving citizens influence over policymakers. It is a study of elections as instruments of democracy.[1]

This work is explicitly driven by a normative concern: the claim of democracies to be governments in which the people participate in policy making. In political systems with many people, such as modern nations, government "by the people" must for the most part be indirect.[2] The people participate primarily by choosing policymakers in competitive elections.[3] Such elections are instruments of democracy to the degree that they give the people influence over policy making. The normative assumption that runs through this book is that

3

such citizen influence is a good thing, that elections should not only provide symbolic reassurance, but also genuinely serve as instruments of democracy.

Elections are not the only instruments of democracy. They must be helped by other organizations and by rules that encourage communication and cooperation.[4] But elections seem to be the critical democratic instruments. They claim to establish connections that compel or greatly encourage the policymakers to pay attention to citizens. There is a widespread consensus that the presence of competitive elections, more than any other feature, identifies a contemporary nation-state as a democratic political system.[5]

The apparent consensus that elections are significant conceals deep disagreements about whether and how they serve to link citizens to policymakers. These disagreements are partially normative; they reflect different ideals of the relationship between citizens and policymakers. They are partially conceptual, reflecting different understandings of how the preferences of citizens can be aggregated. They are partially empirical, grounded in alternative theories about what kinds of institutional arrangements will best serve to link the people and their representatives.

Following a familiar tradition in comparative analysis, I group the approaches to elections and democracy into two great camps: majoritarian and proportional.[6] These are the contemporary expressions of Tocqueville's "two opinions which are as old as the world," quoted above in the epigraph. Majoritarianism tries to use elections to bring the power of the people directly to bear on policymakers. Proportionalism establishes an alternative, positive democratic ideal, rather than just "limiting" majorities, a goal which can be (and has been) espoused by those who are opposed to democracy as well as by those sympathetic to its fundamental aims.

This comfortable language oversimplifies many complex arguments and distinctions, including the roles of electoral laws and policy-making constraints. But it captures some very fundamental assumptions and their implications. Moreover, as we shall see in the next chapter, the two primary types of constitutional designs in contemporary democracies can be understood as having election rules and policy-making rules that reflect either the majoritarian or proportional vision. In the analysis to come I shall try to identify the contrasting elements in the visions and to test their empirical expectations against performance in real elections.

Democratic Visions of Citizens and Policymakers: Concentrated or Dispersed Power?

In writing this book I was (naively) surprised to discover how hard it is to use consistent language about the empirical claim of competitive elections to be instruments of democracy. I was torn between the formulation that elections enabled citizens to *control* policymakers and the formulation that elections enabled citizens to *influence* policymakers. Initially, I thought that the difference was one of magnitude—that control was a claim of greater effect, while influence implied a lesser effect. After much wrestling with the whole array of associated concepts, I have come to think that the language points to a more fundamental divergence in conception of the processes linking citizens and policymakers.

I shall refer to this divergence in conception as involving two visions of elections as instruments of democracy. Each unites a distinctive image of the electorate, a closely associated normative concept of appropriate citizen influence, and an empirical model of the working of electoral and legislative institutions. These constitute ways of looking at election processes as well as theories about how those processes work in practice. In a shorthand that is generally consistent with recent usage in the empirical literature, I refer to these as majoritarian and proportional visions of elections and democracy.

The language of elections as instruments of control seems to be associated with a vision of concentrated policy-making power whose exercise can be made the target of citizen action. The elected officeholders are able to make and implement policies. Responsibility for policy is obvious to everyone. From one perspective the citizens use elections to choose between prospective teams of policymakers. From another perspective the citizens use elections to reward or punish the incumbents. While there are some very important disparities between the forward- and backward-looking views, they both presume concentrated policy-making power exercised by officials who are the objects of citizen electoral behavior. In the use of elections to control these powerful policymakers, it is the citizen majority that should, normatively, prevail over a minority who supports the opposition. It is the domination of the majority that gives such a vision its status as a democracy. In Tocqueville's words, "The very essence of democratic government consists in the absolute sovereignty of the majority" ([1835] 1945, 264). Hence, the term *majoritarian* to refer to this vision.[7]

In the majoritarian vision of citizen control, concentrated policy-making power is not undesirable. In fact, concentrated power is necessary, although not sufficient, for citizen control. If power is dispersed among officials, offices, and issues, then policy making must be the outcome of complex bargaining between winners and losers, ins and outs. As a result of such dispersion, retrospective responsibility can be difficult to pinpoint, and elections may bear only a tenuous relation to the formation of winning policy coalitions. The directness and clarity of the connections that make this vision attractive depend on concentrated political power that citizens can control.

On the other hand, the language of elections as instruments of citizen influence is more often associated with a vision of dispersed policy-making power. In this vision elections play a more indirect role in policy making. The essence of the vision is that the election brings representative agents of all the factions in the society into the policy-making arena. These agents then bargain with each other in a flexible and accommodative fashion. The concentrated, majoritarian approach views elections as mechanisms for tight control, with election outcomes determining directly the makeup of the policymakers who will make all policies between elections. The dispersed influence counterpart emphasizes the representation of all points of view brought into an arena of shifting policy coalitions.[8]

Two important arguments underlie the claim of the proportional influence vision.[9] They offer related but conceptually distinct reasons for dispersing power among representatives of all groups:

1. Elections are clumsy instruments. The intersection of party offerings, citizen choices, and election rules is complex. Many kinds of distortions may intervene between citizen preference and electoral victory. The heated rhetoric of election campaigns may make it difficult to locate the true majority position. Thus, using elections as a one-stage device for concentrating political power is hazardous (especially given the rules used in practice in most majoritarian systems). It is safer to elect a legislature of representatives and let these representatives bargain to find the most preferred policy. This argument is essentially an empirical challenge to the working of majoritarian institutions in practice. In chapters 6 and 8 I shall test its validity.

2. In a democracy the preferences of all citizens, not just an electoral majority, should be taken into account in the making of policies.[10] Even if they represent the citizen majority position on all the issues, a majority of representatives should not ride roughshod over the preferences (especially if intense) of the minority. The best guarantee that the majority will take account of minority preferences is to give the minority some valuable policy-making power (by consensual policy-making rules, regional governments, checks and balances across institutions, and so on). As John Stuart Mill argued, "Human beings are only secure from evil at the hands of others in proportion as they have the power of being, and are, self-protecting" ([1861] 1958, 43).[11] If one accepts its assumptions, this argument requires a different democratic connection, a different standard of democratic performance, from that of the majoritarian or concentrated power vision.[12]

I shall explore various implications of these visions later in the book. At this point I want only to emphasize the presence of these quite disparate general visions of the kind of connection that elections can and should establish between citizens and officials. In part these are two empirical theories about the kinds of arrangements that will usually result in policymakers being connected to the voters. The proponents of concentrated power are more suspicious of the autonomy of elected representatives, less concerned about minorities, more desirous of seeing that elites are clearly accountable to voters. The proponents of dispersed power are more suspicious of majorities (especially those created by elections), less worried about the autonomy of policymakers as long as citizens have had a role in selecting them, and less worried about negotiated inaction.

To some extent one can test predictions about the relation between concentrated or dispersed power arrangements and electoral connections. One can see the extent to which — and why — each vision succeeds or fails. But as two visions having something a little different in mind in conceptualizing the citizen-policymaker relationship, they do not always imply the same hypotheses. The concentrated power vision focuses on majorities, assuming that one can reasonably identify what citizens want — or at least who emerges from the election with the citizens' support — and the problem of elections is to make policymakers follow that citizen directive. The dispersed power vision tends to assume that citizens are not a homogeneous bunch, and the main problem of elections is to see that everybody and everybody's views get taken into account in policy making. To some degree, then, empirical predictions about the nature of the citizen-policymaker relationship will focus on dissimilar dependent variables and not really be alternative theories about achieving the same goal.

Elections and Policymakers: A "Voter's-Eye" View

Conceptions of how elections permit citizens to exert influence are surprisingly varied. Different images of citizen control direct our attention to different aspects of the connection that elections may create between the voters and the elected. Some of these connections may be complementary and mutually supportive. Others require radically diverse, even contradictory, political conditions.

A "voter's-eye" view of elections as instruments of democracy affords a fresh outlook on issues debated in the theoretical literature and will also help build from empirical studies of voters. Assume for the moment that citizens are fully participating in elections and are making the best choices they can.[13] In what ways can these choices influence the basic directing decisions of government? Two dimensions of choice seem suggestive (fig. 1.1).

The vertical dimension of citizen choice involves the target of voting. I am

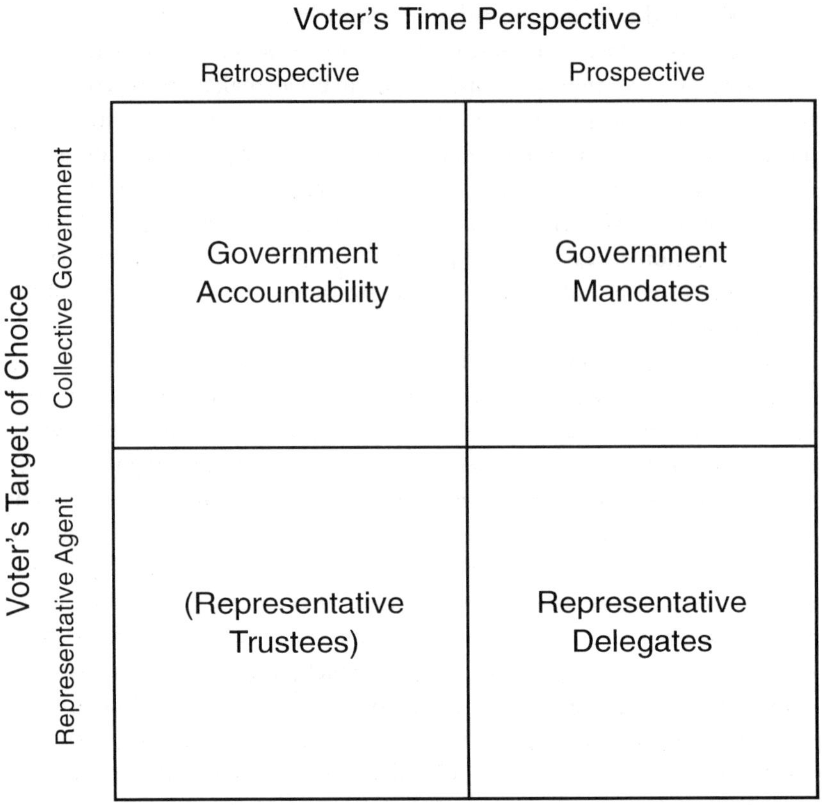

Voter's Time Perspective

	Retrospective	Prospective
Collective Government	Government Accountability	Government Mandates
Representative Agent	(Representative Trustees)	Representative Delegates

Voter's Target of Choice

Figure 1.1. Citizen Control Through Elections: A Voter's Eye View of the Processes

thinking here of the distinction between voting for or against a government with the power to make policies and voting for a representative agent who will not have control of government generally, but who will try to serve his or her constituents in negotiations and coalition building during the period between elections. In the former case the voter anticipates a decisive election whose consequences will directly determine the policymakers. In the latter case, the election will be followed by a process of coalition building (either in a discrete stage or on a continuing basis), and the voter is choosing an agent to represent his or her interests in that process. This dimension corresponds closely to the distinction between the concentrated and dispersed power visions of democracy.

Both opportunities may be in principle desirable to the voter, although not necessarily at the same time. Where the issues are clear-cut and a united citizenry has an overwhelmingly clear set of preferences, voters might well prefer to take most of the choices out of the hands of negotiators and be sure that the election results are in themselves decisive. But where the issues are complex, the citizens divided, and problems that the citizens cannot anticipate arise, each group of citizens may well prefer to be represented by trustworthy agents who can be relied upon to negotiate for their constituents.[14] Citizens who fear being in the minority on the issues that dominate a single election outcome, but anticipate being part of a majority on other issues, may especially prefer to have representative agents bargaining for them anew on each separate issue.

Second, there is the temporal direction of citizen choice: Do citizens look primarily back at the performance of those in office before the election or primarily forward to what they expect new officeholders to do? This is the horizontal dimension of citizen choices in figure 1.1. The language commonly used to describe this aspect of their choices is that of retrospective or prospective voting.[15] In the abstract, both retrospective and prospective views may be valuable in aiding citizens to shape the political process. Retrospective control is helpful insofar as it ensures that great abuses of public power can be checked before they go on too long. Prospective choice is helpful if it directly focuses on the commitments of candidates to take actions that citizens desire to be taken.

Moreover, the two views can be interactively useful and powerful.[16] The anticipation of future prospective voting should encourage candidates in election campaigns to make commitments that will appeal to many voters. The threat of retrospective sanctions against those who betray their commitments should encourage incumbents to keep those promises. Of course, it is not necessary that both prospective and retrospective choices actually be used in a given election. But the threat that either may be used, if incumbents behave badly or if candidates make outrageous commitments, should help keep policymakers more closely tied to the general preferences of citizens.

Figure 1.1 shows the combinations that emerge when these two dimensions of choice are put together. In the upper-left-hand cell of the figure the voters use the election to evaluate the incumbent government. They use their voting choice either to retain the incumbents in office or to "throw the rascals out." The focus is on the incumbents, not on the opposition. In the upper-right-hand cell the voters focus on choosing a future government. They need to estimate the future performance of the competing parties, taking account, perhaps, of the alternative promises and of how credible, as well as how desirable, these seem to be. The past performance of the parties may be one consideration here, although it need not be.

In the bottom cells are the multistage representation (dispersed power) approaches. The voter assumes that the elections are not decisive for policy making, but that bargaining takes place on issues. In the lower-right-hand cell, the focus is on choosing an agent, a delegate, to bargain for the voter in the policy making that will take place after the election. The voter needs to choose an agent who he or she believes will act as the informed voter would have acted if bargaining for him- or herself. Ideally, it should be an agent whose preferences mirror the voter's own across many issues, including issues that have not yet arisen. Presumably, it should be an agent with good bargaining skills.

In the lower-left-hand cell, the voter is evaluating the past behavior of her or his incumbent representative(s) in influencing policy as the voter would have wished. The retrospective focus recalls Edmund Burke's famous letter to his constituents in 1774, in which he argued that they should trust him to act in their best interests, subject only to their retrospective oversight[17] — thus my characterization of this combination as representative trustee. This role is shown in parentheses because it is given little attention in subsequent chapters.[18]

The various visions of the salient features of the election will emphasize different kinds of information for the voter and different kinds of policy-making conditions for them to work well. One can develop these further by explicitly associating them with models of citizen control that appear in theoretical and in ordinary language discussions of the roles of elections in democracy. These models draw attention to intermediate conditions that seem to be necessary if elections are to serve as instruments of democracy.

Accountability, Mandates, Authorized Representation

Later (especially in chapters 3, 4, and 5) I will describe the presence or absence of conditions that several models imply are important for elections. I will sketch them here to prepare for that analysis. This sketch identifies more explicitly the relation between the two great normative and conceptual visions of the role of elections in empowering citizens and the alternative conceptions of electoral processes from the voter's-eye viewpoint.

The simplest and perhaps most fundamental role of elections is the evaluation of the incumbent government. Citizens consider the performance of an incumbent party of policymakers and decide to keep them in office or throw them out. Walter Lippmann wrote more than half a century ago, "To support the Ins when things are going well; to support the Outs when they seem to be going badly, this . . . is the essence of popular government."[19] Elevated into a full-fledged model, Lippmann's argument corresponds to the ideal of elections as enforcing *accountability* on the part of governments. As a model the accountability idea has been attractive at two levels. At the more basic level it has seemed a kind of minimal criteria of what elections must do: they must offer citizens a periodic opportunity to change the policymakers. It is a model that appeals to those who desire clear citizen control yet are skeptical about the capability of the citizens to form opinions on complex policy issues.

The accountability model is also appealing to theorists who find it difficult to accept the collective electorate as able to choose positive policy directions across multiple issues. William Riker (1982a) puts this very plainly:"The essence of the liberal interpretation of voting is the notion that voting permits the rejection of candidates or officials who have offended so many voters that they cannot win an election."[20] Riker argues that we can expect no more of elections than this ability to permit the rejection of incumbents.[21] The complexities of public opinion make it impossible to interpret future-oriented voter choices as endorsing government policies. The minimal veto on incumbents is the essence of elections as instruments of control. Citizens will have an influence because they will be able, at least occasionally, to reject policymakers who are doing the wrong thing. The role of competitive elections as enabling unhappy citizens to throw the rascals out has great appeal. Although many theorists would like elections to do even more, few would want to abandon this role entirely.

To other theorists the simple accountability model can be even more powerful because the anticipation of possible rejection shapes the policies of the incumbents.[22] In this view the power of the voters to throw the rascals out will not only keep obvious rascals from remaining in office, but also create a pressure on all incumbents to worry about the next elections and make policy with voter review in mind. Despite the difficulties that social choice theorists' view of the uninterpretability of elections creates for general applicability of such a model, there are certainly examples in both theory and practice that suggest the power that policymakers' anticipation of citizen desires has.

Part of the appeal of the accountability models is their simplicity and the limited knowledge that is required of the electorate. Citizens do not have to worry about the credibility of proposals and promises. But there is one thing that the citizens do have to know: who was responsible for policy making. They cannot make retrospective judgments about the incumbents unless it is clear which incumbents made the policies. Closely linked to this idea is the notion that the citizens need to have a clear opportunity to vote against those incumbents. The critical condition for this model, then, is *clarity of responsibility,* a clarity that is relevant in electoral terms. If a single, unified party had control of all the policy-making resources and the citizens can vote for or against that party in the election, then clarity of responsibility would be high. But if policy-making resources were divided among numerous parties or groups or if the policy-making coalitions changed from issue to issue, then it would be difficult for citizens to use elections as instruments of accountability. They would not know whom to hold responsible. Moreover, accountability requires that voter rejection of the incumbents be followed by their actually losing policy-making power. In chapter 3 I will explore the degree to which electoral conditions in contemporary democracies in fact offer clarity of responsibility and decisive incumbent replacement.

A second major role of elections focuses on citizens looking ahead to choose future governments (see fig. 1.1). This is the top right cell in the figure: prospective choice and national government as a target. There is a special body of theoretical literature associated with this idea too. It is often called the idea of *electoral mandates*.[23] The focus is not only on the incumbents, but on the opposition party and the policy alternatives presented by both. For example, in an influential statement written nearly fifty years ago, a committee of American political scientists discussed an ideal party system with strong, cohesive political parties, including an effective opposition party that "acts as a critic of the party in power, developing, defining and presenting the policy alternatives which are necessary for a true choice in reaching public decisions."[24]

The origins of this idea are discussed more fully in chapter 4, but for the moment it is enough to note some of the essentials of the model. First, it must be possible for the voters to be able to identify alternative future governments at the time of the election. Although many writers in the tradition of mandates and responsibility have assumed only two parties, this need not be so. One can imagine competing teams of party coalitions. But there should be good reason for the voters to anticipate a tight connection between a vote for a party or team of parties and the governments subsequently formed. If voters think that the formation of policymaker coalitions is disconnected from shifts in their support—either because it is predetermined or because it is incomprehensibly complex—they have little reason to use their votes strategically to shape future policy making.

Second, this model requires that the winning electoral party (or coalition) in fact dominate policy making after the election. If the policy-making rules in the society force the electoral winners to negotiate with the losers after the election, the impact of the voters' choice is weakened or lost. I discuss these issues more fully in chapter 4 and then describe the degree to which mandate conditions are offered in elections in contemporary democracies.

Both accountability and mandates fall within the vision of concentrated power. They are two faces of majoritarian control. The vision of dispersed political power and citizen influence suggests rather different conditions for the voters. The retrospective-prospective distinction is not so powerfully associated with models of representation and influence, although it appears in a limited way in the argument as to whether representatives should serve as trustees or delegates of the citizens they represent.[25] More essential conditions, in my view, focus on each of the two stages involved — the election and the post-election bargaining. These two stages are discussed more fully in chapter 5.

At the election level, as can be inferred from the lower-right-hand box in figure 1.1, voters will be choosing representatives to bargain for them in policy making. In this model it is critical that each group of voters be able to find a candidate or party who will have their confidence and understand their views. Equally significant, the voters' choices must result in the election of representatives in proportion to the size of the group of voters. As the model assumes that policy-making influence begins as the representatives bargain (not as a collective government carries out its promises or anticipates future sanctions), citizen influence will depend directly on all the groups of voters getting proportional representation. These linked concepts of desirable choices and proportional representation for all are so essential to this vision of democracy that they are often valued as if they were democracy in their own right. Mill summarizes this in the title to chapter 7 of *Considerations on Representative Government:* "Of True and False Democracy; Representation of All, and Representation of the Majority Only" ([1861] 1958, 102). He has no doubt that representation "of the majority only" is "false," not "true," democracy. Disproportionate representation is presumed to imply a failure in democracy itself. In chapter 5 I discuss the extent to which proportional representation of votes is achieved in elections in contemporary democracies.

At the postelection stage, the vision of dispersed power and citizen influence tends to assume at least flexibility in forming coalitions among all representatives. There is some tension here, as observed earlier (see note 9 above), between theorists who see this flexibility as a means for allowing different majorities to form on different issues and those who hope that it will allow minorities to have some influence on all issues. In my examination in chapter 5 I fall short of identifying conditions that discriminate between these two views, preferring to look merely at the degree to which authorized representatives of each group of voters are provided with proportionate policy-making influence after the election. This condition of *authorized representation in policy making* is the most removed from the voters of any that I examine. This distance reflects the two-stage nature of the dispersed power and citizen influence vision. It reflects the autonomy that this vision necessarily confers on authorized representatives, who must serve as their voters' agents as new issues are debated.

Responsiveness and Representation

Even aside from the differences between control and influence, questions about elections and the role of citizens are hard to answer, in part because they involve concepts that are slippery to conceptualize and difficult to observe. The past half-century of theoretical and empirical research in political science has taught that such essential concepts as citizens' preferences, political influence, and policy consequences are fraught with exquisitely complex problems for analysis.

I cannot avoid all those problems in this book, but I shall try to dodge some of them by focusing on only part — an essential part — of the larger process: the connection between citizens' preferences and the selection of influential policymakers. The empirical claim of elections as instruments of democracy is that the competitive election forges connections between the wishes of citizens and the behavior of policymakers. Because of these connections, the policymakers take account of citizens' preferences more fully than they would otherwise. I investigate the connections, in theory and fact.

The problem and the process are shown in figure 1.2. At the top of the figure is the general causal claim of elections as instruments of democracy. The causal sequence leads first from the preferences of citizens to their electoral behavior. Below the entry for electoral behavior are listed some important conditions for that behavior that I shall be looking at later. These are divided into two sets, linked respectively to the majoritarian vision (clarity of responsibility, identifiability of future governments) and the proportional vision (diversity of party choices). The election outcomes in turn are hypothesized to affect the influence of the competing parties on policy making. Below the election outcomes entry are shown immediate outcome features associated with the alternative visions: legislative majorities and proportionality of vote representation. Connection D, policy making between elections, is supposed to be determined by the election of a government in the majoritarian vision, but only indirectly shaped in the proportional vision. Thus, under that entry the majoritarian vision implies government domination, while its proportional counterpart implies participation in policy making by authorized representatives. The preferences and official positions of the policymakers shape the general public policies of a democracy, which is the last point in the causal sequence (E), but not a target of analysis in this book.[26]

The direct examination of the full range of relations between citizens' preferences and policy outcomes is too large a task to take on here. I shall disregard critical elements at the beginning and end of the democratic process: the formation of citizens' preferences at one end and the fit between the claims of policymakers and what they do in office at the other. I explore only the A through D linkages of figure 1.2. The task at hand will, however, be sufficiently challenging.

I shall take two parallel approaches to examining the connections between

Proposed Connections

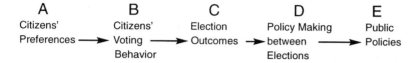

A	B	C	D	E
Citizens' Preferences	Citizens' Voting Behavior	Election Outcomes	Policy Making between Elections	Public Policies

Critical Conditions Implied by Each Vision

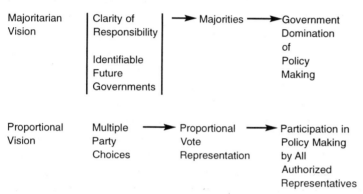

| Majoritarian Vision | Clarity of Responsibility

Identifiable Future Governments | Majorities | Government Domination of Policy Making |

| Proportional Vision | Multiple Party Choices | Proportional Vote Representation | Participation in Policy Making by All Authorized Representatives |

Figure 1.2. Connecting Citizens' Preferences and Public Policies

citizens' wishes and the formation of policymaker coalitions. In each of these the critical role is played by political parties. Insofar as political parties link individual candidates and collective policy commitments — at both the stage of citizen voting and the stage of making policies — they greatly increase the coherence of possible connections through competitive elections. Moreover, parties are in fact critical in the electoral and government formation processes in all the democracies in this study.[27]

The difference between the two approaches to analysis in subsequent chapters lies in what is assumed about citizens' preferences. The first approach (developed in part 2) assumes that all one can know about citizens' preferences is revealed in their voting choices. The choices citizens make in elections are, then, the starting point for assessing whether elections are performing as instruments of democracy. (In this approach the analysis can consider only linkages B through D in figure 1.2.) If the elections are performing this role, there must be a strong connection between citizens' electoral choices and the participation of their authorized representatives in making policies. Elections should lead to the continuation or replacement of incumbent policymakers in a way that is directly responsive to citizens' votes. I shall refer to this connection as responsiveness in the emergence of policymakers.

Focusing on responsiveness defined in this way has both strengths and weaknesses. The great strength is that it builds on firm, largely indisputable evidence about the choices made by citizens. If we find that those electoral authorizations seem to have little relationship to the people making policies, we are certainly justified in being skeptical about the claims of elections to provide citizens with even indirect participation in policy making.

The problem with relying on votes to measure citizens' preferences, however, is that citizens can vote only for the candidates and parties offered to them. Usually they can choose only one party, although sometimes multiple offices and agreements among parties about policy-making participation can expand their options. But not knowing how satisfactory were the options provided by the party system, we do not know how well the party they chose can represent their preferences. We know only that relative to the alternatives and in the given circumstances it seemed the most preferable.[28] We know even less about the parties that citizens did not select. Were some of these almost as satisfactory as their given choice, so that these parties would be acceptable substitutes to represent their position in policy making? Were others totally distasteful? To get at these questions we have to go beyond the simple assumptions that voting choices are all we can know about citizens' preferences. We must measure those preferences directly. (We must incorporate the A to B linkage in figure 1.2, rather than beginning with stage B.)

In the second approach taken below, in part 3, I shall use the device of the left-right scale to attempt to measure citizens' preferences and parties' positions. The left-right scale has huge advantages over simple vote choices. We can see whether the chosen party is really very close to the voters' preference. We can also see if the parties that make policy are very close to the voters, regardless of the specific voting authorization connection. If this measure, which I shall refer to as *representational congruence* between voters and policymakers, is very strong, then elections seem to be performing well as instruments of democracy. On the other hand, if congruence is poor, if the policymakers are quite far from the citizens, then elections are performing less well.

Although representational congruence seems plausible as evidence that elections are performing well as instruments of democracy, it contains hazardous assumptions. The questions or techniques used to assess citizen preferences must yield an accurate measure of those preferences. If the left-right scale used here is not meaningful to the citizens, or if citizens' preferences across many issues are not being adequately aggregated in that scale, or if the citizens are not responding candidly, or if the survey sample is not a good one, or if the placement of the parties on the scale does not reflect the same issue positions as citizens use to place themselves, then one can commit grievous errors. A party may appear to be close to what citizens want when in reality some of its policies are abhorrent to them, and vice versa.

Of course, if both responsiveness to elections in choosing policymakers and the representational congruence between the policymakers' positions and the citizens' preferences lead to similar assessments about the performance of elections as instruments of democracy, then we would be more confident in our assessments. As their likely sources of error vary somewhat, finding common results would be reassuring. As we shall see, there are some grounds for optimism about our parallel findings, but also some serious problems in comparing them.

The Subsequent Chapters

In chapter 2 I continue my introduction to the problem of elections as instruments of democracy by examining the constitutional arrangements under which elections and policymaker recruitment proceed. I link the basic constitutional arrangements to the alternative visions — majoritarian control and proportional influence — of the role of elections in democracy.

Part 2, containing chapters 3–6, examines the electoral experience in democracies over the past twenty-five years to see how frequently the most important conditions for the two visions of the controlling roles of elections were satisfied. It builds on the assumption that citizen voting choices are the critical starting point for evaluating democratic performance. Under the concentrated power vision, the majoritarian view, I shall look in chapters 3 and 4 at accountability, the eviction of unpopular incumbents, and election mandates. Under the dispersed power vision, I shall look in chapter 5 at election choices, proportional outcomes, and authorized representation. I also consider the degree to which realization of these conditions is associated with the constitutional designs discussed in chapter 2.

Scholarly literature and political debate frequently refer to the value to democracy of such conditions as clarity of responsibility, interpretable electoral mandates, authorized representation for all citizens. The first step in my empirical investigation will be to measure the presence or absence of such conditions. The results are interesting in their own right, even before one attempts to assess their relation to the connections of responsiveness and congruence. While these conditions are often valued as good in their own right, in chapter 6 I evaluate more directly the performance of constitutional designs in shaping responsiveness in choosing policymakers, a criterion of democratic performance valued in each of the great visions. As we shall see, the empirical manifestations of each vision are relatively successful in creating responsiveness, but only in their own terms, a result that is encouraging for democracy but does little to resolve competing claims between the ideals.

Part 3 assumes that in analyzing elections as instruments of democracy we can move behind citizens' voting choices and build directly on their political preferences. In this section I seek the sources of the creation or failure of representational congruence. Chapter 7 discusses the left-right scale as a device for measuring citizens' preferences, so that they can be compared to the positions of parties in governments and influential policy making. It also specifies the normative expectations and empirical hypotheses associated with each vision. I shall argue that proximity to the position of the median citizen is a criterion valued in each vision, especially by majoritarians. Chapter 8 examines the successes and failures of the majoritarian designs and processes in linking legislatures and governments to the position of the median citizen on the left-right scale. Chapter 9 revisits the proportional influence processes and shows their strengths and limits in representing the median citizen preference, taking account of the influential policymakers as well as the governments. Each vision expects its ideal electoral process to create good representational congruence between citizens and policymakers. As we shall see, they are not equally successful. The proportional influence designs enjoy a surprising advantage.

Chapter 10 summarizes the findings of the book from a slightly different point of view. Shifting from elections to country averages, it shows the performance as measured by vote and preference connections between citizens and governments and by majoritarian and proportional criteria. It also considers explicitly the relations between desirable outcomes. Consideration of these relations addresses an important puzzle about the writings on elections. On one level, students of democracy assume that competitive elections make a difference. They are loathe to accept a claim of democracy by rulers, however well intentioned, who do not permit electoral competition. On another level, the same students of democracy are perpetually complaining about the failure of democratic elections to provide citizens with adequate opportunities to exert the right kind of control in their society. Americans complain about the confusing paradoxes of decentralized parties and divided government. Italians and Hollanders complain about government coalitions whose formation seems divorced from election outcomes. The English complain about underrepresentation of some voters and government dictatorship between elections by the representatives of others. Some of these complaints are indirect forms of pleading for special policies. Others, however, genuinely point to respects in which elections seem to fail in offering conditions necessary for them to serve as instruments of citizen control.

A conclusion that emerges most forcefully from the approach taken in this book is that even success in using elections as instruments of citizen control (or influence) usually involves a trade-off between desirable processes. Those political systems that have perfected most fully one of the major processes through which citizens seem to use elections for influence do so at the expense of one of the other processes. This trade-off is not only a matter of flaws in constitutional design or human imagination (although we shall see some of these). It is built into the tension between concentrated and dispersed power for policy making and the desirable consequences of each. Students of elections and democracy will always have something to complain about because no set of election arrangements can satisfy conditions for all the desirable electoral roles. We also see, however, that there is much evidence of the relative success of elections performing as instruments of democracy.

2

Constitutional Designs as Visions of Majoritarian or Proportional Democracy

Stable democracies work under a set of rules that specify how policy-makers are to be chosen and how authoritative policies are to be made. These rules, whether embodied in a single document, a body of legislation, or just accepted practices, shape both the context and consequence of democratic elections. I refer to these rules as the constitutional design of a democratic political system. Although these constitutional rules can be changed, such changes are unusual. Most elections in a country are fought under the same rules that governed previous elections in that country.[1] After the election, policies are usually made according to the same rules that shaped policy making before the elections.

In tracing the processes through which elections may serve as instruments of democracy in different countries, it is helpful to begin with the constitutional context. Constitutional arrangements are a useful beginning point for three reasons. First, because constitutions are designs for democracy, and these designs can be understood as reflecting, to varying degrees, the majoritarian or proportional visions. They embody specific theories about democracy that can be tested in subsequent chapters. Second, because I can introduce the twenty democracies whose experiences constitute the basis of this book by describing their basic constitutional arrangements. Finally, because as I examine specific processes in subsequent chapters, valid measurement and interpretation of important variables will depend on taking into account the constitutional rules under which they operate.

The constitution of any national democracy is a many-layered text. It often reflects a historic moment of intense bargaining. It always contains unique elements that express the special values and concerns of the constitution makers. We can, however, identify features of a constitution that are particularly relevant to understanding how elections can serve as instruments of democracy. For our purposes it is the implications of these features for concentrating or dispersing political power that are important, not the intent of the constitution writers.

Two features of the constitutions are of critical interest. First, do the rules of representation encourage the election of legislative majorities that can control the executive? Second, do the rules for making authoritative public policies concentrate political power in the hands of this party "government." If the answer to both questions is yes, then we can characterize the constitution as majoritarian. If the election rules encourage the equitable representation of multiple parties and the decision rules encourage dispersion of power among these parties in policy making, then the constitution embodies the proportional vision.

In his influential book *Democracies* (1984) Arend Lijphart suggests that the two great approaches to representative democracy offer two answers to the question, "To whose interests should the government be responsive when the people are in disagreement?" The answer proposed by the Westminster, or majoritarian, approach is that the government should be responsive to the majority of the people. The answer proposed by the alternative approach is that the government should be responsive to "as many people as possible" (Lijphart 1984, 4). Lijphart's empirical analysis includes many features of the on-going democratic processes of his countries, especially the nature of their party systems. Here, I follow the same distinction between the approaches but begin with the constitutional design.[2]

This chapter prepares for subsequent analysis by classifying the constitutional designs of the twenty working democracies according to their expected implications for the visions of citizen control through elections. The classification is based on the election rules, the policy-making rules, and political science theory about the implications of each. Thus, I begin by summarizing the election rules in the twenty democracies and the majoritarian or proportional implications suggested by the large body of theory about them. While the subsequent chapters will trace the empirical implications more thoroughly, I offer here some initial evidence that the classification is plausible. Then, I do the same for the policy-making rules. The chapter concludes with an overview of the combinations of election rules and decision rules in the twenty democracies. The combinations enable us to classify most of these constitutions as primarily majoritarian or proportional, although other combinations are quite possible.

The Sample of Democracies

The sample of democracies in this study is not a random sample of possible democracies or even a random sample of democracies in the world today. Rather, it comprises all the working democracies for which I could obtain relevant data about citizen preferences and party alternatives for a substantial set of elections in the past twenty-five years or so. Inevitably, this has meant a heavy concentration of democracies from Western Europe, plus the United States, Canada, Japan, Australia, and New Zealand.

These countries share a number of features, including a high level of economic development and (except for Japan) a Western cultural heritage. Democracy is now generally accepted as the appropriate form of political system. They have substantial democratic experience; most of their political parties have been around for most of the relevant lives of most voters. The party leaders have had time to learn the intricacies of the constitutional rules and to develop meaningful national organizations. All of them except the United States operate under some variation of a parliamentary constitution. The party choices offered in electoral competition can be summarized to a substantial extent on a left-right or interventionist-conservative dimension understood by voters and politicians alike.

There are substantial advantages in these commonalities. They control for considerations such as a threat of military intervention or an ongoing civil war that can vitiate the role of elections as instruments of democracy. They ease the problems of finding equivalent measures for some of the interesting variables that connect elections and public policies. Nonetheless, one must be careful in generalizing from the democratic experiences analyzed here to democracies in other settings. This is obvious in the case of some of the large disparities in economic and political conditions. It also applies to new electorates, new party systems, and variations on the constitutional rules. In the concluding chapter I shall try to be more specific about the limitations, as well as the advantages.

The Election Rules and the Visions of Democracy

Elections may be shaped by many kinds of rules. The election rules or election laws refer here to the rules of representation by which the votes of the citizens are aggregated to determine the winning candidate(s). As almost all these democracies are parliamentary systems, I shall concentrate on electing representatives to the popular house of the national assembly, which has the critical authority to authorize public policies.

A large political science literature is devoted to analysis of the consequences of the election laws. The landmark in this literature is Maurice Duverger's assertion in 1954 that single-member district plurality (first past the post) rules tend to produce two-party systems, an observation known famously as Duverger's Law.[3] Under single-member district plurality rules the nation is divided into geographic constituencies; in each constituency candidates compete to win a single representative position. The candidate winning more votes than any other candidate, a plurality, wins the district and becomes the representative. As Riker has shown, effects favoring two-party or two-candidate competition under these rules were widely suspected during the British debates about franchise extensions in the nineteenth century (Riker 1982b). That single-member districts could unfairly disadvantage some candidates or parties was also known sufficiently well to encourage the various nineteenth-century inventions of alternatives — districts with multiple representatives chosen according to some rule of proportional representation. Duverger hypothesized that proportional representation election rules would encourage multiparty systems. Duverger, properly, gets the credit for generalizing these ideas and suspicions into a scientific theory and offering some empirical evidence for them.[4]

The political science election law literature since Duverger contains both theoretical and empirical analyses, although until fairly recently these were seldom found together.[5] There are three elements in the theoretical analysis: the decisions of parties as they offer candidates in the election; the decisions of citizens as they vote; the rules that aggregate the citizen partisan choices to determine the winning representatives. In a given election the election rules are fixed (although they may, of course, be modified over time for partisan advantage or other reasons); the citizen and party decisions interact. The essential element is that the election rules limit the number of representatives from a district, so only slightly more than that number of candidates have a realistic chance of winning.

In a single-member district, only the two leading candidates have much chance of winning, unless the difference in support between the second and third is very slight. If a district has three or four or five representatives, this same logic applies to the fifth, sixth, and seventh candidates. If the citizens know this and know the rough prospects of the candidates, they may vote "strategically," that is, vote only for candidates who have a reasonable chance of winning rather than wasting their votes on candidates who, however appealing their ideas, have no chance. If parties know roughly the prospects of the candidates, and especially if they expect some citizens to vote strategically, they will not waste effort running candidates in situations with poor prospects. Rather, to maximize their overall chances, they will work out agreements with similarly oriented parties to divide the districts in which to offer candidates or join to form larger parties.

In practice there are many possibilities for making strategic mistakes, depending on the information available and the numbers of potential competitors. In early democratic elections we expect all kinds of mistakes by candidates, parties, and citizens, mistakes that can lead to very strange representation. (Striking examples appeared in early elections in Poland and Russia, in which a third or more of the citizens voted for parties that failed to gain legislative representation, even with proportional representation rules and a fairly low threshold.) Eventually, however, we expect in theory that the number of candidates competing in a district will be reduced toward no more than the district magnitude (its number of representatives) plus one (Cox 1997).

Thus, in single-member district elections, we expect theoretically that with the eventual development of an equilibrium of expectations only two serious candidates will run in each district. The greater the magnitude, the more candidates. Moreover, the greater the magnitude of a district, the less the consequences for representation of a strategic mistake concerning a single party. These expectations underpin Duverger's Law and its counterpart hypothesis about large district magnitudes and multiple parties.[6]

Although the theoretical logic underpinning Duverger's Law assumes that single-member district election rules will encourage party competition and voter support to consolidate around only two candidates in a district, these rules still produce only one winner per district regardless of the number competing. Thus, the voters for the losing party are always unrepresented in the district's outcome, even if they constitute 49 percent of its district's electorate. If the same party finds itself in this situation across most of the districts, the collective outcome will find its voters badly underrepresented in the legislature. (The famous American invention of gerrymandering the district boundary lines for the advantage of one party and disadvantage of another takes advantage of this possibility.) For single-member district election rules to avoid serious disproportionality of seats in the legislature the many disproportional outcomes in each district must compensate for each other across all the districts (see the discussion in Powell and Vanberg forthcoming). There is no guarantee that this will happen even if strategic anticipation reduces the numbers of candidates to two in each district.

If party and citizen strategies do not reduce the number of competing parties to two, the effect of the single-member district winner-take-all rules may still greatly reduce the number of parties in the legislature and even create legislative majorities for one of them. They may also create some spectacular distortions in vote-seat relations. The former possibility may be helpful for realizing the majoritarian vision; the latter possibility is disconcerting to the proportional vision. Such majorities and such distortions are also possible with multimember-district proportional representation, but seem less likely. With particular distributions of party support across constituencies, it is also possible that the party winning the most votes in the election will not win the most seats in the legislature. This outcome would be normatively disconcerting to both visions.

There are, of course, many variations on the simple dichotomy of single-member district plurality rules and multiple-member district proportional representation. Single-member districts may use multiround runoffs if no candidate attains some basic threshold (usually 50 percent) in the first round, as in France and in some American primary elections. Or they may allow voters to indicate a larger preference ordering among candidates, with wasted votes of losers (and even winners in some systems) to be transferred to candidates getting more support, as in Australia. Proportional representation systems offer varying district magnitudes (from 3–5 in Ireland to a single, national district of 150 representatives in the Netherlands), multiple tiers of candidates chosen in different ways, alternative formulae for calculating the "unused" remainders of votes, ordinal preference possibilities, and various thresholds of minimal amounts of voter support necessary to achieve representation. Moreover, whatever the system, proportional outcomes will depend on an equitable relationship between the number of voters in a district and the number of representatives assigned to it.[7]

Empirically, we can simplify the many complexities of election rules by drawing on the analysis of election laws presented by Lijphart (1994) in his study of election laws in twenty-seven democracies from 1945 to 1990. Lijphart analyzes each of the systems of election laws used in these elections and combines various features into his concept of the "effective threshold" of representation. The effective threshold attempts to capture the difficulty that a small party faces in achieving legislative representation through elections. The concept is most easily understood when applied to a proportional representation system that literally has a minimum threshold for national representation: in Sweden a party must win 4 percent of the national vote to gain any representation in the legislature; in Germany a party must win 5 percent of the national vote (or three individual district seats) to gain any of the list seats in the legislature. But the size of the districts as well as many other features also determines thresholds for representation. In the 150-person Dutch legislature, which has the whole country as a district, a party that wins .75 percent of the national vote will be guaranteed a seat.[8] In a proportional representation system with only 5 representatives in each district, it might take 20 percent of the vote to be assured of a seat — or even less if there are many parties. Lijphart's estimate of the effective threshold incorporates a variety of features of the election rules.

In general we expect high thresholds to penalize small parties and to reward larger ones. Because of these penalties and rewards, the higher thresholds encourage a smaller number of parties to compete and encourage voters to vote strategically for parties that have a chance of passing the threshold. Moreover, high thresholds should mechanically reduce the number of parties in the legislature, even if strategic competition and voting do not do so. These effects should more frequently result in victories for single parties or at least announced coalitions of parties that will become governments if they win legislative majorities. Systems with low thresholds should encourage more parties to compete (depending on the heterogeneity of the electorate) and to allow many of these parties to gain legislative representation. Furthermore, the low threshold systems should explicitly sustain proportionality in the translation of votes into seats in the legislature. The details of these connections and their relation to preference representation are discussed more fully in subsequent chapters. Also of interest are some other features of election rules, such as those encouraging party coalitions.

THE VISIONS, THE ELECTION RULES,
AND THE ELECTION OUTCOMES

As suggested in chapter 1, the majoritarian and proportional approaches to democracy envision rather different roles for elections in connecting the preferences of citizens and the formation of policy-making coalitions. The majoritarian vision sees elections as enabling citizens directly to choose between alternative governments (incumbent or prospective or both), with the winner taking office and making the policies after the election. The proportional vision sees elections as choosing representatives who can bargain for their voters' interests in postelection policy making. Although all national elections aggregate the desires of thousands of voters into a much smaller number of representative policymakers, the majoritarian view favors much greater aggregation, while the proportional view emphasizes the importance of equitable reflection of all points of view into the legislature.

Thus, there is a fairly clear multiple (strategic and mechanical) connection between the normative expectations of the visions and the empirical consequences anticipated from the alternative types of election rules. Election rules with low effective thresholds should encourage outcomes favored by the proportional vision. Rules with high effective thresholds, making representation difficult for small parties, should encourage election processes and consequences favored by the majoritarian vision.

Table 2.1 divides the twenty democracies examined in this book into three groups and shows after each country the effective threshold that applied in the elections during the period, which is roughly the past twenty-five years. The effective representation scores are averaged if more than one fairly similar electoral system was used. In three countries, France, Greece, and Norway, rule changes were sufficiently sharp that the country is entered in different categories for different elections.[9] The table is constructed so that as we read down the table, we encounter election rules that are expected to be favorable to the majoritarian vision. Within each category the countries are listed alphabetically, so that they can easily be located. The last column in the table (in parentheses) shows the number of elections for each country included in the analysis.

While we shall look much more closely at various connections in subsequent chapters, we can see in table 2.1 that a rough grouping of the countries by the election laws supports the patterns of competition and representation that we might expect from theory and previous empirical studies. At the top of the table are listed eleven parliamentary democracies with systems of multi-member-districts and fairly low effective thresholds for party representation. Except in Switzerland, these effective thresholds for representation are usually around or under 5 percent. These are classified as pure proportional representation (PR) election rules.[10] In the middle of the table is a group of five countries (plus one French election) in which there are multimember legislative districts, but also one or more of the elements of higher thresholds (all except Norway), malapportionment across districts (Norway, Japan, and Spain), and something other than simple proportional representation in allocation of seats (Ireland and Japan). These elements would lead us to expect less proportional representation of parties, perhaps even the creation of legislative majorities. At the bottom of the table are six countries using single-member district election rules. The average effective thresholds in the three groups are 3.8, 13.5, and 35 (the number Lijphart assigns to single-member district systems).

The columns in the table following the effective thresholds report averages for several important features of the parties and their legislative representation in each country:

Table 2.1. Election Rules and Consequences in Twenty Democracies: Fewer Parties and Greater Disproportionality

Legislative Elections Rules[1]		Effective Number of Parties[2]		Vote/Seat Disproportionality[3]	Number of Elections
		Votes	Seats		
Multimember districts — pure proportional representation					
Austria	(2.6)	2.7	2.6	1.5	(8)
Belgium	(4.8)	7.6	6.5	3.0	(9)
Denmark	(1.6)	5.6	5.2	1.7	(11)
Finland	(5.4)	6.2	5.3	3.2	(7)
Germany	(5.0)	2.7	2.6	1.6	(7)
*Greece	(3.3)	2.6	2.4	4.1	(3)
Italy	(2.0)	4.8	4.0	2.6	(7)
Netherlands	(.7)	5.3	4.9	1.4	(8)
*Norway	(4.0)	4.9	4.3	3.7	(2)
Sweden	(4.0)	3.7	3.5	1.9	(10)
Switzerland	(8.5)	6.5	5.7	3.1	(6)
Multimember districts — increased potential distortion					
*France	(12.0)	5.0	3.8	7.2	(1)
*Greece	(16.1)	3.0	2.2	8.7	(4)
Ireland	(17.2)	3.1	2.8	3.3	(8)
Japan	(16.4)	3.8	3.1	6.4	(8)
*Norway	(8.9)	4.0	3.3	5.0	(5)
Spain	(10.2)	3.8	2.7	8.3	(5)
Single-member districts					
Australia	(35.0)	2.6	2.4	9.6	(11)
Canada	(35.0)	3.2	2.3	12.1	(7)
*France	(35.0)	5.2	3.3	14.0	(7)
New Zealand	(35.0)	2.8	2.0	14.6	(8)
United Kingdom	(35.0)	3.0	2.2	14.4	(7)
United States	(35.0)	2.0	1.9	5.9	(6)

*Major changes: Greece in 1989–90 only; Norway 1989 ff, France 1986 (PR). Austria and Sweden used higher PR thresholds only for the very first election covered. Italy 1994 excluded. N=155.

[1]"Effective Threshold" (Lijphart 1994, 25–30) in parentheses.
[2]"Effective Number of Parties" from Laasko and Taagepera 1979.
[3]Gallagher disproportionality measure (Lijphart 1994, 61).

1. *Number of Parties.* As we read the down three groups of election rules in the table, we expect to find fewer parties competing in the elections (anticipating that high thresholds will make it hard for small parties to win) and, especially, fewer parties winning legislative representation. The majoritarian vision of democratic elections usually assumes two-party competition. The election averages show us how well this expectation is met. The numbers in the first two data columns show the effective number of parties winning votes and seats, respectively. For both votes and seats this number is the equivalent of the simple number of parties if their sizes were similar. It is a rough guide to the number of competing parties that takes account of parties' relative size and asymmetry.[11]

The averages in the table fit our expectations fairly well. The (effective) number of parties winning votes generally declines as we read down the categories in the table. However, we see that only the United States is truly a two-party system in this sense. Even in the bottom-most category, the electoral competition is usually between the equivalent of three parties. In chapter 8 we shall see that this seems to create problems in achieving some of the putative benefits of two-party electoral competition. Expectations about parties in the legislature are fulfilled more satisfactorily. In all countries fewer parties win seats in the legislature than run in the election, but the reduction (comparing the first and second columns under parties) is slight in the low-threshold PR systems, quite substantial in some of the countries in the bottom categories. Because of the dual effect of generally fewer parties running and elimination of some party representation, the number of parties in the legislature declines sharply as we descend the categories in the table. There are effectively about 4½ parties in the legislatures of the pure PR systems, 3 to 4 parties in the intermediate threshold cases, and only 2½ parties in the single-member district systems. The correlation between Lijphart's effective threshold and the (effective) number of parties winning votes is $-.43$, while the correlation with number of parties in the legislature is $-.57$. To this extent, we are justified in considering the election rules more likely to encourage majoritarian processes as we move down the table. In chapters 3 and 4 I shall explore this relation in much more detail, moving beyond the number of competing parties to consider accountability and mandates more directly.

We can also see in table 2.1, however, that various special circumstances of history and the nature of the society create interesting exceptions to these strong general patterns. Austria has only an average of 2.7 parties competing in the elections in this period, despite PR with a low threshold;

France has effectively 5 or more parties, even using single-member districts. Constitutional design is not the only factor shaping the party system.

2. *Vote-Seat Disproportionality.* The proportional vision presumes multiparty competition, so that a variety of points of view can be represented, and the fair representation of all parties in the legislature. We have already seen that the number of competing parties does decline as we move down the table. In the third data column, the table shows a measure of the disproportionality of the relation between votes and seats, that is, the degree to which the distribution of party seats in the legislature fails to correspond to the votes won by the parties in the elections. While there are many measures of disproportionality, the number here is based on the ratios of vote percentage to seat percentage for the parties, in a particular formula (Gallagher's) usually considered the best and most widely used in vote-seat proportionality analysis.[12] Various empirical analyses (for example, Rae 1967, Lijphart 1994) have shown the strong relation between effective threshold and vote-seat disproportionality. Therefore, we expect to find more vote-seat disproportionality as we read down the groups of the table. The theoretical relation is somewhat more complex than sometimes assumed, as I shall discuss in chapter 9 (also see Powell and Vanberg forthcoming,) but the expectations here are consistent with the standard findings.

Indeed, the outcomes are strikingly consistent with these expectations and with Lijphart's (1994) results on effective threshold and disproportionality. The average disproportionality numbers for the three groups are 2.3, 6.0, and 11.8. The correlation between effective threshold and disproportionality is .80 (N = 155). It is notable that the single-member district system with the least misrepresentation in vote-seat terms is the United States, whose disproportionality is still higher than that in any PR system with under a 10 percent threshold. Low threshold PR systems are without doubt creating much fairer party representation in the legislature and are, to that extent, encouraging of the proportional influence vision.

I need not add to the large literature on consequences of election laws at this point. Table 2.1 (and the literature discussed above and in the notes) should be sufficient to justify the classification of electoral systems by the election rules. This classification, as well as Lijphart's continuous effective threshold variable, offers a useful starting point as we begin in the next chapter to examine characteristics of the election more precisely linked to the various democratic visions. However, we need also to consider features of the decision rules for the policy-making process that follows the elections.

The Policy-Making Rules and the Visions of Democracy

The elections allow citizens to choose the potential policymakers. But after the elections those representatives act to make policies following another general set of rules. I call these rules about how to make policies the decision rules. As in the case of the election rules, important features of the decision rules may appear in a single constitutional document, in ordinary legislation, or even in less formal norms of behavior. For our purposes, the critical point is that some decision rules encourage majoritarian policy making, while others encourage policy-making processes closer to the proportional vision.

In many ways the twenty countries in this book share quite similar decision rules. They are all democracies in which an elected national assembly has most of the final power to authorize public policies. Moreover, most of them are relatively centralized parliamentary systems with single or similarly elected assembly chambers and limited or relatively inactive judicial review systems. I shall refer to these as pure parliamentary systems. The similarity of the decision rules is helpful in giving us substantial confidence in the comparability of our measures and analyses. However, it limits the applicability of the analysis to democracies with different kinds of decision rules. I shall begin by considering a critical dimension of the decision rule common to all these democracies, the degree of sharing or concentrating power in the assembly. Then, I turn to decision rule features relevant to only a few of these countries.

CONCENTRATION OR DISPERSION OF POWER IN THE ASSEMBLY

Such countries as Britain, Sweden, and the Netherlands are pure parliamentary systems. Authority to make public policies is concentrated in the national assembly. Nonetheless, these countries vary strikingly in the decision rules that shape the policy making of the assemblies. In the usual language of parliamentary politics, these rules regulate the relation between the government, whose cabinet controls the bureaucratic agencies of the executive, and the assembly. They also regulate the relation between the government parties and the opposition parties within the assembly. I want to distinguish between rules that encourage a single parliamentary majority to control policy making and rules that encourage all parties to have influence on policy making and implementation proportional to their size.

I take for granted here that political parties in mature parliamentary systems are generally very cohesive in their voting behavior.[13] Obviously, when legislators in the governing parties frequently break ranks, this lack of party discipline will create opportunities for opposition parties. This feature of legislative politics is given separate consideration later, as I do not consider it, directly, a feature of the constitutional rules.

If the decision rules encourage or require the government parties to negotiate with independent groups in the assembly, especially those representing voters who supported different parties, I want to characterize them as closer to the proportional vision. If the decision rules encourage the government parties to control the executive and the assembly without check or division, I characterize them as majoritarian. It is harder to identify the assembly decision rules and their consequences than the election rules. The assembly rules are complex, often less formalized, and have been less frequently studied in a comparative context. Fortunately, recent scholarship enables us to get some insight into this important set of constitutional features. In a seminal article and subsequent book Kaare Strom (1984, 1990) suggested that to understand how national assemblies function we should look to their committee systems. In some countries the committees are organized to facilitate or even require dispersal of policy-making influence to many groups, including representatives of opposition parties. In others, however, the committees are primarily instruments by which leaders of the government party or parties wield centralized control. As all national legislatures have some kind of committee system to help them carry out their work, the nature of that system can tell us a great deal about them.

Strom constructed a variable he called "influence of the opposition" based on features of the parliamentary committees: the number of standing committees, fixed areas of committee specialization, correspondence between committee jurisdictions and ministerial jurisdictions, restrictions on the number of committee assignments per legislator, and the proportional distribution of committee chairs to legislative parties (Strom 1990, 71). Strom argued that each of these features contributed to opposition influence and constructed an additive scale of opposition influence based on them. Because the features suggested by Strom were systematically described in the Inter-Parliamentary Union's (IPU) *Parliaments of the World* studies (1976, 1986), it was possible to construct this scale for many countries, even if few detailed studies of their legislative politics were available. In-depth analysis of a few countries provided some validation. Very recently, further valuable research, stimulated by Strom's work and by theoretical and empirical studies of policy making in the U.S. Congress, has appeared on West European parliaments and their committee systems. These studies, especially the articles in Doering 1995, make it possible to refine and validate an abbreviated version of Strom's measure for our purposes.

Conceptually, the role of committee systems in providing an opportunity for opposition influence has two elements. First, the committee systems themselves must be influential in shaping policy, not rubber stamps for decisions made by the governing parties in the executive. Second, the committees must provide an opportunity for the opposition, not merely individuals in the ruling party(s), to affect policy. From this perspective, the first four elements of Strom's additive scale seem to be related to the potential influence of the committees relative to the government. More committees, committee specialization, correspondence to government ministries, and member specialization are all expected to enhance the ability of a committee to modify the legislation submitted to it by the government, perhaps even to introduce legislation of its own. The fifth element, the sharing of the committee chairs, is obviously related to the influence of the opposition within the committee system, as the powers of committee chairs to set agendas and otherwise influence committee deliberations are often considerable. The presence of this rule is likely associated with other norms of sharing legislative influence.

The first two columns in table 2.2 show separately these two elements in the formal structure of the committee systems. The first column indicates the number of standing committees and their correspondence to organization of the government ministries.[14] In the countries at the top of the table, there are at least eleven regular standing committees (median fifteen), and their specialization corresponds more or less closely to the structure of the government ministries. We would expect these committee systems to have the capacity to exert some independent influence on legislation. This configuration is also found in the first four countries in the middle group. In the countries at the bottom of the table, on the other hand, there are either many fewer committees (six in France, eight in Greece, nine in Ireland) or the committees are not specialized to correspond to government departments, dealing with bills in a purely ad hoc way that limits the specialized knowledge needed to shape what the government has submitted (France, Greece, Ireland, New Zealand, United Kingdom). Australia has moved toward a more independent and specialized committee system, especially in the Senate,[15] but seems, even with ten somewhat more specialized committees, to remain appropriately in the lower group.

The second column shows whether the committee chairs are given only to the parties in the government or are shared with the opposition parties. Not surprisingly, this feature is itself related to the committee strength; the weak committees at the bottom of the table are dominated by the government in the distribution of chairs also.

In the countries at the top of the table the main opposition parties are given a substantial share of the committee chairs. This is often strictly proportional to legislative membership, once a party exceeds some minimal size, as in

Table 2.2. Legislative Decision Rules: Concentrating Governmental Power

| Country | Formal Committee Structure[1] | | Associated Features of Assembly Rules[2] | |
	Over Ten Standing Committees Corresponding to Government Departments	Committee Chairs to Opposition	Government: Controls Assembly Agenda	Limits Committee Amendment
Rules facilitate opposition influence in legislature				
Austria	Yes	Shared	Medium	No
Belgium	Yes	Shared	Medium	No
Denmark	Yes	Shared	Low	Yes
Germany	Yes	Shared	Medium	No
Netherlands	Yes	Shared	Low	Yes
Norway	Yes	Shared	Medium	No
Spain	Yes	Shared	Medium	No
Sweden	Yes	Shared	Low	No
Switzerland	Yes	Shared	High	No
Rules encourage some dispersal of influence in legislature				
Canada	Yes	No	—	(Some)
Italy	Yes	No	Low	No
Japan	Yes	No	—	(Yes)
United States	Yes	No	—	(No)
Finland	No	Shared	Low	No
Rules support domination of legislature by government				
Australia	No	No	—	(Yes)
France	No	No	High	Yes
Greece	No	No	High	Yes
Ireland	No	No	High	Yes
New Zealand	No	No	—	(Yes)
United Kingdom	No	No	High	Yes

[1]From IPU 1986, except for Greece, which limited number of committees when democracy was reinstituted in late 1970s; see Mattson and Strom 1995, 261 ff. and Damgaard 1995, 311.
[2]From Doering 1995, 225 (I–III = High; IV = Med; V–VI = Low), based on expert assessments; Doering 1995, 236; parentheses are my interpretation, based on Doering's original source (IPU 1986, table 33.4). For Canada also see the special issues of *Parliamentary Government* 43, 44 (June and August 1993).

Belgium, Denmark, Norway, and Sweden and the popular houses in Germany and the Netherlands. Variations on this arrangement give more committees to the government, but still a substantial number to the opposition in Austria, divide committee chairs only between the two major parties in Spain, and give each substantial party exactly two chairs in Switzerland. Thus, in the top group the combination of many committees whose specialization corresponds to government departments and sharing chairs with the opposition suggests substantial opportunities for the opposition to influence legislation.

In the other countries, the opportunities seem to be fewer. The middle group may have stronger committees, but the government dominates the committee chairs. Only intraparty or intracoalition divisions (admittedly fairly common in Italy, Japan, and the United States, as we shall see later) can spread opportunities for the opposition members. Finland shares the committee chairs, but the committees themselves are weak.

In the countries at the bottom of the table, we find the combination of committee systems that are greatly disadvantaged relative to the government and committee chairs largely in government hands. (In a few countries some special committees, such as committees overseeing particular government procedures, may be given to the opposition.) We would expect that in these countries the opposition should have little opportunity to influence legislation unless it can persuade the government of the rightness or electoral appeal of its arguments.

The two columns on the right of the table present additional information about the assembly rules that offer some validation of our expectations and the classification. We do not use them for the classification itself as most are available only for the European countries included in the Doering (1995) volume. Legislative rules that directly bear on the power of the government versus the committees in shaping legislation can show the strength or weakness of the classification based simply on number and jurisdictional specialization. The analysis of Mattson and Strom (1995) suggests two dimensions of committee influence, one linked to control of the assembly's agenda and the other linked to the ability of the committees to amend legislation submitted by the government. The two features shown explicitly here lie at the heart of those two dimensions and are fairly self-explanatory.

The analysis by Doering (1995, 225) classifies the government's control over the assembly agenda on a seven-step ordinal ranking from most government control (I = government alone determines the plenary agenda) to least government control (VII = chamber itself controls the agenda). The table collapses those into a Low-Medium-High classification. There is a fairly good fit with the general committee structure. The government dominates the legislative agenda in all the countries in the bottom group in the table, while elsewhere only in Switzerland is there more than moderate government control over the agenda. (In Switzerland, over 80 percent of the legislators are members of parties directly represented in the government.)

The column on limitations on the committee amendment powers is also drawn from Doering's analysis, but here he interprets the 1985 IPU reports rather than experts in his own study. I have put in parentheses my interpretation of the same data, after reviewing Doering's classification. The main distinction in the rules is whether the committee can completely replace the government's initial wording with a new draft text or whether it is restricted to amendments of the government's original text within general constraints. In most of the countries in the top group and even in the middle group, the committees are free to substitute their own drafts for the government's original language. In Austria a substitute text may be offered, but it must be considered against the original, as in the U.S. House. The exceptions are committees in Denmark, the Netherlands (despite the maximum agenda freedom of the legislature shown in the previous column), Japan, and to some extent Canada. In contrast, committees in all the countries in the bottom group are severely constrained to work with the government's original text. The purpose of committees in most of these countries is not primarily shaping of policies but oversight of the government bureaucracy. Thus, the government's capacity to control the assembly agenda and to limit committee amendments generally coincides with the organization and chair distribution arrangements that were used to classify the committee systems.[16]

INSTITUTIONAL FEATURES THAT CAN DISPERSE POWER
OUTSIDE THE NATIONAL ASSEMBLY

Most of the democracies studied here are parliamentary systems featuring relatively centralized political authority. In such democracies the main features that organize the concentration or dispersion of power are the election rules and the rules for making policy inside the legislature, which I have been discussing. The dependence of the executive on the legislature in parliamentary systems fuses control of both and contributes to high levels of legislative voting cohesion in governing legislative parties. The election rules help shape the formation of governments; the committee rules help determine whether the legislative opposition will have influence on government-originated legislation. I have devoted most attention to these two types of rules because they dominate our sample of democratic constitutions. In a few of these democracies, however, the decision rules offer points of institutional influence outside the assembly. When one party or coalition of parties controls the legislature and another controls some outside veto point, then shared influence — if only in the form of deadlock — is inevitable. Several of these possible veto institutions are worth brief comment:

1. *Independent Executives.* The most famous constitutional distinction in democracies is, of course, that between parliamentary and presidential systems, a contrast complicated by the explosion of mixed legislative-executive arrangements in many of the new democracies of the 1990s. A separately elected executive with independent policy-making powers (such as a veto over legislation, authority to issue decrees, or ability to dismiss the legislature) can give rise to divided government situations with dispersed opportunities for influence. (See Shugart and Carey [1992, 155] for a list of presidential powers in different systems.) Among our twenty systems, however, only the United States clearly has a strong presidential constitution. The French president has had a sufficiently independent role to be considered a point for opposition influence under the "cohabitation" situations of the late 1980s and mid-1990s.[17] In both cases we must take account of divided government possibilities in examining the role of elections as instruments of democracy in policy making.

2. *Separate Legislative Chamber with Independent Selection Base and Veto Powers.* Many democracies have more than one legislative chamber. For our purposes, these are interesting as a strong basis for opposition influence only if the second house can effectively veto legislation passed by the first and if its basis of election is likely to create different majorities (see Lijphart 1984, chapter 6). The British House of Lords and the Canadian Senate no longer have serious veto influence. The Belgian and Italian upper houses were elected by PR with rules very similar to those of the lower houses and simultaneous elections, thus resulting in similar party balances. In four of our democracies — Australia, Germany, Switzerland, and the United States — the upper house has sufficient power to influence policy significantly if controlled by the opposition. Australia and Germany offer a number of instances of such opposition control that we shall have to consider in analyzing the postelection situations.

3. *Federal Systems.* Regional governments with independent bases of election and policy making can be sources of influence for opposition political parties. Where such governments are represented directly in the upper house, as in Germany, we shall already have captured some of the effect. But regional governments also have some direct influence over policy making and its implementation in Germany as well as in Australia, Austria, Canada, Switzerland, and the United States. Regional governments have

also been developed fairly recently in France, Italy, and especially Belgium. Unfortunately, we do not have good measures of possible regional government influence for the opposition, apart from control of the upper house, and shall generally bypass this influence venue in our discussions.

4. *Judicial Review*. A number of democratic systems provide for review of the constitutionality of legislative actions, either by the ordinary court system or by special constitutional courts. At times these courts can provide a point at which opposition political parties can challenge and even defeat government legislation. The Supreme Court in the United States is a prime example: it defeated or at least delayed parts of the New Deal programs of a Democratic president and Congress in the early 1930s. The judiciary is especially likely to be a limiting force on the power of newly elected governments that promise major political change. The evidence suggests that constitutional courts are becoming increasingly active in setting the bounds of legislative action in a number of countries, notably in Germany and France.[18] Yet the connection between judicial activism and the dispersion of political influence among political parties and factions is, at best, extremely complex. I shall not take systematic account of it in the following chapters but leave that task to a future agenda.

A Constitutional Overview

Constitutional designs need not partake exclusively of proportional or majoritarian features. It is possible to combine proportional election rules with government control of committees, as in Greece in 1989–92, and vice versa (no cases here, however). Theoretically, whether such combinations are desirable depends on whether the designers wish to maximize or mix the advantages and disadvantages of each approach. I shall return to this theme in the concluding chapter after having investigated the empirical consequences in more detail.

The constitutional designs in the countries considered here do tend to fall into either proportional or majoritarian combinations of electoral and legislative rules. The majoritarian electoral classification in table 2.1 is strongly associated with the government dominance of the legislature in table 2.2. The correlation coefficient between the two trichotomized variables is .77 for the twenty countries. This association is displayed in table 2.3, which reproduces the classification of electoral rules on the left-hand side (vertical dimension) and the legislative committee rules across the top (horizontal dimension). The eight systems in the top left group are highly proportional on both dimensions: proportional representation election rules with low thresholds are combined with

Table 2.3. Two Dimensions of Constitutional Rules:
The Potential to Concentrate Power

Legislative Election Rules[1]	Legislative Committee Rules[2]		
	Opposition Influence Facilitated in Committees	Mixed: Weak Committee with Shared Chairs or Vice Versa	Government Domination of Committees
Pure proportional representation	Austria Belgium Denmark Germany* Netherlands Norway Sweden Switzerland	Finland* Italy — — — — — —	Greece 1989–92 — — — — — — —
Multimember districts with increased distortion potential	Norway pre-1989 Spain	Japan	Ireland Greece France 1986
Single-member districts	— — — —	United States* Canada — —	Australia* France* New Zealand United Kingdom

*The upper houses in Australia, Germany, and the United States and the presidencies in France and the United States occasionally provide added possibilities for dispersed power in policy-making. Legislation involving increased taxes required a two-thirds majority in Finland until 1992. Committee systems were mixed in Denmark before 1973 and Sweden before 1970.

[1]Classification from table 2.1
[2]Classification from table 2.2.

committee rules facilitating opposition influence in the legislature. On the far lower right are four systems that are strongly majoritarian on both dimensions, having single-member district elections and committee rules facilitating government domination of the legislature. More than half of the countries fall into these "pure design" cells through most of the analysis period considered here.

The association between the two dimensions is also marked by the paucity of systems in the extreme off-diagonal cells. We have no cases of majoritarian election rules and rules encouraging substantial opposition influence through committees. The United States is the closest, but the party with the legislative majority holds all the committee chairs. Greece in the brief period of 1989 through 1992 offers the only example of the extreme opposite possibility — purely proportional election rules and government domination — although Ireland comes close. The constitution makers, or gradual adaptations of electoral and legislative rules over time, seem to have favored either a decisively proportional or a decisively majoritarian approach, rather than a mix.[19]

Using table 2.3 and the other information about the associated rules for elections and policy making, we can classify the constitutional designs in most of these countries fairly definitely. On the proportional influence side are the eight countries in the upper left cell (Austria, Belgium, Denmark, Germany, Netherlands, Norway, Sweden, Switzerland), to which could probably be added comfortably most of the cases in the neighboring cells (Finland, pre-1994 Italy). Finland's requirement of a supermajority to pass tax increases (at least until 1992) and Italy's strong and secret committees, as well as the low disproportionality of votes in each, helped compensate for committees that are (for different reasons) only moderately helpful to the oppositions. Norway fits especially well after the modification of its election rules for the election of 1989, when addition of second-tier seats limited the effect of malapportionment; but even before 1989 its very inclusive decision rules (Strom 1990) and marginal electoral distortion place it in the proportional category. Spain is in all respects more doubtful as a proportional design system.[20]

At the other end of the scale, Australia, France, and especially New Zealand and Britain had strongly majoritarian constitutional designs. Their single-member district election rules created great distortion in vote-seat relations and also many legislative majorities, even single-party majorities, that were not based on vote majorities. Despite the aberration of the French legislative election of 1986, when the Socialist majority tried unsuccessfully to stave off decisive electoral defeat by introducing PR election rules, and some impact from the upper house in Australia, the constitutional rules in these countries encouraged decisive linkages between voting outcomes and the formation of policymaker coalitions.[21]

Some of the countries in neighboring cells also qualify fairly comfortably as having had predominately majoritarian constitutional designs. Despite its stronger committee system, Canada belongs in this group, with single-member districts, high vote-seat distortion, and government control of committee chairs. Discussion of the role of Canadian committees emphasizes the predominantly British flavor, with committees oriented more toward oversight than legislation, even after the reforms of the 1980s.[22] Greece was highly majoritarian after its reconstruction as a democracy in the late 1970s, and quite deliberately so at both electoral and legislative levels. Except for the tumultuous election years of 1989 and 1990, the effective threshold in Greece was the highest of any PR system in our group and consistently created single-party majority governments that could use the legislative rules to control the assembly. In the 1989 to 1993 period, however, Greece was a truly mixed constitutional system.

The designs in the remaining countries are more problematic to classify on a single proportional-majoritarian dimension. The United States is constitutionally unique in this group. Having very strong independent powers in both the executive and the legislature and a host of other points featuring possible sharing of power, it does not imply strong majoritarianism in its decision rules. The executive has a hard task in implementing its policy commitments even when it has congressional majorities. On the other hand, the United States uses single-member district election rules — but separate presidential and legislative elections — and yields all committee chairs to the party with a majority in the legislative chamber, so on the surface it is not a very proportional design either. (Dahl's [1956] account of the Madisonian compromise prepares us for this situation.) We shall have to look closely at the role specific combinations of elections, institutional control, policy-making rules, and patterns of party discipline play in the U.S. policy-making linkages. Ireland and Japan, too, can be categorized as predominately majoritarian only with difficulty. In the chapters to come, I shall treat them, like Greece in 1989–93, Spain, and the United States, as mixed systems in shorthand references to their constitutional designs. Yet given the diversity of arrangements in these countries, we should be careful not to think of mixed as a homogeneous category in the way that we can more comfortably classify the other constitutional designs.

This discussion leads to the following classification of the constitutional designs of the twenty countries:

Predominately Proportional	Mixed	Predominately Majoritarian
Austria	Ireland	Australia
Belgium	Japan	Canada
Denmark	Spain	France
Finland	USA	Greece
Germany		New Zealand
Italy		United Kingdom
Netherlands		
Norway		
Sweden		
Switzerland		

In general, then, it will be fairly straightforward to see whether on the basis of its constitutional design we would expect proportional or majoritarian performance from a particular political system. Individual elections and associated postelection periods in France (1986–88) and Greece (1989–92) deviate sufficiently from the general country designs that, where included in the analysis, they have to be treated separately as forms of mixed designs. For some purposes, of course, we can analyze individual elections and individual features of electoral rules or committee systems, rather than general design classifications, to test some of our expectations. In such analysis we can also more easily handle such varying features as the control of a strong upper house or influential presidency by the nongoverning party. We can even make some effort to disentangle the effects of electoral rules, committee rules, and party systems, although the convergence of powerful design features on proportional or majoritarian emphases makes it difficult.

Consequences

Although I begin the empirical discussion of elections as instruments of democracy by describing the constitutional setting, I do not mean to imply that constitutional rules are unmoved movers in the process. They are neither entirely unchanging nor independent of the nature of the citizen-policymaker connections. In several of these democracies unsatisfactory experiences with one system of constitution rules led to revisions to deal with the problems that emerged under the old rules. France and Greece in 1958 and 1974, respectively, radically altered both election rules and decision rules to make them much more majoritarian. High threshold election rules were instituted, the number of committees was cut drastically, and committee powers were curtailed. Both countries conducted elections under much more proportional rules in the late 1980s, then reversed themselves again. Norway became more electorally proportional with the rule changes of 1989. Italy became more majoritarian in 1994, slightly after the period of this analysis; New Zealand introduced PR in 1996. Smaller changes take place quite often; Lijphart's book counts fifty-eight domestic electoral systems (plus more for European Community elections) in his twenty-seven countries. Small changes in committee rules take place continuously, often as committees seek influence and governments seek to limit them. If we had better over-time measures, we could no doubt see these changes more clearly.[23] I do not assume that constitutional rules are unchanging and have, indeed, tried to note the large changes.

Nonetheless, it remains true that the general thrust of the constitutional design changes between elections in only a handful of cases. The designs are usually sustained because the incumbents, having won under the current system, tend to be favored by it and are reluctant to open a less certain future for short-term advantage. Perhaps the current rules are sustained, too, by the supportive logic of majoritarian and proportional design and the values they reflect. Those favoring the current system have a ready-made body of arguments and "horrible examples" of features associated with the alternative design to support the present rules against proposed changes. Polls suggest that as long as citizens are reasonably satisfied with the system, they tend to disapprove of the short-term manipulation of constitutional rules for partisan advantage, even where this is not difficult. Major citizen disaffection toward the current political system is a notable feature of most of the major changes mentioned above.

Continuity of the constitutional rules means that as citizens and parties approach an election they usually know a great deal about how votes will translate into seats and about what capacity the winner will have to impose its policies. The parties' short-term tactics and even their long-term strategies will be shaped by that knowledge. Unless they can transform the system itself, their roads to power and policy are quite different under proportional or majoritarian arrangements. For the citizens, too, the constitutional rules shape in the short run the ways their votes seem likely to translate into policy influence.

For our primary purpose of understanding the alternative approaches to using elections as instruments of democracy, and the successes and failures of those approaches, it is not essential whether the constitutional features here identified are exogenous causes of those consequences or merely part of a policy-making equilibrium. Of course, if we wish to advise on the consequences of constitutional change, we shall need to try very hard to get the causal connections specified as fully as possible. But at the moment it is sufficient to determine whether indeed the approaches work as envisioned. Do we find clarity of responsibility, evicted incumbents, directly elected majorities for policy mandates in the majoritarian systems? How often do we find them elsewhere? Similarly, do we find proportional influence by authorized bargainers in the proportional designs? Which approach better connects citizens' preferences and responsive and representative policy making? When does each fail? I turn to these questions in the following chapters.

PART II

*Responsiveness: Connecting Votes,
Governments, and Policymakers*

3

Accountability: Conditions for Citizen Control

Few contrasts between dictatorship and democracy are sharper than this one: in a democracy the citizens can vote the leaders out of office. The citizens' ability to throw the rascals out seems fundamental to modern representative democracy because it is the ultimate guarantee of a connection between citizens and policymakers. It enables the citizens to hold the policymakers accountable for their performance. Such accountability is a keystone of majoritarian democratic theory.

Throwing the Rascals Out: Do Votes Count?

Let us begin with the fundamentals. In chapter 2 I discussed the constitutional designs in twenty countries assumed to be democracies. We would not call them democracies if their citizens could not vote against the incumbents. But how frequently do democratic citizens vote against the incumbents? Much more important, when they do so, do those votes make a difference in retaining or replacing the policymakers?

To look first at governments, table 3.1 shows some simple evidence that voters often vote against the incumbents and that those votes do make a difference. In the 153 elections[1] held in our twenty democracies across a quarter of a century, the party or parties in office lost votes much more often than

Table 3.1. Incumbent Vote Losses and Subsequent Government Changes

| | Change in Government Parties After Election | | | | |
Incumbent Vote Change	None	Some Change	All New Parties	Total Percent	Cases*
Loses over 5%	34%	17%	49%	100%	(47)
Loses 1–5%	51%	28%	21%	100%	(67)
None or gain	69%	21%	10%	100%	(39)

*Cases: 153 legislative elections in twenty democracies, from 1969 through 1994. Also includes elections in 1967 and 1968 in France, Italy, and Sweden. United States includes only congressional elections in years of concurrent presidential elections. Elections in Norway 1973, Italy 1994, and Spain 1982 are excluded because the configuration of parties changed so much between elections that it was not possible to calculate gains or losses of governing parties.

not. The average government lost about 2 percent of the vote. We can see from the number of cases in the right-most column of the table that in 31 percent (47/153) of the elections they lost over 5 percent. In only a quarter of the elections did the incumbents actually gain votes. Citizens in these countries are not shy about showing their disapproval of incumbent officeholders.

Moreover, the table shows a strong relation between the incumbent parties' gain or loss of votes and their being retained or replaced in office. When the incumbent parties gained or broke even in votes, they were retained in office 69 percent of the time, partially replaced 21 percent, and fully evicted only 10 percent of the time. When the incumbent parties lost over 5 percent of their voting support, they were retained in office only 34 percent, partially replaced 17 percent, and fully evicted 49 percent of the time. Clearly, the elections do make a difference. This is in a general sense reassuring for the status of the countries as democracies. We would not expect that a 5 percent vote loss would evict the incumbents half of the time in authoritarian systems, even if citizens were allowed to express their disapproval so freely.

Obviously vote losses are not the only thing that shape eviction of incumbents. Half of the governments losing 5 percent or more are retained in office at least in part; a third of them are retained in entirety. And what is one to make of the fact that incumbents who *gained* votes are still replaced, at least in part, a third of the time? For the visions of concentrated power and citizen control through elections, the whole concept of partial replacement seems somewhat suspicious. Some parties stay in office while others are evicted.

In fact, empirical performance is consistent with this normative predisposi-

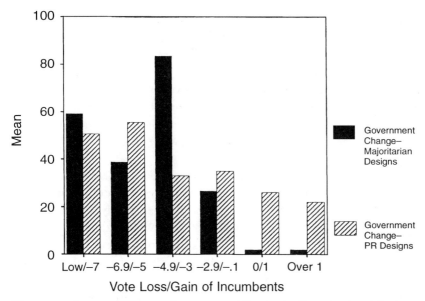

Figure 3.1. Impact of Vote on Government Change, by Constitutional Design

tion. The countries whose constitutional designs are primarily majoritarian seldom experience such partial changes. In the six majoritarian design countries identified in chapter 2, governments were retained in office after 60 percent of the (45) elections and evicted after 40 percent. They were almost never retained only in part. To some extent this all-or-nothing pattern reflects single-party governments which must be either retained or evicted, but even the party coalitions in Australia and France stayed or departed as a unit. In the predominately proportional countries, on the other hand, partial changes occurred after 38 percent of the (81) elections. (Incumbents were retained without change in 44 percent of the elections and completely replaced in only 17 percent.)

This divergent pattern of all-or-nothing changes reminds us that the two great visions of citizen control or citizen influence have differing ideals about how citizen vote choices should translate into policy-making power. I shall develop these ideals and their realizations more explicitly in chapter 6, when I can also distinguish governments from the full group of policymakers. However, we can get some sense of the way that incumbent eviction fits into the larger picture by considering the change in relation to vote for the incumbents (fig. 3.1). The figure shows the average change in government on a 0 to 100 scale, where no change is 0, partial change is 50, and full change is 100, for increasingly improved government voting support. The solid bars represent elections in the majoritarian systems. There is some correspondence to the ideal of all-or-nothing change, with lots of change in governments that lose a good deal and no change for incumbents who were vote winners. This pattern generally corresponds to what we might expect for majoritarian accountability. There is also a lot of jaggedness on the government loser side, some of it caused by distortions in seat-vote relations, more of it reflecting varying margins of government support at the time of the election, so some governments can lose 5 percent and still be the largest party, while others can lose 3 percent and fall behind.

On the other hand, the proportional systems, the second set of bars, show quite a different pattern. There is a rather gradual, linear decline in government change as the governing parties do better. Statistically, the fit between vote change and government change is fairly good. While it does not show the sharp break at the point where incumbents start to lose votes that the ideal majoritarian view of accountability would imply, the proportional vision may find this a more appropriate pattern. I shall explore the different normative perspective on vote change and government change in analyzing responsiveness in chapter 6.

If we broaden our perspective from governments to the full policy-making structure, the impact of votes on the fate of policymakers would generally be blurred when the opposition parties share power. If the opposition parties are allowed to share power — by their acquisition of political bargaining power against minority governments, by their control of secondary policy-making institutions such as an upper house of the legislature, or by providing permanent minority influence through strong committees and the like — then eviction of incumbent governments will mean much less severe loss of policy-making influence.[2] This outcome implies, in turn, less impact of voters' choices in holding incumbents accountable for their policy performance.

Clarity of Responsibility and Government Accountability

As suggested in chapter 1, democratic theorists have diverse expectations about what elections can accomplish. For proportional theorists elections are primarily an occasion to reconsider and rebalance the opportunities for influence; accountability does not loom so large in this vision. For some majoritarians an occasional all-or-nothing rejection of the incumbents, perhaps based on citizens' contradictory evaluations and concerns, is all one can expect of democratic elections (for example, Riker 1982a). They have little hope of seeing substantive connections between citizens' preferences and government policies. For other, perhaps most, majoritarians the possibility of throwing the rascals out is essential in order to retain policymakers who do what the citizens want and evict those who stray from citizens' preferred policies. Perhaps more than the occasional evictions themselves, the threat of eviction should encourage responsible behavior.

But if retrospective control is to play a significant part in linking what citizens want and what policymakers do, citizens must be able to cast reasoned votes based on the performance of the incumbents. What must we expect from the electoral and policy-making setting if citizens are to use this powerful instrument of democracy appropriately and effectively? A first condition is that citizens must know who is responsible for making policy. A second condition is that they must have a fair opportunity to cast a meaningful vote for or against the policymakers. Given these two conditions, they could use their votes to retain the good policymakers and send the bad ones packing.

In a dictatorship the first condition is usually satisfied and the second is not. Citizens know who is responsible for the policies, but they are not allowed to throw them out if they dislike the results. In a democracy it can be the other way around: citizens are allowed to throw somebody out, but they do not really know who is responsible for the policies. If citizens in a democracy cannot identify responsibility for policy, they cannot use elections precisely to hold policymakers retrospectively accountable for their actions. When policy responsibility is unclear, the incentive for policymakers to anticipate what citizens want and work to achieve it is also lessened. Clarity of responsibility, then, is an important condition if elections are to serve as instruments for citizen control in a democracy.

Unified Control and Clarity of Responsibility: Majority Status of the Government

My analysis of clarity of responsibility builds upon a simple assumption. If all the resources necessary for policy making are controlled by a unified, identifiable set of elected officials, it will be easy for citizens to perceive accurately that those officials are responsible for the policies made. On the other hand, if the resources necessary for policy making are dispersed into the control of numerous groups and individuals, citizens cannot identify who is responsible for policies.

In a modern democracy the most important resources for policy making usually lie with the national legislature and the chief executive. The most important vehicle for unified identifiability for citizens is the political party, which, conveniently and critically, is the prime organizing vehicle for citizens' electoral choices as well. Clarity of responsibility is greatest when a single, unified political party controls both the national legislature and chief executive. If control of these critical policy-making points is dispersed among various parties or among individuals not firmly connected by political parties, then it will be much harder for citizens to determine who should bear the responsibility for policy success or failure and to use their electoral resources effectively as instruments for reward or retribution.

MAJORITY STATUS OF THE GOVERNMENT: FROM MINORITY
GOVERNMENT TO SINGLE-PARTY MAJORITY

The first and most important element in determining clarity of responsibility is the majority status of the government. By *the government* I mean, of course, the party or parties who occupy the main offices of the executive — usually a prime minister or president and his or her cabinet. The status of that government depends on its control over the votes needed to make or ratify policy in the national legislature. When the leaders of a single party hold the chief executive and cabinet offices and also command enough seats (usually a simple majority, sometimes more) in the legislature to initiate or change policies at will, citizens are provided with the maximum clarity of responsibility. This situation existed, for example, in Britain in the 1980s, when the Conservative Party led by Margaret Thatcher occupied the prime ministership and the cabinet and commanded a disciplined majority of seats in the House of Commons.

At the other extreme, a party may occupy the prime ministership but be well short of enough votes to control the legislature. In Denmark after the chaotic election of 1973, in which all the major parties lost badly to various protest parties, the Liberal Party assumed the government with only 13 percent of the seats in the legislature. Such a government can be turned out of office at any time by a combination of other parties voting against it. In order to gain enough votes to make positive policies it is dependent on gaining the support of other parties. These outside parties are not identified to the electorate as policymakers because they do not hold positions in the executive. It will be very difficult for voters to ascertain who should be held responsible for policy outcomes. The party or parties in a minority government can always claim that their best efforts were blocked by other parties, that policy failures must be shared by them. Sometimes these claims are true.

From the point of view of clarity of responsibility, we can identify five conditions of government majority status. These are listed below in order of increasing clarity of responsibility:

1. *Minority Government.* The government is dependent on other parties for its continuation and its policies. It could be evicted if other parties did not support it. Policy responsibility will be hard to identify, although these governments are usually single-party governments.
2. *Minority Government with Outside Support.* Such a government does not itself command a legislative majority, but it can consistently rely on the backing of some other party or parties that have agreed to keep it in office. When challenged at election it may be able to diffuse responsibility by referring to its formal minority status, its supporters, or both.
3. *Majority Government Negotiated After the Election.* Such a government is composed of several parties. *After* the election these parties agreed to share cabinet posts and collectively control a legislative majority. The policy responsibility of such control is clearer than in the minority situation. But because the parties ran against each other and made individual policy proposals before forming a government, it may be difficult to attribute responsibility within a government made up of competitors, who can blame each other for failures.
4. *Multiparty Preelection Majority Government.* Such a government is made up of several parties sharing cabinet positions and collectively controlling a legislative majority. But here, the coalition parties had announced *before* the election that brought them to office their intention of formulating policy and working together. While disagreements between the coalition partners may obscure responsibility, the tighter bonds between the parties (which may include joint policy programs, candidates withdrawing in each other's favor, and the like) make responsibility much clearer to voters.[3]
5. *Single-Party Majority Government.* A single political party controls the national executive and the legislature. If the party is unified, this government status condition provides the greatest clarity of responsibility.

This fivefold classification is based on the formal majority status of the government, the number of parties sharing government power, and the competitive relation between those parties. Although these properties can be investigated independently, the five combinations considered here contain enough cases for examination and seem to capture the major variations that affect clarity of responsibility.

I have no absolute verification that the fivefold classification of government status conditions is linked to increasing levels of clarity of responsibility. But there are two pieces of supportive evidence. One of these has to do with the behavior of voters. Incumbent governments generally lose votes; it seems easier to be blamed for failures in office than to exploit successes. But majority governments tend to lose more votes than minority governments; single-party majority governments lose the most of all. Over the full set of elections in this book, minority governments lost a little over 1 percent of their vote in the average election; single-party majority governments lost about 4.5 percent; coalition governments collectively lost somewhat over 3 percent.[4] The increases are not quite linear, but they show generally the pattern we would expect from minority governments to majority coalitions to single-party majorities. Furthermore, in a study of the impact of the economy on voters' choices, Guy Whitten and I found that both positive and negative economic conditions seemed to have less impact on voters' assessments of governments in political systems in which accountability was less clear according to the status of the government (Powell and Whitten 1993).

Inferring perceived clarity of responsibility from the behavior of voters is not easy because voters may worry about future promises as well as past behavior, may be concerned about multiple issues (even different dimensions of the performance of the economy), and must always choose among the specific party choices offered to them. For example, it may make a difference to leftist voters whether there are other leftist alternatives outside the government.[5] Thus, the voter evidence is encouraging, but not decisive.

A second piece of evidence draws on the assessments of political experts of the influence of opposition parties in the legislatures of their country of expertise. It is, of course, largely the potential influence of the opposition that blurs the clarity of responsibility of the government incumbents. Michael Laver and W. Ben Hunt (1992) surveyed a number of experts in each of our countries in 1989, asking them to rate the influence of the opposition on a 1–9 scale. It seems reasonable to assume that when the experts gave high scores to opposition influence, the clarity of responsibility of the governing parties was lessened. They report the results for nineteen of our twenty countries, all of them except Switzerland. As we have only this single point in time, we have to use these data with caution. But they are relevant to the question of government responsibility. We should expect a strong negative relation between our categories of government status and the reported influence of the opposition parties in the legislature. The difference between minority governments and single-party majorities should be especially clear.

If we look at the government in power at the time of Laver and Hunt's February 1989 survey and compare its majority status with the average expert estimates of opposition influence, we find in fact a very strong relation. Table 3.2 shows for sixteen parliamentary systems the majority status scale on the left and the average influence of the opposition score on the right.[6] The reputed influence of the opposition is twice as great in the pure minority governments

Table 3.2. Majority Status of Incumbent Governments and Reputed Influence of Opposition Parties in Parliamentary Systems, 1989

Majority Status of Incumbent Government[1]	Rating of Influence of Opposition Parties on Government Policy[2] (Average Score) (1 = No Impact 9 = High Impact)	Number of Countries
Pure minority	5.8	3
Supported minority	5.2	1
Postelection majority coalition	4.7	3
Preelection majority coalition	3.6	2
Single-party majority government	2.9	7

[1]The government status of the countries in 1989 was a follows: pure minority = Denmark, Ireland, Norway; supported minority = Sweden; postelection coalition majority = Austria, Belgium, Italy; preelection coalition majority = Germany, Netherlands; single-party majority = Australia, Canada, Greece, Japan, New Zealand, Spain, United Kingdom. Because of debatable majority status, Finland, France and the United States are not included here. (See text note 6.) For individual country scores, see table 5.3 below.

[2]The opposition ratings are averages from a survey of experts in each country, initiated in February 1989; because of too few respondents, results were not reported for Switzerland (Laver and Hunt 1993).

at the top as in the pure single-party governments at the bottom. The relation is attractively linear, creating a series of stepping stones. As we move up the five stages of majority status, the Laver-Hunt scores decline from 5.8 to 5.2 to 4.7 to 3.6 to 2.9. The simple correlation between the two variables is about −.65. This is stronger evidence than that provided by voter behavior of the relation between government status and clarity of responsibility.

GOVERNMENT MAJORITY STATUS IN TWENTY DEMOCRACIES

Table 3.3 shows the status of the incumbent government at the time of the election in more than 150 elections in twenty modern democracies in the past twenty-five years. The number of elections is shown in parentheses at the far right. Each succeeding column shows the government status conditions, from minority governments, which promote the least clarity of responsibility, to single-party majority governments, which promote the greatest clarity of responsibility.

Reading across the bottom of table 3.3, we can see the frequency of each type of condition across the full set of elections. In more than a quarter of the

Table 3.3. Majority Status of Incumbent Governments in 156 Elections, 1969–94

Country[1]	Majority Status of Incumbent Government					
	Pure Minority (20)	Supported Minority (40)	Postelection Coalition Majority (60)	Preelection Coalition Majority (80)	Single-Party Majority (100)	Average Majority Status Score
Australia	0	0	0	5	6	91 (11)
Austria	1	0	3	0	4	75 (8)
Belgium	0	0	9	0	0	60 (9)
Canada	2	0	0	0	5	77 (7)
Denmark	8	1	1	1	0	31 (11)
Finland	0	2	5*	0	0	54 (7)
France	1	1	2	3	1	65 (8)
Germany	0	0	2	5	0	74 (7)
Greece	0	0	2	0	5	89 (7)
Ireland	2	1	2	1	2	60 (8)
Italy	1	1	6	0	0	53 (8)
Japan	0	2	0	0	6	85 (8)
Netherlands	0	0	6	2	0	65 (8)
New Zealand	0	0	0	0	8	100 (8)
Norway	5	0	1	1	0	34 (7)
Spain	1	1	0	0	3	72 (5)
Sweden	4	5	0	0	1	38 (10)
Switzerland	0	0	0	6	0	80 (6)
United Kingdom	1	1	0	0	5	80 (7)
United States	0	0	5**	0	1	67 (6)
Totals	26	15	44	24	47	67(156)
Percentage	17	10	28	15	30	100

*Some of these governments held legislative majorities but fell short of the two thirds required to pass legistlation requiring tax increases, hence their majority status is more doubtful.
**This category refers to the U.S. "divided government" situation in which one party controls Congress, the other the presidency.

[1]Elections in 1967 and 1968 in France, Italy, and Sweden are included. The numbers in parentheses on the far right are the numbers of elections in each country. All elections are legislative. The number under each majority status category is the clarity of responsibility score assigned to that category (from 20 to 100).

elections the voters were confronted with a minority incumbent government of either pure minority or supported types. In about another quarter of the elections the voters faced a multiparty majority not built on preelection coalitions. In 15 percent of the elections the incumbent government was a coalition elected as a precommitted team. In only 30 percent of the elections were voters able to evaluate a single-party majority government.

The conditions of the government at the time of election varied greatly in the democracies. The penultimate right column shows the average country experiences. In order to give plausible and easily interpretable meaning to the averages, the different government status conditions are assigned the values of 20, 40, 60, 80, and 100 for the five categories. The bottom value is 20 rather than zero to remind us that even the most hapless minority government has some policy control, through executive actions and through a blocking role, and carries some distinctive responsibility for policy outcomes. (Recall that the average influence of opposition parties facing pure minority governments was only 5.8 on Laver and Hunt's 1–9 scale.) The average scores on my 20–100 scale range from 31 in Denmark, where voters were usually faced with minority governments throughout this quarter century, to 100 in New Zealand, which was the only country that always had single-party majorities. (New Zealand's string came to an end in 1996, under new election rules.)

The presidential systems, especially that of the United States, do not fall as easily into this scale of comparison as the parliamentary systems. By definition, the chief executive in a presidential system has a separate base of election and distinctive political resources that do not depend on control of the legislature. An American president whose party is in a minority in the Congress has nonetheless the power to veto legislation, which can be overridden only by a two-thirds majority of both legislative chambers. The president has been elected (indirectly) by the people, not by the legislature, and can be forced from office by the legislature only under the most unusual circumstances (as in the case of Richard Nixon in 1974). The cabinet, too, once confirmed, is relatively unremovable. In all these ways, the American "minority" president has far more power and hence far more clearly observable responsibility than a minority government in a parliamentary system. Yet the president remains unable to pass new legislation without negotiating with leaders of the opposition political party in the legislature.

In general, the situation in which one party controls the presidency and the other controls the Congress seems most comparable to the parliamentary situation of a majority coalition government.[7] There is substantial governmental responsibility, more than in a pure parliamentary minority situation. The fact that voters can vote for the legislative and executive offices separately allows them to express their assessments of responsibility separately. They can hold the president more responsible for foreign policy, less responsible for the domestic economy, for example. But the situation is also more blurred than in single-party government because the voters must decide whether the president or Congress is more responsible for good and bad outcomes that involve their interdependent powers.

American election campaigns under conditions of divided government (typified by those of 1948 and 1996) often involve just this dispute over responsibility. In the election campaign of 1996 the Democratic president and the Republican congressional majority blamed each other for the bargaining deadlock that had shut down the federal government twice in the winter of 1995/96, as well as for other policy failures. When the president gains control of one or both legislative houses, of course, his power and responsibility increase. The American case is treated in that fashion in table 3.3. (Because they vote separately for the chief executive and the legislature, voters may distinguish their ability to assess responsibility in the two types of elections.)

In some countries — for example, Belgium, Switzerland, and New Zealand — the voters faced similar conditions of government majority status in most elections and, hence, clarity of responsibility. But in other countries the conditions varied sharply from election to election (see table 3.3). Voters in Ireland, for example, were sometimes confronted with weak minority governments and sometimes with preelection or single-party majorities and even with a postelection coalition. Voters in Canada tended to face either of the extremes: minority governments or single-party majorities. Their circumstances vary widely from election to election. Eventually, we shall need to explain the differences in variability across countries as well as differences in average government status.

Diffusing Government Responsibility: Intraparty Divisions, New Governments, Inclusive Policy-Making Rules

The majority status of the incumbent government is the critical point from which to begin assessing clarity of responsibility. It is a condition that is meaningful in policy making, frequently emphasized in election campaigns, and easily identifiable by voters. As shown in table 3.1, it was strongly negatively related to expert assessments of the influence of the legislative opposition. There are further conditions, however, that serve to intensify or diffuse clarity of responsibility.

Table 3.4 shows various conditions that could modify the basic clarity of responsibility offered by the government's majority status. This set of factors is obviously not exhaustive. For example, it may well be that developments in

Table 3.4. Additional Conditions Diffusing Government Responsibility

Country	Government Party Lacked Cohesion	Months Government in Office[1]	Federal System	Bicameral Opposition	Committee Influence[2]
			Constitutional Arrangements		
Australia	No	29	Yes	Frequently	No
Austria	No	34	Yes	No	Yes
Belgium	No*	25	Some	No	Yes
Canada	No	29	Yes	No	Some
Denmark	No	23	No	No	Yes
Finland	No	22	No	No	Some
France	No	25	No	No	No
Germany	No	32	Yes	Sometimes	Yes
Greece	No*	27	No	No	No
Ireland	No	28	No	No	No
Italy	Yes	14	No	No	Some
Japan	Yes	32	No	No	Some
Netherlands	No	29	No	No	Yes
New Zealand	No	36	No	No	No
Norway	No	31	No	No	Yes
Spain	No*	29	No	No	Yes
Sweden	No	29	No	No	Yes
Switzerland	Yes	36	Yes	No	Yes
United Kingdom	No	28	No	No	No
United States	Yes	34	Yes	Sometimes	Some

The table header also carries the overall span: **Conditions Diffusing Government Responsibility**.

*Belgium parties experienced divisions on the language issue in the late 1960s and 1970s, eventually leading all the major parties to split. Disputes in the Greek New Democracy Party precipitated an early election in 1993. In Spain the UDC disintegrated into contending factions between 1979 and 1982 and did not contest the 1982 election as a united party.

[1]Months in office is figured from the last election or from the time the government was formed, whichever is less, to a maximum of thirty-six months.
[2]Opposition parties share legislative committee chairmanships and committees have significant influence (see chap. 2).

the European Union after 1992 will make devolution of policy responsibility to international organizations an important factor in diffusing clarity of responsibility. Further attention to semiautonomous government agencies or to the judicial system may also be appropriate. The general problem is, of course, to identify these various factors as well as to weight their importance.

Column one shows a critical feature already alluded to: cohesion of the incumbent parties in the government. I suggested that multiparty coalition governments diffuse responsibility to some degree because of potential interparty differences. When single parties are themselves internally divided and lose control of policy because of those divisions, voters have trouble knowing how to apportion credit or blame. *Party* is usually the unifying cue on the ballot. If the party does not act as a reasonably coherent unit in policy making, the voters' task in enforcing accountability is harder.

Comparable statistics on the voting cohesion within the main governmental parties are scarce. For some countries — Australia, Denmark, Finland, France, Germany, New Zealand, Sweden, and Britain — I have been able to obtain data on the Rice cohesion index of party voting in the legislatures.[8] These data provide evidence of very cohesive party voting, representatives of the same party voting together 95 percent of the time or more in divided votes. In other cases I have had to rely on impressionistic reports, either because data are not recorded on most votes (as in Italy) or because I have not yet discovered it. In most parliamentary systems, representatives of the same party vote together.

The exceptions that appear in the literature seem to be Italy, Japan, the United States, and Switzerland. In each of these countries, especially in the first three, the candidates often compete somewhat independently of the party as a whole. The major political parties in Japan and Italy are well known for their internal factions. These have often blocked the policies of government majorities. In Italy such lack of cohesion within the Christian Democrats is believed to have led to the overthrow of governments (voting was secret on votes of confidence through most of this period, so it is hard to be sure). Lack of party cohesion is also a primary factor in the failure of Japanese governments to pass more than 76 percent of the legislation they introduced in 1978–82, despite having single-party majority governments throughout that period (*Parliaments of the World* 1986, 915). In the United States the tendency of geographic constituency factors to diffuse party coherence is well documented. Observers of Swiss politics note the failure of representatives of party groups to vote consistently with party affiliation (Lanfranchi and Leuthi 1998). The table also notes lack of cohesion by the governing parties at specific time points or on specific issues in Belgium in the early 1970s, Spain in 1979–82, and Greece in 1993. In the absence of other information, I have assumed cohesive party voting in the other countries in table 3.4.

A second plausible condition for responsibility is the length of time a government has been in office when the voters have the chance to vote for or against it. All else being equal, it would seem to be easier to assess responsibility in a durable, long-lived government than in a brief, new government. One reason is that in the complex governments of modern democracies it takes time for any set of new leaders to gain real control of the bureaucratic machinery and to pass legislation on complex issues. It takes even longer for the effects of their policies to become apparent. Because of the presence of its majority governments and the absence of other diffusing conditions, Britain is a good example of the time factor. After a decade of Conservative control it seems clear that it took at least two or three years for the Thatcher government to get her policy "revolution" under way. On the other hand, if a minority government remains in office for several years voters may perceive that whatever its formal status, it has found a reliable (even if shifting) support base and may not unreasonably attribute greater responsibility to it.

Column two in table 3.4 shows the average number of months the incumbent government had been in office at the time of the election — its durability. The maximum time allowed between elections varies substantially from country to country. To make the comparison more meaningful, I have cut the maximum time back to thirty-six months — the time between elections in New Zealand and Sweden — in all cases. (Only the congressional elections in the United States have a fixed time interval of less than thirty-six months.) No matter how long a government had actually served, its contribution to the average was only thirty-six months.

Across all the democracies, the median durability of governments had been about twenty-nine months, over three-quarters of the possible maximum. The shorter durations are caused either by new elections being called well before the maximum allowed time or by the breakdown of the first government formed after the election and formation of a new one(s). In some countries, especially in Italy, the average duration was much shorter, and many countries had at least one relatively new government at election time. While these effects are partially captured in the absence of majority status of the incumbent government, there are variations created by other party system factors as well, such as levels of extremist representation in the legislature (Powell 1986). Constitutional arrangements also have a role to play, as noted in chapter 2. Italy stands out here, however, with its average government having been in office only fourteen months when the election was held.

Clarity of responsibility may be diffused also by constitutional arrangements that provide other bases for political power than simple majority control of the executive and legislature. When the opposition political parties can influence policy substantially because of such alternative resources, power and hence responsibility are diffused. Columns 3–5 of table 3.4 draw attention to three elements of the decision rule (the rule about how to make decisions) in the national political system.

First, some constitutions explicitly give an important role in policy making to regional (state) governments. In these *federal systems* the national government's policies may be blocked in some policy areas if opposition parties (or dissident factions of the governing party) gain control of regional governments in which many voters reside. In West Germany, for example, the educational programs of the majority Social Democratic Party/Free Democratic Party (SPD/FDP) coalition in the 1970s were fully implemented only in the Land governments that they controlled and largely ignored in parts of the country where the Land government was controlled by the opposition Christian Democrats (CDU/CSU). Among the countries considered here, Australia, Austria, Canada, Germany, Switzerland, and the United States have formally federal systems, and Belgium has introduced some federal elements since the mid-1970s. Lijphart (1984, 178) draws attention to a particularly significant share in governmental tax receipts collected by local and regional governments in the United States, Germany, Canada, and Switzerland. The considerable policy making outside the federal level in these systems could diffuse responsibility of the federal government, at least in some policy areas. Yet it is not clear whether voters would be affected by this diffusion when they vote in the national elections. Thus, while federal arrangements can be important, their relation to the issues of concern here remains somewhat ambiguous.

Often closely linked to federal arrangements, the national constitution may also provide a second house in the national legislature, such as the Senate in the United States and Australia and the Bundesrat in West Germany. Some second chambers in the national legislature — the House of Lords in Britain and the Senate in Canada and France, for example — are afforded powers too weak to make them a major force in blocking government policies. In other countries, as in Belgium, the Netherlands, and Italy, the second chamber is elected on a similar basis as the first and is almost always controlled by the same party or coalition. But in Australia, Germany, Switzerland, and the United States the second chamber has both real powers and a distinctive basis of election, which make it a potential source of blurring of political responsibility. (Lijphart 1984 calls this property "strong bicameralism"; see chapter 6, especially p. 99.)

In fact, as indicated in column 4, this bicameral opposition power was noticeably present during specific governing periods in Australia, Germany, and the United States. In Australia the Labor Party governments of the early 1970s and mid-1980s had to contend with lack of control of the Senate, whose consent was needed to pass the national budget. In West Germany from 1972 to

1982 the incumbent SPD/FDP coalition commanded a majority in the lower house, the Bundestag. But for most of that period the upper house, the Bundesrat, had a majority of representatives of states (Lander) with CDU governments. A number of government policies, especially in the area of education, were blocked by the CDU-controlled Bundesrat. In the late 1980s and 1990s the reverse situation prevailed, with CDU/CSU governments blocked in some policy areas by an SPD-controlled upper house. In the United States in 1980–82 (as in 1952–54) the Republicans controlled both the presidency and the Senate but still faced a Democratic Party–controlled House of Representatives.

Finally, as discussed in chapter 2, one of the most acute observers of minority and majority politics (Strom 1984, 1990) has emphasized the varying importance of the systems of legislative committees in democracies. In some countries, such as Ireland and France, there are relatively few committees in the legislature. In these and some other countries, committees do not correspond closely to bureaucratic departments, making it more problematic to oversee the formation and implementation of the government's policies. In addition, in many of these countries the chairmanships of all committees are controlled only by the parties in the government. On the other hand, in systems such as those of Norway and Germany rule making involves scrutiny of legislation by many committees, specialized to fit with the structure of the governing bureaucracy, and whose chairmanships are distributed proportionally to all political parties. This last point would seem to be especially critical because in combination with the others it explicitly offers the opposition parties some bases of power.

In systems of the first type, the committees typically do little more than rubber stamp policies initiated by the government (or negotiated between a minority government and opposition party leaders). In the second type, the committees are a major area of debate and negotiation over policy, with government legislation emerging (if at all) in altered form and the committees themselves even serving as major policy initiators. (See the discussion in chapter 2 above and the essays in Doering 1995.)

For my purposes here, the point is that whatever the virtues of strong committee systems for policy analysis and for representation of diverse citizen interests (see chapter 5 below), their role can blur responsibility for policy making. Even the most attentive observers may be hard put to say which party should bear the major responsibility for the final shape of a particular piece of legislation. In Germany, for example, the government succeeds in getting about 85 percent of its initiated legislation passed by the Bundestag,[9] but it is very often amended and altered in many ways to reflect a variety of specialized interests.[10] The Bundestag committee system as well as its relation with the

Bundesrat plays an important role in such alteration, which in effect diffuses political power.

Column 5 in table 3.4 builds on table 2.2 to indicate countries in which the committee system can provide a base of resources for the opposition parties, even when facing a majority government. The committee systems that provide a strong resource for the opposition are those with proportional sharing of chairmanships with the opposition, plus more than ten committees and committee specialization corresponding with government departments. Committee systems with either strong committees or sharing of chairs with the opposition, but not both, are rated as having some influence. Under these conditions we would expect legislative power even of majority governments to be somewhat diffused.

As in the case of government status, there is little previous work or theory to help identify the importance, or even validity, of these plausible candidates for diffusing clarity of government responsibility. However, table 2.2 and the associated text drew on the new findings in Doering et al. to consider some additional legislative rules, and some expert assessment of party–committee member relations that help support the assessments. Whitten and I also found that government vote losses seemed to be fewer where government party cohesion was lower, strong committee chairs were shared with the opposition, and there was politically significant bicameral opposition. All these relations except bicameral opposition were statistically significant at at least .05 level in regression analysis, even taking account of government majority status (Powell and Whitten 1993). We also tried to include these considerations collectively in our analysis of the effect of economic voting.

Similarly, despite the limited time frame, simple analysis of the Laver-Hunt "influence of the opposition" variable suggests that opposition influence is greater where governments are less durable, government cohesion is less, and strong committee chairs are shared with the opposition (bivariate correlations in the .33 to .41 range). The effects of all these variables are much weaker than government status and short of statistical significance, but in the expected direction. Association with bicameral opposition and, especially, federalism are much weaker (not surprisingly, as the question was asked about influence in the national legislature). These results further enhance the face validity of these factors as shaping clarity of responsibility.

Clarity of Responsibility: Provisional Overview

Some evidence indicates that all of the features discussed except federalism are associated with lower levels of clarity of government responsibility.

However, a number of them are associated with each other. Government status and the durability of governments, for example, go hand in hand, as minority governments are generally less durable than majority ones. The consistency of constitutional design, as noted in chapter 2, tends to put election laws enhancing single-party government majorities together with committee rules allowing little role for the opposition. Thus if we add the considerations in table 3.4 to the status of the government we shall certainly be "double counting" some features.

In principle, what is needed here is regression analysis to consider the alternative factors simultaneously. We can then assess their significance and relative weight more confidently. Unfortunately, neither of the possible dependent variables in such statistical analysis — government vote losses and reputed opposition influence — is without problems. The voting analyses are shaped by the party context and alternatives available to the voter, as well as by voter perceptions of how well the government has been doing. The opposition influence analysis is based on a single survey of experts in 1989. Both approaches do seem to agree on the significance of the distinction between majority and minority government and on the importance of cohesion of the governing parties. These factors show up clearly as significant in both types of regression analysis. On the other hand, the relations with federalism are weak or nonexistent. Bicameral opposition, as best we can see, is important when it occurs but is pretty rare across the set of democracies (although common in a few countries).

The regressions are less consistent in the treatment of different types of party coalitions and coalitions versus single-party governments. These variables show up very powerfully in the influence analysis (as we might expect from table 3.2), less consistently in the voting analysis. Recent work on voting (Stevenson 1997) suggests that voters facing coalition governments may focus more on the party of the prime minister than on the other parties, which blurs the distinctions considered here. The committee system variable is significant in the voting regressions but varies with the particular specification and classifications in the influence analysis.[11]

Given these results, my judgment is that our best overview of clarity of responsibility will be strongly based on the government majority status at the time of the election, taking further account of the cohesion of the government party. Roughly speaking, lack of cohesion of the governing parties is worth about 30 points, equal to 1½ government status categories, on the 0–100 scale to which I transformed the government status variable.[12] Effects of the committee system may have some independent effect but are certainly weaker than these. We would not, however, wish to be very confident about either the

Table 3.5. Clarity of Responsibility: A Preliminary Overview

Country	Average Majority Status of Incumbent Government	Diffusion of Responsibility Due to Lack of Government Party Cohesion	Modified Average Clarity of Responsibility
New Zealand	100	None (some post-1993)	100
Australia	91	No (some bicameral)	91
Greece	89	1993 only	84
United Kingdom	80	None	80*
Canada	77	None	77*
Austria	75	None	75
Germany	74	No (some bicameral)	74
Spain	72	1979–82 only	68*
France	65	None	65
Netherlands	65	None	65
Ireland	60	None	60*
Japan	85	Substantial (−30)	55
Finland	54	None	54
Belgium	60	Early 1970s only	53
Switzerland	80	Substantial (−30)	50
Sweden	38	None	38
United States	67	Substantial (−30)	37
Norway	34	None	34
Denmark	31	None	31*
Italy	53	Substantial (−30)	23

*In these countries there were often sharp differences in government majority status from election to election. (Standard deviation over the cross-national average of 30.)

relative importance or the causal relation between the intermediate coalition types versus the committee system. Table 3.5, then, shows an overview of average clarity of responsibility that is based on the government status from table 3.3, modified only by the government party cohesion variable.

At the top of the table, in such countries as New Zealand, Australia, Greece, and Britain, the voters usually had an excellent opportunity to rely on political accountability as a way of controlling policymakers. These are in fact countries with majority design constitutional arrangements in both election rules and policy-making rules. Canada ranks nearly as high, but more frequent minority governments have blurred its accountability.

The countries in the middle of the table, from Austria through Ireland, have mixed conditions from the point of view of clarity of responsibility. They have generally good party cohesion. Most of them frequently have majority governments, but coalitions rather than single parties. In the Irish case, as already noted, we find virtually every combination of government type.

At the bottom of the table are most of the Scandinavian countries with proportional designs producing frequent minority governments and many opportunities for the opposition, despite high party cohesion. We also see the countries such as Japan, Switzerland, and the United States, where lack of governing party cohesion, sometimes together with other factors, blurs the clarity of responsibility. Italy appears at the very bottom of the table, with both lack of governing party cohesion and infrequent majority government. Frequent turnover of governments both reflects these conditions and further obscures clarity of responsibility.

Indeed, in Italy, continuing blurred clarity of responsibility seems seriously to have weakened political accountability as an instrument for voters to use in shaping public policy. Such a country may remain a democracy, but the conditions for using elections to discipline unpopular policymakers are seldom available. Events in the mid-1990s in Italy showed that it was virtually necessary to repudiate the entire political system to bring about turnover in policymakers — and at least in the first instance the courts played a larger role than voter sanctions.

Accountability: Overview

We shall be exploring a number of these issues from the forward-looking majoritarian view in the next chapter. At the moment it is sufficient to conclude with three observations:

1. There is good evidence that the outcomes of elections do make a difference. Incumbent governments that lose a substantial percentage of votes are more likely to be replaced than those who lose less or actually gain votes. The probability of replacement increases especially sharply in the majoritarian countries at the point where incumbents start losing votes.
2. Various factors contribute to obscure clarity of responsibility in our twenty democracies. These factors include minority governments, coalition governments, intraparty divisions, and various constitutional rules offering influence to opposition parties. Only a fairly small number of elections offer voters undiminished governmental responsibility for policy according to our measures (which seem fairly well validated by expert assessments

and vote loss patterns). Only five countries had average scores over 75 on our 100-point scale. In about half of the democracies the average clarity of responsibility score was over 60, suggesting at least some relative degrees of clarity of responsibility for the voters. In the other countries citizens have less opportunity for retrospective majority control.

3. The constitutional designs discussed in chapter 2 generally seemed to deliver the expected empirical consequences. Changes of government were of the all-or-nothing" sort in the six countries we identified as having relatively majoritarian constitutional designs; partial changes were common in the proportional design systems. Five of the six majoritarian design countries were the top five in our clarity of responsibility overview (see table 3.5); multiparty France was ninth with a score of 65. At the other extreme, of the ten countries with predominately proportional designs, only three made the top ten, and four were in the bottom five. (See also figure 4.1, which shows the average accountability by constitutional design type.) I shall explore the complexities of responsiveness in government replacement/formation in chapter 6. The initial evidence suggests substantial consistency with the expectations from the majoritarian vision in the systems with majoritarian constitutional designs, an alternative (but not necessarily undemocratic) pattern in the proportional design systems.

4

Conditions for Mandates:
Identifiability and Majority

The idea of party mandates seems to have appeared at the end of the nineteenth century as the first mass political parties, usually Socialist parties, were mobilizing new electorates in Western Europe.[1] The organizers of these new parties offered radical proposals for transforming the government and politics of their societies. They promised that if the voters would bring them to office, they would not only provide more equitable and sympathetic management of government, but use the power of government for change. They argued, moreover, that, having made policy commitments to the electorate, they were both authorized and obligated to carry out those policies once in office. This formulation translated the older concept of majoritarian or populist democracy into terms that took explicit advantage of the enfranchisement of mass electorates and the emergence of mass political parties.[2]

The idea of mandates for policy has been appealing to many citizens, politicians, and democratic theorists. To citizens it offers the prospect of influencing policy in advance, of setting at least the general directions of future government action. Such prospective shaping of policy is a powerful addition to accountability after the fact. To politicians it offers a justification for determined action in carrying out election promises they desire. To democratic theorists it has seemed to establish a clear connection between citizens' desires and government policies. The mandate idea has often seemed particularly appealing to

American political scientists who have been frustrated by the weaknesses of their political parties and the general diffusion of power in their government.[3]

On the other hand, the concept of policy mandates has also been subjected to harsh criticism by theorists (and losing politicians and citizens) for its insensitivity to the complex multiplicity of political issues and political majorities. It is obviously troubling to discover instances in which a party has used its mandate, based on aggregate voter support and a set of electoral pledges (probably unread by many voters and including elements of varying popularity), to put into effect some specific policies that are not in fact favored by most voters. The renationalization of the steel industry by the British Labour Party in 1966 is a frequently cited example.[4]

The party mandate, like accountability, is a virtue and a linkage strongly associated with the majoritarian vision of citizen control. Where the conditions are appropriate, its appeal is undeniable. A clear majority of voters chooses the package of policies they desire. Any other outcome blocks the will of the majority, allowing a minority to prevail. Democratic theory requires majorities to prevail over minorities. Mandates offer decisive evidence of democracy in action. For majoritarian theorists, mandates add a second valuable linkage between citizens and policies. Citizen control need not be limited merely to an occasional rapping of the knuckles of transgressing policymakers; through mandates, elections can be linked to the future.

Many of the criticisms, too, are familiar ones that we associate with a more proportional vision of democracy (see chapters 1 and 2). On one hand, we find the problem of multiple majorities on multiple issues. Mandate elections assume a single decisive choice. But if multiple dimensions are involved, then do we not need a more complex pattern of bargaining and negotiation to build new majorities as issues are addressed in policy making? On the other hand, we find the familiar problem of the views of the minority. Should they not be taken somehow into account, although not allowed to control, in the course of policy making? Should there not be an opportunity for minority representatives to present their arguments and urge intensity of belief against the blind counting of numbers?[5] I shall return to these arguments in juxtaposing the two visions in later chapters, especially chapter 6 (responsiveness) and chapters 8 and 9 (representation). But let us first take the mandate linkage proposed by majoritarianism on its own terms. In this chapter I identify and measure its conditions, summarize their presence in the elections in our study, and consider the role of the constitutional designs in creating them.

I begin, as usual, with the voter. The mandate approach assumes that the voter will be looking forward and that he or she will be considering possible national governments as the target of voting choice (recall fig. 1.1). The focus on national governments committed to policy directions throughout their postelection tenure in office reminds us of the considerations of coherent policy making that we examined in thinking about national government accountability. The voter needs to be able to anticipate either a single-party majority government or a majority party coalition announced before the election, if she or he is to be able to use the vote to determine postelection policies for a national government.

In terms of the achievement of conditions for control through mandates, then, we may think of two stages. First, the voter needs to be able to identify the prospective future governors and have some idea of what they will do if elected. This condition is necessary if the voters are to make good prospective choices. Second, the outcome of the election should bring into office a coherent government committed to policies that correspond to the voters' anticipations and capable of carrying them out. A mandate process requires, then, identifiable prospective governments at the time of the election and a responsively formed working majority after the election.[6]

Identifiability of Future Governments

IDENTIFYING FUTURE GOVERNMENTS IN MULTIPARTY SYSTEMS

If two and only two parties compete in the national elections, it is easy for everyone to identify the future government. Most democracies do not offer their voters a straight two-party choice. Among the democracies studied here, only in the United States did the two largest parties consistently win more than 90 percent of the vote in legislative elections. In the other nineteen democracies, it was very unusual for a single party to win a majority of the votes. In fact, it occurred in only 5 of the 150 elections (Austria in 3 elections in the 1970s, Sweden in 1968, and Ireland in 1977). The prospects for identifiable future governments usually rested on one of three other possibilities.

First, the working of the electoral laws in converting votes to legislative seats may consistently create legislative majorities by overrepresenting the large parties at the expense of small ones. This distortion may be well known to the voters, who expect that the election will usually result in a majority government of one of the large parties. Britain and New Zealand in the 1980s and early 1990s offer good examples. In each country the two larger parties together received less than 80 percent of the vote, but over 95 percent of the seats in the legislature. One of them always had a governing majority. The election rules in Australia, Canada, Greece, Japan, and Spain also frequently "manufactured" single-party governing majorities in this fashion.[7]

Second, alternative future governments may be offered to the voters by explicit preelection coalitions between the political parties.[8] Australian voters faced a choice between the Liberal/National-Country Party coalition and the Labour Party alternative in each election in this era. In every election from 1976 through 1994 German voters were presented with an announced preelection coalition agreement between the small FDP and one of the two larger parties. The voters have known that if the FDP and its partner won a legislative majority, they would form a government. Such was in fact the outcome of each election. In 1981 voters in France were offered a choice between a Socialist-Communist coalition and a Gaullist-UDF (Union for French Democracy) coalition. Indeed, on the second round of voting (in the many districts where no candidate won a majority) the voters were offered only one representative of each coalition. Some version of this choice, with varying strengths of connection between the coalition partners, has been offered in most French elections since 1967. The nature of preelection coalition agreements varies across countries and elections. In many cases the parties present the voters with joint statements of their policy intentions as well as their intention of governing together.[9] In some elections in France and elsewhere, there were asymmetric situations, in which one side of the spectrum explicitly offered a coalition and the other featured multiple competing parties.

Yet a third possibility is that a much less certain, but still important, degree of identifiability may emerge when strong expectations develop about postelection coalition governments and the way that elections will influence them. In some of the multiparty countries there was no explicit agreement, but the relations between the parties led to strong expectations that some parties would govern together and that the voting outcomes would influence this outcome in well-known ways. In Sweden in 1976, for example, the three conservative parties made it fairly clear that if they won a collective legislative majority they would govern together in a coalition and replace the long-dominant Social Democrats in power.[10] Such implicit preelection coalitions seem to have been fairly common in Austria, Denmark, the Netherlands, Norway, and Sweden, although they did not appear in every election, and when they did appear they did not always succeed in winning electoral majorities.

In contrast to voters in the countries with two-party systems, distorting election laws, or preelection coalitions (implicit or explicit), the voters in some democracies have little explicit information on how the election outcome will shape the government to be formed after the election. In Finland and Italy (until 1994) the voters were offered a wide range of parties, and they had good reason to expect that at least seven or eight of them would win legislative representation. No preelection coalitions were announced, although some parties occasionally called for such alliances. At most, certain postelection combinations were denied (as in Italy in 1979 when the Christian Democrats (DC) said during the election campaign that they would not bring the Communists into the government). Neither did the parties present joint promises about what they would do if elected together. In Belgium, only one election (1985) featured a preelection coalition, when the governing parties announced they would continue together if their majority was sustained.

The elections in these countries were typically followed by substantial and relatively unpredictable periods of bargaining between the parties to form a coalition government. The voters' support for a party was not irrelevant to its chances of becoming part of the government. A party denied legislative representation could not participate. The largest party was often given first chance at attempting to form a government.[11] But there was no strong link between gains of a package of parties and its ability to form a commanding parliamentary majority. It may be true that if a party had won a majority it would have taken office alone, but this outcome seemed very unlikely to all observers. In these countries most of the time, and in Austria, Denmark, Greece, Ireland, and the Netherlands in several elections, we would characterize the preelection identifiability of future governments as low or nonexistent from the point of view of needs of the party mandate model.

IDENTIFIABILITY IN TWENTY DEMOCRACIES

Table 4.1 presents my coding of the identifiability of future governments at the time of the election in our twenty democracies in the past twenty-five years. The table divides the countries and elections in two ways. First, from the top down, it divides the countries into three large groupings and several subgroupings by the levels of identifiability of the future governments at the time of the election. Second, the two columns on the right show the countries, with the number of elections in parentheses. The first country column shows countries in which most elections fell into that identifiability category. If a country appears in that column and only there, which is the case for thirteen of our twenty countries, then its citizens usually faced a similar level of government identifiability from election to election. The second column shows countries with less than the majority, but at least two, elections in the category. Seven countries show up somewhere in this column; their citizens faced different levels of identifiability in different elections. Two countries (Austria and Ireland) show up only in country column 2 — their electoral conditions varied so much in different elections that we cannot characterize a predominant pattern.

Reading from the top of table 4.1, we first find Belgium, Finland, and Italy, where many parties competed and won seats in the elections with almost no announced preelection coalitions. Election results were followed by bargaining between most of the parties. The party gains and losses had only indirect

Table 4.1. Identifiability of Prospective Governments Before the Election

Usual Level of Identifiability Before Elections		Basis of Prospective Governments	Countries	
			Most Elections[1]	Some Elections
Low	(23%)	Negotiations between parties after the election	Belgium (8) Finland (7) Italy (7)	Austria (3) Denmark (2) Greece (2) Ireland (4) Netherlands (2)
	(4%)	Long-range agreement apparently independent of elections	Switzerland (6)	—
Moderate	(15%)	Implicit/asymmetric preelection coalitions	Japan (7) — —	Austria (2) Denmark (3) Ireland (2) Netherlands (4) Norway (3) Sweden (4)
High	(4%)	Two parties only	United States (6)	—
	(26%)	Single-party majority expected in legislature	Canada (7) Greece (5) New Zealand (8) Spain (5) United Kingdom (7)	Austria (3)
	(28%)	Explicit preelection coalition or single-party majority expected in legislature	Australia (11) Denmark (6) France (8) Germany (7) Sweden (6)	Ireland (2) Netherlands (2) Norway (3)
Total	(100%)			
Cases	(156 elections)		(111)	(41)

[1]Countries with single election in another category: Low ID: Norway 1993; Moderate: Belgium 1985; High: Italy 1994, Japan 1993.

impact, at best, on the formation of governments. Sometimes the connections between party gains/losses and their exclusion/inclusion in governments seemed quite perverse.[12] As shown in the far right column, government formation in five other countries also was marked, at least occasionally, by postelection bargaining.

Switzerland is unique among these democracies, but in my opinion belongs in the top group. A large four-party coalition of Catholic Conservatives, Radical Democrats, Social Democrats, and Farmers controlled over 80 percent of the parliamentary seats and faced only a very weak and fragmented opposition. The coalition itself did not present negotiated preelection policy proposals; neither did it operate as a disciplined policy-making group in either legislature or executive (Lanfranchi and Leuthi 1999). Shifts in voting support did not alter the composition of the government, whose members were elected individually by the legislature. The voters might have known the likely postelection government, but they also knew that the voting outcomes were unlikely to affect it. Belgium, Finland, Italy, and Switzerland usually depart very far from the conditions needed for citizens to use choice of prospective governments to influence policy. Occasionally, Austria, Denmark, Greece, Ireland, and the Netherlands similarly failed to approximate mandate conditions.

At the bottom of the table we see the elections in which voters could quite reasonably be expected to know the consequences of their votes for the formation of party governments. In the countries in the left column, they could be certain of this most of the time. In the United States, of course, one party always gained a majority in presidential and in congressional elections (although often those two key policy-making sites were divided between the parties). In Canada, Greece, New Zealand, Spain, and the United Kingdom the contests were seen as largely two-party struggles for future government control, and elections frequently returned single-party majority governments; the election rules had a lot to do with this majoritarian perception (see below). In all elections in Australia and Germany (from 1972 through 1994) and in most elections in France and Sweden, the voters were offered packages of party alternatives with good reason to expect the winning package to form a government. These ten systems offered their voters good prospects for an authorization of party mandates. Moreover, a substantial number of elections in Austria, Ireland, the Netherlands, and Norway also offered the voters reasonably good identifiability of a future government by a single party or negotiated party coalition. Over 70 percent of all the elections presented reasonably clear mandate potential.

The pre-1993 Japanese situation also fits some aspects of the requirements of the party mandate model and helps reveal its nature. The voters knew what the future government was likely to be, could locate the LDP's general policy stance, and could vote for or against that future government. But the absence of a credible alternative government, owing to the divided opposition and lack of support for the hard-line Socialists that would apparently be the main alternative governing party, seems to weaken the model substantially. For this reason I considered Japan to have only moderate preelection identifiability for the purposes of voter control through mandates. The presence of varied factions within the LDP also weakens it, a point to which I shall return shortly.

In other countries changing relations between potential coalition partners were critical for identifiability of future governments. In Ireland, the Fianna Fail party formed one continuing government possibility, but the two main opposition parties (Fine Gael and Labour) sometimes were able to offer the voters a preelection package and sometimes were in serious conflict. Similarly, in Sweden and Denmark the left was usually dominated by a large Social Democratic party that offered a prospective government, but the right had to build coalitions among three or four parties to create a credible alternative. Sometimes this happened (Denmark 1979, 1981, 1984; Sweden, 1973); sometimes it did not happen (Denmark 1973, 1975; Sweden 1970); sometimes it happened to a limited degree (Sweden 1976–82).

The middle of table 4.1 lists these complex, mixed, partial identifiability electoral situations. They usually involved implicit coalition alignments without formal electoral, policy, or governing pacts. Sometimes there were explicit agreements on one side of the spectrum and not on the other. Most commonly these situations pitted left parties versus right parties with varying kinds of agreements within the ideological groups. Sometimes this lack of agreement stemmed from the presence of an extreme left or right party, which might support the more ideologically proximate moderate party(s) against a common foe but would not join, or would not be allowed to join, in a coalition government.

Despite the complexities that perturb easy categorization, it is difficult to understand the campaigns and, especially, the subsequent government formation in the elections in the middle category without paying attention to the strong expectations about potential governing coalitions. And, very loosely, one could argue that these expectations made it much easier for citizens in this grouping than for those in the top grouping to identify future governments and thus generate mandates.

Electing Government Majorities

Identifiability to the voters is necessary, but not sufficient, to create the linkages assumed by the mandate model of forward-looking citizen control. For a government to claim a mandate it must win a majority. There are two reasons majority support is important for the idea of citizen control through party mandates. First, at the level of normative theory, democracy is based in part on the idea that a majority (or more) will prevail over a minority, not vice versa. Even if they have been elected in a free and competitive election, the failure of governing parties to have secured majority support would seem to deprive the government of the essence of a democratic mandate. Such a minority government should be bargaining with other minorities, not imposing its will.

Furthermore, the implementation of the policy mandate is problematic for a minority government. If neither of the prospective governments secures a majority, it seems unlikely that they will have sufficient control of the policy-making process to carry out their promises. At best, they must find allies who did not join them in their initial commitments to the electorate. This postelection expansion of the coalition weakens the direct voter-government connection that is critical to the mandate control model, although it might still leave room for substantial citizen impact on policy if the alliance is a strong one and is based on similar policy stances.

DEFINING AND ELECTING A GOVERNING MAJORITY

What is majority support? It would be nice if such support meant a majority of the citizens of voting age actually voted for the party that forms the government. In practice this kind of a mandate almost never appears, except in a few cases of preelection coalitions in countries with very high voter turnout (Australia in 1977; West Germany close in 1976). In practice two compromises are made. First, we usually consider only voters who participated in the election. In the United States we speak of the Roosevelt, Johnson, and Nixon landslides of 1936, 1964, and 1972. In each of the elections the majority party got about 61 percent of the voters — but under 40 percent of the potential electorate. Of course, if nonvoters and voters have similar preferences on most issues, this compromise will not make much difference for citizen control.[13]

A compromise that seems to weigh more seriously against the normative underpinnings of the party mandate model is to consider majority support in the legislature, not in the electorate, sufficient for the government to claim a mandate. We have already noticed that most single-party majorities and in fact many preelection coalition majorities are created by the distortions of the electoral laws. Particularly in single-member district electoral systems, the smaller parties that spread their support across a number of districts are badly underrepresented. A consequence of such underrepresentation is often the creation of legislative majorities for one of the larger parties. Table 4.2 shows elections that might (generously) be considered to meet the two mandate criteria of identifiability and majority — and demonstrates how important the election rules are in creating mandate "authorization" in our twenty democracies in the 1970s and 1980s.

At the top of the table we see first that in about a quarter of the elections,

Table 4.2. Authorizing Government Mandates: Preelection Identifiability and Elected Majorities in 156 Elections

Can Electorate Identify Alternative Governments Preelection?	Does an Identified Government Receive a Legislative Majority?	Elections	Countries
No	No	27% (N=42)	Austria, Belgium, Denmark, Finland, Greece, Ireland, Italy, Netherlands, Norway, Switzerland
Yes	No	22% (N=37)	Canada, Denmark, France, Ireland, Japan, Netherlands, Norway, Spain, Sweden, United Kingdom
Yes	Yes — Legislative majority only[1]		
	Preelection coalition	8% (N=13)	Australia, France, Germany, Ireland, Italy, Norway, Sweden
	Single party	26% (N=40)	Australia, Canada, France, Greece, Japan, New Zealand, Spain, United Kingdom, United States
Yes	Yes — Voter Majority		
	Preelection coalition	10% (N=14)	Australia, Austria, Belgium, France, Germany, Netherlands, Sweden
	Single party	6% (N=10)	Austria, Ireland, Sweden, United States
Total percent		99%	
Cases		156 Elections	

[1]In seven of these cases the legislative majority was won by the party or coalition that finished second in the voting. See text n. 15 and also the discussion in chapter 6.

including all of the elections in Finland, in pre-1994 Italy, and in Switzerland and six of seven in Belgium, the electorate was not presented with identifiable future alternative governments. These cases, and the similarly low identifiability situations in specific elections in another five countries, have already been discussed in connection with table 4.1 above. About a quarter of all the elections in our study fail to meet assumed conditions for mandate linkages.[14]

In the second major category in table 4.2, we see that in another quarter of the elections neither of the potentially governing parties or preelection coalitions actually won a majority of either votes or seats. In some of these cases, especially in the Netherlands, one of the coalitions was expanded after the election to include more parties; more frequently, a minority government was formed. But the critical mandate conditions that combine identifiability and majorities were not achieved. About half of the elections, then, failed to meet the two minimal criteria for the control through mandates model. In addition to the four countries already mentioned, most elections in Denmark, Ireland, the Netherlands, Norway, and Sweden, several in Austria, Canada, France, Greece, Japan, and Spain, and one in the United Kingdom failed one or both criteria.

The importance of election laws in converting votes into legislative seats to create majorities appears clearly in the next large category in table 4.2. In about a third of all elections one of the contending parties or preelection coalitions failed to get a majority of voters but did obtain a majority of the legislative representation. Over three-fourths of the single-party majorities, including all those in Canada, Greece, Japan, New Zealand, Spain, and Britain, and nearly half of the coalition majorities were built on these electoral law effects.

Of course, in some cases the governing parties did not fall very far short of a voter majority. In Sweden in 1976 the three conservative parties captured a legislative majority on the basis of 50.8 percent of the vote. In 1979 these three parties held on to their legislative majority by one seat with 49.0 percent of the vote, still more than the 48.8 percent gained by the Social Democrats and Communists. The Christian Democrats, another relatively conservative party, gained 1.4 percent, and another .8 percent went to other parties. Whatever difficulties the looseness of the three-party coalition may have presented for the voters, it is hard to be very concerned about the magnitude of difference between the majorities in 1976 and 1979.

On the other hand, we can see potential concerns about this kind of party mandate government. If the government's support is well under 50 percent, if the main alternative governments are far apart (a substantive issue I shall be addressing in chapter 8), if the government's support is distinctively different from the majority's, then we may find some outcomes that are quite troubling for mandate theory. Far from constituting a mechanism for majority citizen control, such a government could be a mechanism for minority control.

If we examine the backing of the governments emerging in the elections that had legislative majorities but not voter majorities, we find that in nearly half of them (21/54) the governing party's legislative majority was based on only 45 percent or less of the popular vote. Such majorities required a 5 percent bonus, or more, from the election rules. In this category are four of the five majorities in Canada, three of the five in France, two of the three in Spain, and five of the six in the United Kingdom. Even more problematic mandates were found in seven elections, in which the winning party required a 10 percent bonus from the election rules to gain a parliamentary majority.[15] The most extreme example of an electoral bonus creating a legislative majority was New Zealand in 1993, when the National Party gained only 35.1 percent of the vote but won fifty of the ninety-nine seats in the legislature. (Opposition vote in New Zealand in 1993 was divided between the Labour Party, with 34.7 percent of the vote and forty-five seats, the Alliance with 18 percent of the vote and two seats, New Zealand First with 8.4 percent of the vote and two seats, and some smaller parties that won no seats.) These examples underline the frequency and extent to which so-called majoritarian mandates rest on the mechanical operation of the election rules rather than on coherent majority sentiment.

In addition, as mentioned in the table note, seven of the fifty-six manufactured mandates were created for a party other than the plurality vote winner.[16] Such distortions can easily be created in close contests, especially with single-member districts. The "wrong winners" appeared in Australia, France, and New Zealand, all majoritarian design countries that give strong government control to the party controlling the legislature. Such instances of unchecked control of government delivered to the vote runner-up are difficult to justify in any democratic theory. As discussed further in chapter 6, they represent an infrequent but unmitigated failure of majority design in practice. If we remove these cases from the successful mandate conditions groups, then slightly fewer than half of all elections meet basic mandate conditions.

The final category in the table shows that in only 16 percent of the elections did single parties or coalitions preidentified in the election win an absolute majority of the voters who went to the polls. In Australia, Belgium, Ireland, and the Netherlands such majorities occurred in a single election. In Sweden, the Social Democrats won an absolute majority in 1968; the three parties of the "bourgeois bloc" (although their preelection coalition was not well defined) won an absolute majority in 1976. In Austria the Socialists won an absolute majority three times in the 1970s; the implicit grand coalition between the Socialists and the People's Party (OeVP), twice in the 1990s. Only in

Germany and the United States did the party or preelection coalition consistently win a majority of votes. If we confined our identification of mandate conditions to governments with preelection identifiability and vote majorities, we would find very few mandates in practice. If, as suggested by table 4.2, we consider identifiability and legislative majorities sufficient (as do the governments in most of the countries in the third large category in the table), we "find" more mandates, but their credibility and consequence remain to be explored.

Table 4.2 shows one other important point: the significance of preelection coalitions in the mandate creation process, especially in multiparty systems and systems with election laws featuring proportional representation. Preelection coalitions that won (at least) legislative majorities accounted for about a third of all the governments that met the two mandate conditions. Among the countries with proportionally oriented election laws, they accounted for most of the mandate situations except for Austria in the 1970s. Such preelection coalitions were also very important in creating mandate conditions in elections in Australia and France.

While majoritarian theory has tended to focus on single-party governments, preelection arrangements have the potential to give voters similar power to shape government policy and constitute a significant part of the democratic experience. However, as shown in the second block in the table, even with such preelection coalitions it can be hard to win parliamentary majorities with permissive election laws and multiple parties. Elections in Denmark, Norway, and Sweden quite frequently offered the voters fairly clear choices between alternative future governments, but (much) more often than not, neither side won a majority, and postelection bargaining and negotiation were still needed to build policy coalitions.

Problems: Diffused Power in Making Policy

THE PROBLEM OF DIFFUSION OF MAJORITY POWER

The problem of voter minorities transformed into government majorities is normatively disturbing because election mandates are supposed to act as mechanisms for control by a citizen majority, not by a distinctive minority. The opposite problem arises for the mandate model when various factors diffuse and limit the ability of majority governments to put their policies into practice. A government may claim formal mandate authorization based on preelection identifiability and an election majority, yet be constrained in its ability to carry out its electoral commitments. The political factors that constrain it are precisely those examined vis-à-vis clarity of responsibility in chapter 3: short-lived governments, weak cohesion of the majority party, opposition in the other legislative house or between executive and legislature, federal systems, and strong legislative committees.

Short-lived governments can be disposed of in short order. Majority governments based on single parties or preelection coalitions almost always lasted until another election, giving the voters the opportunity to renew or deny the mandate.[17] It may well be true that governments do not have enough time in a single term to implement major policy commitments, but in a democracy it must be left to the voters to make the judgment as to whether or not they have had enough time. If the authorized mandate government endures until the voters are consulted again, that is probably as much durability as this control mechanism requires.

The other elements that diffuse majority control do limit to various degrees the ability of the government to carry out its promises. The internal divisions of majority parties in Japan and the United States limited their abilities to carry out policies. Opposition control of the Senate in Australia on various occasions limited the ability of the government to carry out policies and in 1975 actually brought down the Labour government, despite its majority in the lower house. Opposition control of the German Bundesrat blocked a number of policy efforts of the SPD/FDP coalition in Germany between 1976 and 1982 and blocked some important policies of CDU-CSU/FDP governing coalition in the 1990s. Divided executive-legislative control has frequently limited the ability of the president's party to carry out policy in the United States and imposed a (less significant) limitation on the policy-making ability of the conservative coalition in France in 1986–88. As discussed in chapter 2, there is also good reason to believe that the internal rules of legislative policy making enhance the ability of some governments to carry out their election commitments but limit and constrain others.

It is difficult to assess how much these government limitations and opposition advantages attenuated the ability of citizens to control policy making through the mandate process. Here, I offer a multistage assessment that treats all these constraints as roughly equivalent and the presence of any of them as moving an otherwise mandate-authorized government (identifiable before the election and controlling a legislative majority) about a quarter of the way down the 100-point identifiability (and accountability) scale. (Yet the specific weights assigned here, unlike those examined in the next chapter, are not used in subsequent analysis and are presented only to help readers visualize the problems of carrying out the mandates.) Thus the overview of mandate linkages in table 4.3 shows three columns, taking increasing account of the attenuation of mandate linkages because of postelection governing problems.

Table 4.3. Problems Attenuating Conditions for Party Mandates Linkage Even Where Future Governments Were Identifiable and One Received a Majority

Countries Ordered by "Basic" Mandate Conditions Only: Identifiability and Majority	Basic Mandate Score[1]	Blocked Mandate: Subtract 25 When Opposition Controls Block Point[2]	Net Mandate: Blocked Score Less 25 for Committee System[3]
Denmark	0	0	0
Finland	0	0	0
Switzerland	0	0	0
Belgium	6	6	3
Italy	13	9	8
Norway	14	14	11
Sweden	25	25	19
Ireland	31	31	31
Japan	34	19	11
Austria	50	50	34
Netherlands	50	50	31
Spain	60	60	45
Canada	71	71	63
Greece	71	69	69
France	75	69	69
United Kingdom	86	86	86
Australia	100	86	86
Germany	100	79	54
New Zealand	100	100	100
United States	100	75	63

[1]Average identifiability of future governments at time of each election scored as follows: low = 0, moderate = 50, high = 100 from categories in table 4.1; if government does not command a legislative majority after election, basic mandate score is 0.

[2]Subtracts 25 points from basic mandate score if, after the election, the opposition controls strong upper house or strong presidency, or main government party lacks legislative cohesion. Minimum is 0.

[3]Subtracts an additional 25 points from blocked mandate score if majority government faces strong legislative committees sharing chairs with opposition, 12½ if mixed system (from table 2.2.) Minimum is 0.

In the first column the countries are ordered by the basic mandate situation, from low to high. The basic mandate variable, whose score is shown in column 2, assigns a value of zero if the government does not command a legislative majority at the time it takes office after the election. If the government does have a majority, the basic mandate score is 0, 50, or 100, depending on the identifiability of the governing alternatives during the election, from table 4.1. For convenience the countries are divided into four groups. In the first group of six countries, as discussed earlier, it was rare for citizens to have mandate processes linking their voting choices and their governments. In the second group there tended to be different circumstances in different elections, but there were mandate connections possible from a quarter to over half of the elections. In the last two groups, the average election typically offered mandate possibilities. (Note that taking account of the wrong party winners does not alter the groupings, as these did not occur in over a quarter of the elections in any country.)

The next column diminishes that basic mandate score by a maximum of 25 points if any of the following conditions were found that might have enabled the opposition to block government election commitments: divisions within the governing party (Japan, United States), opposition control of a strong legislative upper house (Australia, Germany, United States), or strong presidency (France, United States). These blocked mandate scores subtract 25 points in any election in which these conditions faced the newly elected majority government. In comparing columns 2 and 3, we can see how much effect these blocking potential conditions have on the ordering of the countries. Although a few countries are reordered, their general positions do not usually change greatly.

The final column subtracts an additional 25 points if the government majority faced a strong committee system mandating sharing of committee chairs with the opposition. (A mixed committee system, as per table 2.2, subtracts half as much.) This net mandate score is the most realistic, in taking account of all of these potential conditions, but also forces us to assign mandate attenuation based not on additional evidence but on our knowledge of the operating constitutional rules in the legislature. A primary reason for separating the committee system attenuation is to maintain some ability to examine the relation between mandates and the constitutional designs independently of the measurement overlap.

The most important point about table 4.3 is that while the additional attenuation considerations are important in some countries, the overall reordering from the first to last column does not change the picture much. If we read down the countries in the first and last columns, we find little difference for the first eight countries. The absolute levels are diminished fairly sharply in the next four, but only Japan changes its relative position in the list. They remain distinctively superior to the first group.

The countries whose relative mandate positions would change most because of the attenuation conditions are Germany and the United States. In both cases there are multiple factors diminishing the control of identifiable government majorities after a number of elections: control of the upper house and a strong committee system in Germany; intraparty divisions, moderately strong committees, and divided presidential/legislative control in the United States. But both remain in the superior eight; their average net scores (supported by consistent legislative majorities and good identifiability in the two-party U.S. and German preelection coalitions) remain over 50.

The net mandate score is consistent with our general impression of the role that mandates can play in elections in the different democracies. It identifies New Zealand, Australia, and the United Kingdom as the only countries with averages at or above 85. Greece belongs in this group except for the 1989–93 period. Appropriately, the United States and Germany fall behind this very best group, while still demonstrating substantial potential for mandate elements in their elections and policy making.

Overview of Conditions for Majority Control: Constitutional Design, Accountability, and Mandates

The vision of majority control offers, as we have seen, both accountability and mandates as electoral linkages between citizens and policy making. Ideally, these are mutually reinforcing, as in majoritarian systems the threat of accountability helps hold policymakers to their mandate promises. In practice, we did often find them together in our analyses. The ranking of countries on average accountability of the previous government (see table 3.5) is fairly similar to the average mandate conditions for the incoming government in table 4.4. (If we use the individual election as the unit, the correlation is .46, significant at .01, between accountability and net mandates.) They are not perfectly related; for example, an outgoing (accountable) government majority may be replaced by a minority government in the following election and vice versa. But both require concentrated government power linked to the election process, so we should expect to find them associated in practice as well as in theory. (These relations are even stronger, of course, if we allow some of the additional features that limit control of policy making by governments to be incorporated into both majoritarian process measures.)

In considering the total majoritarianism of a given election, we could combine accountability and mandates in several ways. We might argue that a really majoritarian election should offer both accountability and mandates and require some minimal level of each. Or we might argue that these are two somewhat different ways in which elections can link citizens and policy, so each can play a role without the other. In this view, we could argue that either condition is sufficient for majoritarian linkage and measure the majoritarianism of an election by taking the larger of the two. Or we might think of each as making a contribution and average the two. A case can be made for any of these formulations. But in fact whichever we choose has a marked effect on estimations of the absolute level of majoritarian linkage but does not greatly alter the relative rankings. It also turns out that they relate similarly to the national constitutional designs.

As I discussed in chapter 2, one way of understanding constitutional designs is by examining their encouragement of concentrated or dispersed political power. The analysis of the election rules and policy-making rules in that chapter found that most of the twenty democratic countries have constitutional features that could be classified as broadly proportional or majoritarian. We expect in general that the majoritarian constitutions will be more successful in establishing conditions for accountability and mandates than their proportional counterparts. Of course, other features come into play in shaping these linkages, most notably the number and cohesion of the parties and the coalition decisions of the party leaders.

Figure 4.1 shows the relation between the overall constitutional design and several aspects of majority linkages. The first bar for each constitutional design type shows the average clarity of responsibility level of the incumbent government at the time of the election; the score reflects the majority status of the government less a penalty for lack of legislative coherence of the governing party (from table 3.5) The second bar shows the average level of identifiability of alternative future governments at the time of the election (scored as low [0], moderate [50], and high [100], as in table 4.1). The third bar combines mandate conditions by requiring at least moderate identifiability, plus a majority for the new government, and the absence of major blocking conditions, such as intraparty division or opposition control of a major institutional checkpoint outside the legislature (see table 4.3). The three linkage conditions are certainly not identical. The majoritarian systems always had high government identifiability but might lack a government majority in a specific government or otherwise fail the mandate conditions. The proportional design systems were much more likely to have incumbent majorities or at least moderate identifiability of future governments in the election than to meet combined mandate conditions. If we also took account of the problems that strong,

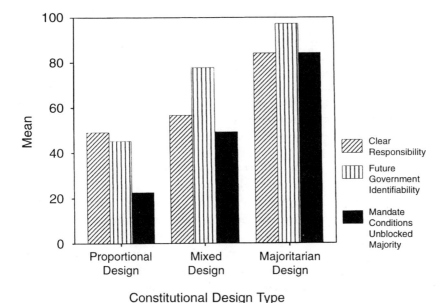

Figure 4.1. Majority Control Conditions, by Constitutional Design

power-sharing committee systems can create for mandate implementation, their scores would be reduced even further on the last bar. (By definition, of course, all the proportional designs have at least fairly strong power-sharing committees, as shown in table 2.3).

By far the most important point about figure 4.1 is that whatever the formulation of mandates and of combining accountability and mandates, we see the expected relation with the constitutional design. The bars indicating higher majority control linkages all rise consistently as we move from left to right, from proportional to majoritarian designs, across the figure. The rise is steepest for the mandate conditions (even without committee attenuation), but is consistent in the other measures, too. The contrast between the pure proportional and pure majoritarian constitutional designs in terms of the provision of accountability and mandates is quite striking. In absolute terms, by all these measures the majoritarian systems are providing control opportunities for their citizens in three-fourths of their elections while, depending on the exact measure, the proportional systems are doing so only half or a third as frequently.

The relations can also be summarized statistically by means of correlation and regression methods. Correlations between the three-category constitutional design measure from table 2.3 and the two key processes of the majoritarian vision are as follows:

	Correlation with Majoritarian Constitutional Design	
Process Measures	156 Elections	20 Countries
Majority Status of Incumbents	+.47**	+.62**
Identifiability of Future Governments	+.55**	+.64**

The double asterisks mean the correlations are significant at the .01 level for the 156 and the 20 cases, respectively. The similar correlations with the country averages show that the results are not being biased by the greater numbers of cases for some countries and the significance is not being overstated by autocorrelation. If we attempt to separate the two constitutional variables and examine their effects independently with regression analysis (admittedly a somewhat doubtful enterprise, given the high correlation of .80 between them), we find that only the election rules have a significant net effect on either majority status of incumbents or on identifiability of future governments. (We shall see in the next chapter that the committee system measure has more direct effect on the influence of authorized representatives.)

The effect of the election rules operates in part through the party system. The effective threshold has a −.42 correlation with the effective number of parties winning votes. The number of parties, in turn, has a negative correlation of −.36 and −.61 with majority status and identifiability of future governments, respectively. In multiple regression, both election rules and number of parties have independent and significant effects on the majoritarian processes.[18] Features in the social structure of the society, its historical experiences, and the organization efforts of political leaders that increase the number of parties independently of the election rules make it more difficult to achieve majoritarian connections.[19] Yet the electoral threshold continues to have a significant direct effect on government status and especially on identifiability, even if the number of seriously competing parties is taken into account.[20] In part this effect is related to the specific way in each election in which it shapes the conversion of votes into seats. But it is no doubt also strong because the election rules shape the general expectations of the voters about the probability that vote outcomes will determine governments. These direct and indirect effects are consistent with the patterns that were expected from the theoretical discussion in chapter 2 and emerged in the more detailed examination of the majoritarian connections in chapters 3 and 4.

5

A Vision of Dispersed Political Power:
Authorized Representation in Policy Making

One of the foundations of modern democracy is the assumption of the intrinsic equality of its citizens.[1] A closely related, but not identical, idea is that individuals are the best judges of their own interests and more likely than anyone else to want to protect those interests. Dahl suggests that these assumptions imply that in a democratic government "at the decisive stage of collective decisions, each citizen must be ensured an equal opportunity to express a choice that will be counted as equal in weight to the choice expressed by any other citizen. In determining outcomes at the decisive stage, these choices and only these choices must be taken into account" (Dahl 1989, 109).

This principle of democratic government leaves undetermined what should be considered the "decisive stage" and what decision rule should be used in determining the outcomes at that stage. The majoritarian vision of democracy, whether focusing on accountability or mandate models of citizen control, has promoted the election itself as the decisive stage at which citizens should enjoy equality and at which the choice of the majority should prevail in setting the guidelines of public policy. Power is concentrated in the hands of a coherent government, whose formation and retention are determined by the electorate. Thus, the electoral decision becomes the decisive stage for applying majority rule. (Clarity of responsibility and identifiability of future governments are, as discussed in the two previous chapters, conditions that help citizens use their opportunities effectively.)

Proponents of the alternative, dispersed power, vision of democracy accept the principles of citizen equality and participation at the decisive stages of public policy making. But they challenge both the majoritarian focus on the election as the sole decisive stage and the validity of simple majority rule as the appropriate decision rule (see chapters 1 and 2 above and especially Lijphart 1984). The election is too early in the decision process and too blunt an instrument to be the only decisive stage. Decisions on many issues must be made between elections. Freezing policy alternatives through the elections, as presumed in mandate models, is too insensitive to the complex nuances of policy. It may exclude various policy combinations prematurely. It offers insufficient opportunity for affected groups and individuals to articulate their concerns as the implications of potential policies evolve. Moreover, elections seldom result in the winning ticket securing backing of even a true majority of voters, let alone of citizens.

Many advocates of dispersed political power are suspicious of simple majorities. Tocqueville referred to "two opinions that are as old as the world . . . the one tending to limit, the other to extend indefinitely the power of the people" (*Democracy in America* [1831] 1945, 183). Proportionalism is the contemporary democratic face of the tendency to limit the power of the people.

The power of the people may be limited in many ways. Theories of guardianship and histories of authoritarianism offer many antidemocratic approaches.[2] But democrats, committed ultimately to the intrinsic equality of citizens, have fewer legitimate choices. Devices encouraging delay and reflection are common enough. Beyond them lie requirements that larger percentages of the citizens must assent if policies are to be made. This requirement may be spelled out explicitly, as when a two-thirds vote of the legislature is required to change the constitutional rules themselves, or developed implicitly through the introduction of institutions that may be controlled by diverse aggregations of the people, as in differently elected upper and lower legislative houses.[3] The checks and balances of the American political system epitomize such institutional constraints, eloquently justified by the authors of the *Federalist Papers*.[4] The prevalence in modern democracies of legislative assemblies, separate upper houses, provincial governments, judicial review, supermajority provisions for constitutional modification, and the like implies that suspicion of direct, unrestrained majority rule is widely shared.[5] Most of these secondary institutions have in practice operated at most to delay and constrain the power of the popular house of the legislature, rather than to force its majorities to share power with minorities.[6]

The most important democratic institution for expressing or limiting the power of the majority is, of course, the representative assembly itself. Both its election rules and its own decision rules are critical. As one of the traditional ideas about representation was to describe or map the population to be represented, extension of the suffrage soon brought advocacy of election rules that would create accurate reflection of citizens' votes.[7] For those suspicious of majority rule, true democracy required representation of the full range of citizen opinion in deliberations about policy making. Mill argued that "the rights and interests of every or any person are only secure from being disregarded when the person interested is himself able, and habitually disposed, to stand up for them" ([1861] 1958, 43). Practically and politically, the political battles over the extension of the franchise encouraged the adoption of some version of proportional representation as a compromise to protect the interests of the old majorities, which were now potentially minorities.[8] Advocates of proportional representation in legislative assemblies argued successfully in many countries — although not in England, despite the efforts of Thomas Hare and Mill — the need to give all factions of opinion the opportunity to speak.

In the nineteenth-century context having a voice in the legislature may have seemed sufficient.[9] But the emergence of extremely cohesive legislative parties and the dominance of many parliaments by their executives imply to those concerned about them the desirability of giving minorities some greater weight in policy making than merely the opportunity to be heard in (largely irrelevant) legislative debate. Juerg Steiner, arguing the general proportional position on the basis of the Swiss experience, makes the argument very succinctly: "A roughly proportional distribution of influence in policy problems can usually only be assured if the decision is bargained over with the participation of all groups" (Steiner 1971, 63). If the real bargaining is to take place in the cabinet or between the prime minister and his colleagues in specific policy areas, then minorities will need influence within the executive, or the executive must be forced to deal with representative legislative committees and the like.

In the positive vein, the fully developed vision of democratic proportional influence generally assumes the necessity of at least two genuinely representative stages. First, citizens would choose an elected assembly — perhaps supplemented by other institutional devices — that represents the full range of citizen preferences. Through the vote, every citizen could choose one or more authorized representatives to that assembly to work for his or her interests. At the second stage the assembly members would then participate actively in policy making by choosing a government and continuing to work with that government in the formation and oversight of public policies. Thus, the introduction of both a later decisive stage and a decision rule that is larger than a simple majority. Because the full ranges of citizen preferences would be represented in the assemblies and because all the representatives would have some influence at the later decisive stage of actually making policies, true majorities could be constructed (sometimes different majorities on different issues) and minorities could enjoy better opportunity to protect their interests.

The specific weighting of minority preferences varies according to the conceptualizations and systems, ranging from limited persuasion and oversight opportunities to the right of minorities to veto policies with which they disagree (consociational systems).[10] A full right of minority veto, however, raises serious normative problems for many proportionally oriented democrats. Is a minority to be allowed to block policies strongly supported by a majority? Is this not a blow to democratic equality? Do not supermajority decision rules, with unanimity as their extreme expression, privilege the status quo and disadvantage unfairly the advocates of change?[11] There may be deeply divided societies or even a few issues in many societies on which such constraints are necessary to keep a democratic community whole. In addition, some may argue that the larger groups will generally prevail in practice, given their advantages of size and resources, and giving constitutional advantages to minorities merely will push them toward proportional influence.[12] But few democratic advocates of limiting the power of the people are comfortable with unanimity as an ideal normative standard.[13] The most clearly articulated and defended norm is that all the representative groups in the assembly should have influence on policy making in proportion to their size, which itself reflects the proportion of voters who supported them. Thus, the equal opportunities for influence by each citizen would be carried right through the policy-making process.

The distribution of cabinet portfolios among governing parties roughly in proportion to the legislative size of the parties has been frequently observed empirically, suggesting that a proportionality norm is widely held.[14] Insofar as cabinet ministers greatly affect the shaping and implementation of policy in the area of their ministry, the proportional distribution of ministries implies proportional distribution of influence. But we do not know a great deal about the way government coalition partners make substantive policy decisions among themselves, an important problem for empirical research.[15] As observed in chapter 2, the practice of sharing legislative committee chairs proportionally among all the substantial political parties, rather than assigning them to a single party or to members of a government coalition, is also quite widespread. As we shall see, however, it is rare that all the legislative parties or even most of the large ones are invited to share executive power. Although other arrangements can augment minority influence, in most parliamentary systems the origin as well as the implementation of most policies lies in the cabinet and its ministries.

In this chapter I want to consider the most important conditions that would encourage citizen influence through their elected representatives. There are important elements at each of the two stages. The electorate is made up of groups of people defined for our purposes as having similar tastes on all issues. Ideally, at the first, or electoral, stage each group would elect a number of representatives proportional to the size of the group. The group members through the election authorize the representatives to participate in policy making on their behalf. Proportionality in legislative representation has been widely studied, and I can allude briefly to the large literature on the topic as well as to results in our specific set of elections.

At the second, or policy making, stage the representatives would negotiate with other representatives as each new policy arises. Ideally, there would be no specialized government or every party would be a proportionate part of the government. In practice, most working democracies have specialized governments, and few of them are explicitly grand coalitions. Yet opposition influence may be greatly enhanced through minority governments or particular legislative institutions. The more the influence of the opposition is enhanced in the direction of a fair share in policy making,[16] the more encouragement for the proportional influence vision and the less satisfactory for the majoritarian approaches.

Empirically, it is very important for both visions (for opposite reasons) to determine the extent to which the opposition is effectively represented in policy making. As we have rather little research in this area to guide us, it is necessary to be inventive. Most of the rest of this chapter is devoted to that task.

Conditions for Influence Through Authorized Representation I: Proportional Representation in the Assembly

My approach to meaningful authorized representation begins as usual with the voter and with political party as the basis of the voter's decision. I shall assume that voting for a party creates a connection of authorization. The voter is authorizing the elected legislator(s) of that party to act in his or her interest in policy making. Given the party cohesion that prevails in most contemporary democracies, it is essential as well as convenient to begin with the party connection as the main authorizing link between the voter and policy making.

The world of representative democracies departs from the ideal of the representative influence model in a number of ways. One problem is that each group of electing citizens may be quite diverse. If a representative is elected from a geographic district of some four hundred thousand people, as happens in the American Congress, the constituency will contain a wide range of preferences. Even within groups who voted for the representative there may be agreement on some issues and wide disagreement on others. In the latter case, it will be problematic for their representative to match their collective wishes very closely. We shall set aside for the moment the problem of the matching of citizen policy preferences and representative's positions and focus on the process that creates equal and effective authorized representatives. As in the other chapters in part 2 of this book, I shall here simply assume that all we can know about citizens' preferences is revealed in their party voting choices. But I shall return to the policy connection when I introduce a measure of citizens' preferences in part 3.

Given, for the moment, that citizens' preferences are appropriately articulated by the parties they choose to support in the election, there remain two conditions: that each party win fair representation in the assembly and that it have fair influence in policy making. Thinking of these as two stages, we find potential problems at each stage. The problem at the first stage is that groups of citizens may not receive proportionate representation in the legislature and in other policy-making bodies. If some of the electorate vote for a political party and it receives no legislative representation at all, as happened to the 3.5 percent of the French electorate who voted for the Ecologists in 1988, this is a stage 1 problem. Or if a large percentage of citizens voted for a party but it received a much smaller proportion of seats in the legislature, as happened to the 25 percent of the British electorate who voted for the Liberal/Social Democratic Alliance in 1983 and received only 3 ½ percent of the parliamentary seats, this is also a stage 1 problem.

Of course, the literature on representativeness of the legislature in relation to votes cast is quite large. (See chapter 2 and the discussion and references to the literature on election laws.) Lijphart (1994, 58–62) summarizes the various measures of (dis)proportionality and their advantages and disadvantages. Fortunately, all the measures give roughly similar results at the present level of analysis. The current presentation, however, highlights conceptually the comparative representation of voters at the different stages, emphasizing the particular advantage in representation for voters whose party enters the government, who are assumed, even at stage 1, never to be underrepresented. The measure is simply the proportion of voters who voted for parties that become part of the government, plus the lesser of the proportion of votes or seats received by parties not in the government. The conceptual idea is that voters for government parties are always fully represented in the legislative process, but that voters for opposition parties are represented only to the extent that they hold proportionate seats.

Thus in Britain after the election of 1983, the 42 percent of the electorate who voted for the (governing) Conservatives are counted as fully represented (regardless of their 61 percent of the seats); the 28 percent who voted Labor are also fully represented (32 percent of the seats); but the 25 percent who voted for the Alliance received only 3 ½ percent of the seats and are considered represented only to that extent; another 2 ½ percent comes from the lesser of votes/seats for various small parties, giving a total legislative representation score of 76.

The average proportionality scores for our set of twenty democracies in the elections of the past quarter century are shown in the far right column in table 5.1. Of course, we are not surprised to find, from theory in chapter 2 and the work of Douglas Rae, Lijphart, and others (as well as the data in table 2.1), that the electoral systems had a powerful influence on the degree of proportionality in legislative representation in these developed democratic party systems.[17] This is shown by grouping the countries in table 5.1 by their election rules (from table 2.1). The middle column shows the standard Gallagher disproportionality measure from chapter 2. As we read down the table, we see that the effective thresholds rise and so does average disproportionality. Our measure of legislative representation declines.

Legislatures in nations at the top of the table, with pure proportionality rules and low minimum thresholds for representation of parties, represent all parties rather effectively. As we move toward the bottom of the table, parties competing under the "potential distortion" and, especially, the single-member district election rules frequently experience sharp disproportionality in representation. Except for the case of the purely two-party U.S. system, about 15 percent of the electorate is being deprived of representation in the single-member district systems, in contrast to the 2–4 percent in most of the purely proportional representation systems. To think of it another way, in choosing to vote against the eventual governing parties, a large chunk of the opposition in these systems (about 1/3 of it) loses all chance to influence policy at later stages. While numbers may not be terribly disturbing and show a good deal of successful accommodation to the different rules by the parties and voters in all of these working democratic systems, they show markedly differing degrees in meeting the first-stage conditions for authorized representation.

Table 5.1. Average Proportionality in Legislative Representation, 1969–94, by Election Rules

Legislative Election Rules[1]	Country (Effective Threshold)	Vote-Seat Disproportionality	Proportionality of Representation (Government and Opposition)[2]
Multimember districts — Pure proportional representation	Austria (2.6)	1.5	98
	Belgium (4.8)	3.0	94
	Denmark (1.6)	1.7	96
	Finland (5.4)	3.2	96
	Germany (5.0)	1.6	98
	Greece (3.3)	4.1	97
	Italy (2.0)	2.6	96
	Netherlands (.7)	1.4	97
	Norway (4.0)	3.7	94
	Sweden (4.0)	1.9	98
	Switzerland (8.5)	3.1	93
Multimember districts with increased potential distortion	France (12.0)	7.2	89
	Greece (16.1)	8.7	87
	Ireland (17.2)	3.3	95
	Japan (16.4)	6.4	91
	Norway (8.9)	5.0	90
	Spain (10.2)	8.3	84
Single-member districts	Australia (35)	9.6	87
	Canada (35)	12.1	85
	France (35)	14.0	80
	New Zealand (35)	14.6	82
	United Kingdom (35)	14.4	82
	United States (35)	5.9	94

[1]Elections included and all measures of rules, parties, and disproportionality as in table 2.1 and text in chapter 2. N = 155.

[2]Calculated: The share of votes won by the parties in the government, plus the *lower* of the share of votes or seats won by each other party. When there are multiple governments between elections, the shares are weighted by the time the different governments were in office. Each country's figure is then the average of the elections.

Conditions for Influence Through Authorized Representation II: Proportional Representation in Policy Making

The second major problem in authorized representation is that some of the elected representatives, even if they have numbers proportionate to their citizen support, may not have much influence on policy making. In the ideal model of authorized proportional and effective representation, all the representatives have an equal chance to shape policy and form new policy-making majorities on each new issue. Thus, the parties have opportunity in proportion to their size in the legislature. In practice, the organization of policy making in democracies deviates to varying degrees from this ideal. In parliamentary systems the legislature elects an executive, a government, that tends to dominate the policy process at all stages, including implementation. In presidential and mixed systems these relations are more complex, but the executive still plays a critical role. When that government has a solid majority and that majority has the cohesion usually necessary to sustain a parliamentary government, the representatives of the opposition party may have little impact on policy making. (This is the well-known situation in Britain.) On the other hand, the nature of the committee system in the legislature and other special features of the policy process can involve various levels of decentralization and autonomy that enhance the possible bargaining power of each party.

At the level of the whole political system, I consider authorized effective representation in policy making between elections to be high when each voter was represented proportionally by an authorized agent in the final stages of the policy-making process. Authorized representation is low when many voters find themselves without effective agents in policy making. Seats in the legislature are not enough. In contrast to the large literature on the measurement and explanation of legislative representation, there has been little systematic and comparative work on effective representation in policy making. There is both the opportunity and necessity for creative analysis. Because this work is relatively innovative, I spend a good deal of time in the rest of this chapter developing and preliminarily validating the measures of opposition influence on policy making. While much remains to be done, I hope to persuade most readers that these measures are both plausible and generally on the right track.

Given the decision to focus on the party connection in authorized effective representation, we can begin by considering three sets of party voters. Because we know that the government headed by the prime minister dominates policy making in parliamentary systems, the first distinction is between those who voted for government parties and those who voted for other parties.

1. *Voters who supported parties that became part of the cabinet government.* These voters are regarded as receiving effective representation in policy making as well as in the assembly. They can be reasonably certain that their party or parties will take part in policy making as long as the government of which they are a part remains in power.
2. *Voters who supported parties that are recognized as outside support parties of a government* and receive regular consultation on policy making because of this role. This set of voters does not play as effective a role as the first because the actual formation and implementation of policy will likely take place primarily in the cabinet — but supporters of such parties can be assured of a substantial amount of indirect participation in policy.
3. *Voters who supported parties not in the government or formally linked to it.* Effective representation for such voters depends on three legislative conditions: (i) seats in the legislature at least proportional to their share of votes, (ii) "political" governing control conditions that may encourage the incumbent government to negotiate with them, (iii) "structural" features of the policy-making rules that offer opportunities for the opposition to influence the final nature of policies through, for example, the committee system. Or such voters may gain meaningful representation through control of an independent executive or a second legislative chamber with at least substantial veto powers.

An overall assessment of the level of effective authorized representation will combine the size and effectiveness of the representation of each of these three groups. I shall first consider them independently and then turn to the problem of combining their representative contributions.

Voters Represented by the Government Parties or Support Parties

All representatives of all parties are not equal in policy making. The greatest distinction is between parties who are a part of the government and those who are not. In every system the parties of the government will have continuous participation in the formation and implementation of public policy. Even in a relatively weak minority government, the parties of the government will always be guaranteed the opportunity to negotiate in the interests of their supporters. Their ministerial portfolios guarantee that they will be intimately involved in shaping policy alternatives in at least some issue areas. Their seats in the cabinet guarantee that they can have the opportunity to bargain over policy choices.[18]

The first and usually the largest component of effective authorized representation comes for the voters who supported the parties of the government. These voters have a guaranteed connection of authorized representation into policy making. If all oppositions were trivial, which they are not, the measure of representation would be defined simply by the percentage of the electorate that supported the parties of the government. Table 5.2 illustrates by showing the percentage of voters who supported the parties holding cabinet seats in a selection of governments in the twenty democracies in the early 1980s, about halfway through the period of our analysis.

The voters who supported the governing parties may themselves be quite diverse on some policy issues. They cannot count on the parties representing their views on every issue, even if the parties are genuinely committed to do so. The larger the party, the more likely that its supporters will be divided on some issues. A majority of them may disagree even with some official party position. But it is likely that the positions of the average supporter and the party will correspond in a general way.[19] The exceptions may be interesting and important. But as long as we expect only general correspondence, we shall not go too far astray at this point in assuming that the backers of the governing parties are receiving very substantial representation in policy making.

THE VARYING LEVELS OF REPRESENTATION
THROUGH GOVERNING PARTIES

In order to illustrate the range of representational situations, the governments shown in table 5.2 are from slightly varying time periods, but generally from the early 1980s. They are listed in order of decreasing voting support received by the parties in the government. The range in the table is from 78 percent received by the four parties in the Swiss government after the 1983 election to the 32 percent won by the Conservative minority government that took office in Norway after the 1981 election.

The Swiss government offers by far the largest representation of the electorate through the governing parties. This is the closest empirical approximation of the proportionally ideal system of authorized effective representation for all voters. The four governing parties together, representing nearly 80 percent of the voters, continue to share seats on the collective executive, as they have since 1959. Although the voters no doubt expected that coalition to continue, there was no preelection pact regarding joint policy commitments or common candidates. It was expected that policy negotiations would take place between representatives of the parties in the government after the election. The alignment of deputies and parties may well shift from issue to issue, even though they continue, through elaborate negotiation, to share the positions on the

Table 5.2. Vote Received by Parties Sharing Governmental Power Immediately after Election in Twenty Democracies, Early 1980s

Country	Year of Election	Parties in Government After Election	Majority Basis of Government[1]	Vote Basis of Government Parties
Switzerland	1983	CATH/SOCD/RAD/FARM	Majority coalition	78%
Finland	1983	SOCD/AG/SW/RURAL	"Majority" coalition*	60%*
Germany	1983	CDU-CSU/FDP	Preelection coalition	56%
Italy	1983	DC/SOC/PSDI/REP/LIB	Majority coalition	55%
France	1981	SOC/COMM	Preelection coalition	54%
Austria	1983	SPOe/FPOe	Majority coalition	53%
Ireland	1982	FG/Labour	Preelection coalition	52%
Netherlands	1982	CDA/VVD	Majority coalition	52%
United States	1980	Republican**	**	51%**
Spain	1982	Socialist	Majority	49%
Greece	1981	Socialist	Majority	48%
Belgium	1981	CHR(2)/LIB(2)	Majority coalition	48%
Japan	1983	Liberal Dem	Majority	48%
Sweden	1982	Social Dem	Supported minority***	46%***
Australia	1980	Liberal/NAT	Preelection coalition	46%
United Kingdom	1983	Cons	Majority	42%
New Zealand	1981	National	Majority	39%
Canada	1979	Cons	Minority	36%
Denmark	1981	Social Dem	Minority	33%
Norway	1981	Cons	Minority	32%

*The Finnish coalition commanded a majority of the seats in the legislature but fell short of the two-thirds needed to pass financial legislation and some other bills.

**The Republicans controlled the presidency and the Senate; the Democrats controlled the House of Representatives. The 51% is the percentage of vote received by the Republican candidate in the presidential race.

***The Social Democratic minority government was informally supported by the Communists, who received 6% of the vote. For illustrative purposes, this is shown in tables 5.2–5.4 as a formally "supported" government.

[1] "Majority coalition" refers to a coalition that was negotiated after the election and whose members include a majority of legislative seats. "Preelection coalition" majority is a coalition that was explicitly announced to the voters before the election and whose members include a majority of legislative seats.

National Council (the collective executive, whose chairman rotates) (see Lanfranchi and Leuthi 1999). Moreover, the party representatives on the collective executive are expected to be sure that as well as party interests the interests of their language groups and cantons are taken into account.

No other country comes close to Switzerland in the representation of so many voters through parties in government after every election in the past twenty-five years. (Austria did have some grand coalition governments in the late 1980s and early 1990s that were as large.) But the table shows a number of governments that represented over 50 percent of the voters. Notably, these are all coalition governments, not single-party governments. Some of these, as in Finland, Italy, and Austria, were constructed from party negotiations after the election. Others, as in Germany, France, and Ireland, were based on pacts negotiated before or during the election (as discussed in the previous chapter).

In the middle of the table are the governments (some coalitions and some single party) based on parties representing 45–49 percent of the voters. These are all majority governments, except for the supported minority in Sweden (see below).

In the bottom group are the governments that received the support of less than 45 percent of the voters. In the United Kingdom and New Zealand these were single-party majority governments whose legislative majority was created by the working of the single-member district election laws on the voting outcome. The New Zealand National Party had actually .2 percent fewer votes than its main rival, the Labour Party. The Liberal-National coalition in Australia benefited similarly from the election laws.

In Norway, Denmark, and Canada, the limited electoral base of the governments reflects minority governments, whose continuation in office and making of policy were contingent on continuing negotiations with other political parties. In none of these three cases, in fact, did the governments last very long. In Norway the government was expanded after eight months to a majority coalition that included two additional center-right parties. In Denmark the Labour government was replaced by a conservative coalition. In Canada the Conservative minority government was unable to sustain legislative support and a new election was called after its defeat in a vote of confidence. These events testify to the fact that not only the voters who backed the government, but also supporters of other parties had bargaining influence after the election. (I shall return to this theme below.)

GOVERNMENT SUPPORT PARTIES

A special role is accorded to parties that have a regularized and recognized role as support parties of the government. In a number of democracies at various times we find parties that, even though not sharing cabinet seats, have agreed, more or less officially, to sustain the government against votes to overthrow it. In exchange, the governing party usually agrees to consult with the support parties on various policy matters. The British Labour Party developed this arrangement with the Liberals in 1977, after they had lost their single-party majority in by-elections. The government may not always defer to the support party's wishes. On some issues it may seek support from other parties, parties that hold positions closer to its own, if it can do so without bringing about the downfall of the government through a vote of confidence.

A party offering support from outside the executive cannot expect to have as much influence as a member of the government. It will not ordinarily be involved in the development of legislation. It will not have the informational and participatory advantages of weekly cabinet level discussions. On the other hand, it can expect to receive at least special attention to its views, although the specific arrangements vary widely. Examples of these outside support party arrangements are found at various times in Britain, Denmark, Italy, Norway, and Sweden. Although their total impact is not very great, no account of representational performance can afford to ignore them.

For our purposes, I assume that voters for such a support party cannot count on representation as surely as supporters of the governing parties. But their probability of having influence is greater than that of parties outside the government. I shall assign them a weight of .75 for their probability of influence. While across all the democracies such support parties have a rather limited role, receiving an average of less than a percent of the vote, in a few countries they are consistently important. Sweden in 1982 (see table 5.2) illustrates such a situation, assuming the Communists act as a support party for the Social Democrats. The Social Democrats had received the support of 46 percent of the voters. To get a total "representation through governing parties" score we would add to that 46 percent the vote received by the Communists multiplied by .75. As the Swedish Communists received 6 percent of the vote in 1982, we multiply $6 \times .75 = 4.5$ percent. The total Swedish representation through governing parties score in 1982–85 would be 50.5 (see table 5.4).

Voters Represented by Opposition Parties

After elections in many democracies, the authorized representation of the majority of voters depends on the degree of meaningful participation in policy making achieved by parties who did not become part of the government. The average vote for governing parties in all the elections in our twenty countries was 49 percent, while formal support parties received slightly less than another percent. These figures imply that on average nearly as many voters must rely on opposition parties to provide authorized representation of their preferences as rely on governing parties. Because of underrepresentation at the election stage, however, in the average country the opposition parties held only 41 percent of the seats in the legislature. To analyze the effective representation of these large parts of the electorate, we need to look at both the representation and policy-making role of the opposition.

ACHIEVING PROPORTIONAL LEGISLATIVE REPRESENTATION

The first question for opposition voters is whether their parties succeed in achieving reasonably fair representation in the legislature. If an opposition party with 20 percent of the vote is shut out of the legislature or receives only a handful of seats, its views are hardly likely to receive serious consideration in policy making. Table 5.1 shows the degree to which opposition parties were in general penalized in various countries. Overall, they received about 41 percent of the seats on the basis of nearly 50 percent of the vote. But the degree of proportionality in representation varied rather sharply from country to country.

OPPORTUNITY FOR OPPOSITION INFLUENCE:
GOVERNMENT CONTROL

Legislative representation is an essential condition for meaningful representation in policy making through the opposition parties. The greater the opposition's size in the legislature, the greater, generally, its ability to challenge government policy proposals, offer amendments and alternatives, criticize the implementation of laws by the bureaucratic agencies. But sheer legislative representation goes only so far. Under conditions of a united majority government and a weak committee system, opposition party representatives may do little more than use the legislature as a forum for mobilizing public opinion. This forum can be significant as a means of getting the government to modify policies because of concern for citizen actions at the next election. But it is far less useful in shaping public policy on the full range of issues than is continuing participation in the process.

I shall consider initially two factors within the legislature that enhance the opposition's opportunity for influence. One is the political strength of the government. The great contrast is between majority and minority governments. Government majorities usually need bargain only with their own factions. Minority governments must bargain with the opposition. The second major factor is structural — the nature of the committee system. A committee

Table 5.3. Opportunity for the Opposition Parties to Bargain in the Legislature, February 1989

Country	Opportunity for Influence: Bargaining with the Government[1]	Opportunity for Influence: Legislative Committee Structure[2]	Opportunity for Influence: Total: (Sum of Previous)	Expert Rating of Influence: Laver and Hunt Survey[3]
Australia	.20	0	.20	.41
Austria	.10	.25	.35	.39
Belgium	.10	.25	.35	.20
Canada	.10	.13	.23	.31
Denmark	.50	.25	.75	.69
Finland	.50	.13	.63	.49
France	.50	0	.50	.30
Germany	.20	.25	.45	.31
Greece	.10	0	.10	.15
Ireland	.50	0	.50	.39
Italy	.10	.13	.23	.76
Japan	.10	.13	.23	.21
Netherlands	.10	.25	.35	.33
New Zealand	.10	0	.10	.29
Norway	.50	.25	.75	.73
Spain	.10	.25	.35	.13
Sweden	.20	.25	.45	.53
Switzerland	.10	.25	.35	n.a.
United Kingdom	.10	0	.10	.13
United States	.50	.13	.63	.64

[1]Depends on government's majority status. Probability for the opposition parties facing majority government is only .1; facing minority government (or with legislative majority against strong U.S. president) = .5; facing supported minority government = .2, also assigned if opposition controls important upper legislative house (Australia, Germany) or independent weak presidency (France), against a majority government. Opposition facing a simple majority government where decision rules require two-thirds majority is counted as facing minority government (Finland).

[2]See table 2.2 and the associated discussion.

[3]From Laver and Hunt 1992. Recomputed 1–9 scale = (score − 1)/8, as discussed in text.

system that largely rubber stamps the government's proposals offers little role for opposition. A committee system that is a genuine area for policy debate and modification offers important scope for meaningful representation.

Table 5.3 lists our democracies in alphabetical order and refers, for reasons that will be clear in a moment, to the situation in the late 1980s. The first column after the country shows the probability of political bargaining factor assigned to that type of government. If the government formed after the election is changed, I calculated new probability numbers for each government and computed a weighted average based on the proportion of time between elections that the government was in office.

If the government has a clear majority (however achieved), I gave the opposition a probability of political bargaining success of only .1. This is greater than zero to remind us that the opposition can use the legislative forum to try to shape the government's actions by arousing public opinion. Various examples of successful influence come to mind, although most legislation is not affected by it.[20]

At the other extreme, if the parties sharing cabinet positions in government controlled only a minority of legislative seats, I assigned a probability of political bargaining factor of .5. It is still far better for a voter to have his or her parties in the government (1.0) than in the opposition (.5). The government parties can at least negotiate on every issue; they will probably be a part of nearly every winning coalition. But in a minority situation they must find allies, sometimes from one party and sometimes from another. In some situations the support will come from one part of the ideological spectrum or one particular party. But often the partners change with the issue. For example, the minority Socialist government in France in 1988 formed policy coalitions sometimes with the Communists on their left and sometimes with the UDF on their right. In their first budget, they negotiated successfully with both (see Huber 1996, chap. 6). In assigning a .5 probability to the opposition parties, I assume that the average representative of an opposition party facing a minority government is half as likely to have influence as a representative of a governing party. (See the Appendix to this chapter for an alternative approach to opposition parties facing minority governments.)

If the government is a supported minority, we drop the probability of political bargaining factor for the opposition to .2. In this situation the government is usually drawing support from its known support party; the situation is not so fluid. But it is usually more fluid than in the clear majority cases. There is a reason the support party is not directly in the government, whether from its own choice or because of the unacceptability of some of its policies to the other parties. This fact implies that some of the time the government party(s) will need or want to find their support elsewhere. I also increased the political bargaining power of the opposition from .1 to .2, following similar logic, if the opposition controlled an important secondary point in the institutional policy-making rules, such as the upper house in Australia or Germany.[21] These are listed in the table notes and vary over time.

OPPORTUNITY FOR OPPOSITION INFLUENCE: COMMITTEE SYSTEM

Column 2 in table 5.3 shows the second factor to be used in determining the influence of the opposition: the nature of the committee system. Here, I draw on the analysis in chapter 2 (originally stimulated by Kaare Strom [1984, 1990]) to weight the importance of the opposition in the continuing legislative policy-making process. Admittedly, the specific weights are somewhat arbitrary. (The weighting is discussed further in the next section.) But their relative ranking is not. As shown in table 5.3, I assigned a weight of .25 if the legislature has both strong committees and divides the committee chairs among all the larger parties, not just the governing parties. Many legislatures have some minimum size requirement for parties to qualify for membership on committees and other legislative privileges. I assign a weight of .125 if the legislature has a mixture of strong committees chaired by the governing parties or weak committees with shared committee chairs. (See tables 2.2 and 2.3 for a summary of these arrangements and some additional supportive materials.)[22]

The third column in table 5.3 adds the two probability numbers to get a probability of opposition influence in the particular country and government conditions in question. I recognize that the absolute numbers are simply estimates, based on reasoned analysis of the conditions and on knowledge of policy making in some countries. It is likely that more detailed studies of policy making in these countries would lead to their being modified to some degree. (Also see the validation discussion below.)

But the final weighting seems reasonable on the basis of what we do know. Recall that the government parties have, in effect, a probability weight of 1.0 — they will always be able to give their supporters substantial influence on policy making. Indeed, all their voters will have this indirect influence, regardless of the seats in the legislature. The overall minimum probability of impact by the legislative opposition representatives is .1 in the case of weak, rubber stamp committees, a solid government majority, and no sources of influence through control of other institutions. This is the usual situation for oppositions in Britain and New Zealand (weight .1). In these cases the opposition parties can use the legislature primarily as a forum to take their case to the public.[23]

The maximum probability of opposition party influence in this scheme is

.75, assigned in the case of a very strong and opposition-encouraging committee system and a minority government. As shown in table 5.3 this situation was approximated in Denmark and Norway in the late 1980s; Finland and the United States also have scores over .60. In these cases the opposition party members have a very strong likelihood of influence, although still not as much as the government parties.[24] Again, this seems plausible from what we know about policy making in these systems.

The intervening numbers reflect various combinations of committee systems and bargaining possibilities under different types of governments. In Austria, Belgium, and the Netherlands during this period, for example, the majority governments had strong formal control, but internal legislative arrangements encouraged some opposition participation in policy making (weight = .35). Ireland gave its opposition few opportunities through the committee system, but the government in this period (Fianna Fail in 1987–89) was a minority government.

ESTIMATING THE INFLUENCE OF THE OPPOSITION: VALIDATION

I am concerned about two elements in the weighting of the influence of the opposition. On one hand, the specific weights, although plausible, have a disturbing arbitrariness about them. On the other hand, the use of the same committee system analysis here that was used in chapter 2 creates an overlap of measures between our constitutional classification and one component of our analysis of the probability of influence of the opposition. This overlap, while theoretically sensible as a causal connection, limits the inferences we can draw about the impact of the constitutional arrangements on legislative policy making.

Fortunately, data collected by Laver and Hunt (1992) in a survey of political experts provide a completely independent check on the measures.[25] In February 1989 Laver and Hunt wrote to experts on the politics of each of our twenty countries (and some others,) asking a number of questions about politics and the party system in these countries. They eventually collected 355 responses; they report the results from all of the countries except Switzerland, for which too few evaluations were received. Among the questions asked was, "How much impact do parties in the parliamentary opposition have on government policy? No impact = 1; high impact = 9." (Laver and Hunt 1992, 125). We cannot, of course, be sure just what the respondents had in mind by "high impact" or exactly what time period they had in mind, although presumably it was the recent one (as the question is in the present tense). Moreover, we have only the evidence from this single survey question, which has not, as far as I know, been widely used and validated.

But Laver and Hunt did give their respondents a clear baseline: 1 = no influence. This corresponds conceptually to a score of .0 probability of influence in my analysis. In fact, the lowest scores awarded by the Laver-Hunt experts were close to 2 for opposition influence in Britain, Greece, and Spain. This fits with my formulation that an opposition always has some influence through the legislature as a forum for argument. Their highest reported scores were around 7 (of a possible 9), in Italy, Norway, and Denmark. If we assume that "high impact" means "as much impact as parties in the government," we can transform the Laver-Hunt "opposition influence" range of 1–9 to my 0–100 scores by subtracting 1 and dividing by 8, so that the scores are a percent of the maximum possible. This yields the highest reported scores in the area of .70–.76, which is the top end of my conceptual (and empirical) analysis — minority government and strong committee system — also.

It seems reasonable to assume further that the current or recent legislative sessions were reference points for the analysis. For that reason the first three columns in table 5.3 show my probability estimates (bargaining, structural, and total) for the opposition in the legislature at the end of 1988. The last column in table 5.3 shows the average replies from the country experts reported by Laver and Hunt for each country, subtracting one unit and dividing by 8 to get probability numbers conceptually equivalent to those discussed in the previous section. (Note that this transformation makes the conceptual scales roughly equivalent, but it does *not* force the empirical minimum, maximums, or ranges to show the correspondence that they do.)

The comparison of the Laver and Hunt results with my analysis is remarkably reassuring. Only the case of Italy, where Laver and Hunt's experts apparently assessed the influence of the Communist and MSI party opposition to the five-party majority government as being very large, is highly discrepant with my estimates. It seems likely that my scheme underrates the role of the Italian committees and, especially, the effects of the discordant relations inside the government parties. On the other hand, in 1989 the experts might not be discriminating between the situation of five-party government in the late 1980s and earlier periods of fluctuating opposition roles for some of the parties currently in the government. Otherwise the results of the two approaches — comparing the last two columns in the table — seem quite similar. Denmark, Norway, and the United States offer the greatest influence to opposition in both analyses; the United Kingdom and Greece are close to the bottom end in both. The overall averages (around .40) are very similar.

Moreover, the two approaches give quite similar overall assessments in several respects. Consider the average levels of opposition influence for the alternative types of constitutional designs at the end of 1988:

Constitutional Design Types (Table 2.3)	Powell Estimate: Total Probably Opportunity for Opposition Party Influence (Bargaining + Structural)	Laver-Hunt Expert Assessment: Impact of Parliamentary Opposition On Government Policy	Elections
Majoritarian	.20	.26	(6)
Proportional	.48	.49	(9)
All Systems	.38	.39	(19)

Not only are the overall averages for all the systems similar in the two approaches to calculating opposition influence, but each shows roughly twice as much influence for the opposition in proportional design systems as in majoritarian designs. The correlation is .63 between my combined influence measure in column 3 and the Laver-Hunt survey measure in column 4 (see table 5.3). Excluding Italy, by far the largest outlier, the simple correlation is .81. Moreover, regression analysis shows that bargaining and structural variables are each statistically significant predictors of the Laver-Hunt scores. Bargaining, primarily the majority status of the government, is significant at .01, and the committee variable is significant at .05. The magnitudes of the unstandardized coefficients show that the two approaches assess their relative importance similarly, although the Laver-Hunt results suggest the even greater importance of government status.[26] Given the completely unrelated types of measures of the underlying concept of opposition influence, these relations seem to confirm decisively that we are on the right track.

Contributions to Effective Representation

We can now combine the components of conditions for effective representation by adding up the influence probabilities that affect each of the groups of voters. This is done in table 5.4, which shows the conditions for effective representation following the same early 1980s elections described in table 5.2. On the left we see the country and a given election. The next columns show (1) the vote for governing parties from table 5.2; (2) the representation of opposition party voters *multiplied by* the total probability of opposition influence from table 5.3 to get an effective representation of opposition score; (3) the sum of the two previous columns to get the total score of conditions for effective representation. The countries are listed from those with greatest effective authorized representation after the election to those with the least.

Table 5.4 shows two main facts about conditions for effective authorized

Table 5.4. Contributions to Effective Representation after the Election, Twenty Democracies in the Early 1980s

Country	Year of Vote	Voters Who Voted for Parties Now in Government[1]	Voters Who Voted for Parties Supporting Government from Outside	Voters Who Voted for Parties Now in Opposition				Total Conditions for Effective Representation
				Opposition Representation[2]	×	Probable Influence[3]	= Opposition Effective Representation	
Finland	1983	60	—	(39	×	.63)	= 24	84
Switzerland	1983	78	—	(14	×	.35)	= 5	83
Denmark	1981	35	—	(62	×	.75)	= 47	82
United States	1980	51	—	(41	×	.63)	= 26	77
Sweden	1982	46	(6 × .75) = 5	(46	×	.45)	= 21	71
Germany	1983	56	—	(43	×	.35)	= 15	71
Austria	1983	53	—	(43	×	.35)	= 15	68
Canada	1979	36	—	(51	×	.63)	= 32	68
Netherlands	1982	52	—	(45	×	.35)	= 16	68
Norway	1981	41	—	(51	×	.52)	= 27	68
Italy	1983	55	—	(41	×	.22)	= 9	64
Belgium	1981	48	—	(42	×	.35)	= 15	63
Spain	1982	49	—	(38	×	.35)	= 13	62
Ireland	1982	52	—	(45	×	.10)	= 5	57
Japan	1983	48	—	(43	×	.22)	= 9	57
Australia	1980	47	—	(41	×	.20)	= 8	55
France	1981	49	—	(37	×	.10)	= 4	53
Greece	1981	48	—	(40	×	.10)	= 4	52
United Kingdom	1983	42	—	(37	×	.10)	= 4	46
New Zealand	1981	39	—	(41	×	.10)	= 4	43

[1]From table 5.2, except that in Denmark, France, and Norway the governments did not last the entire period between the elections. The scores for these three countries are time-weighted averages for each government formed after the election.

[2]Lower of percentage of votes or seats received by opposition parties.

[3]The sum of political bargaining opportunity and committee structural opportunity, as in table 5.3, for the appropriate years and situations (as in note 1, table 5.3).

representation. First, there is quite a range across the democracies. The possible range would be from about 35 or 40 to 100. Although technically the minimum is 0, it is hard to see how authorized representation could be much under 35 in a system that by our definition is a democracy. (We know of plenty of dictatorships, however, with scores around zero.) Even in that case we would have to imagine, first, a democratic government that somehow got a legislative majority on the basis of less than a third of the votes and, second, an electoral system that badly underrepresented an opposition that had little opportunity for influence anyway. The 100 score would imply a government formed of all the parties that received voting support. In fact the range is from New Zealand's 43 to Switzerland's 83 — not quite as startling as the maximum possibilities, but about two-thirds (40/60) of the theoretically plausible range. Some countries are doing much better than others in providing their citizens with conditions for effective authorized representation.

At the top of the table the effective representation scores in Finland, Switzerland, Denmark, and the United States are about 80. The next group includes six countries with scores in the high 60s and low 70s. We could reasonably say that these ten systems are offering their voters good conditions for meaningful authorized representation between elections. The next three countries show less effective representation but are around the midpoint of the plausible range.

At the bottom of the table, in New Zealand and the United Kingdom, the scores after these elections are well under 50. Conditions for effective authorized representation are certainly poorly met in these systems. Virtually all the representation is achieved by supporters of the governments, a group that constitutes less than 45 percent of the voters. France, Australia, Japan, Ireland, and Greece do somewhat better for authorized representation between elections, primarily because their government support bases are làrger, but they are still in the lower half of the possible range.

The second interesting fact is that the good representation scores come from two somewhat different patterns of composition. We can see this especially clearly by comparing the government voter basis (first column after the election year, from table 5.2) and the opposition's effective representation (next to last column). In one type, of which Switzerland is the extreme case, the governing parties represent many voters, and we get pretty good total effective representation scores even if the opposition voters do not have much influence. Indeed, there can't be many opposition voters if most parties are in the government. Thus, Switzerland is near the top of both tables 5.2 and 5.4

The other pattern is very different. Denmark is at the bottom of table 5.2. Its minority governments were based on only a third of the electorate. But very large numbers of voters are getting effective representation through the opposition parties, whose strong bargaining positions and strong committee systems encourage opposition influence. Important opposition influence through the divided Congress/president also lifts the United States toward the top of the table. In all these countries such strong opposition representation is quite typical throughout this period. This fact is not only substantively important, but it emphasizes the need to take account of both elements in citizen achievement of effective authorized representation if we are going to compare political systems with very different patterns of policy making and government formation.

Authorized Representation and Constitutional Design

Table 5.4 also shows clearly that the general constitutional designs discussed in chapter 2 have sharply diverse effects in creating the conditions for effective authorized representation. Most of the countries with the highest authorized representation scores, such as Switzerland, Denmark, and Norway, have constitutional designs that emphasize proportional representation in elections and proportional influence in policy making. The countries with the lowest scores, such as Britain and New Zealand, have constitutional designs that are highly majoritarian in strategy.

Figure 5.1 allows us to show the effect of the constitutional designs and simultaneously to assess further the robustness of our measure of effective authorized representation. As usual, the figure groups the constitutional designs into the three classes, proportional, mixed, and majoritarian. The vertical dimension shows the average effective authorized representation score after all the elections in the past twenty-five years. The bars show four calculations. The first bars show the average level of proportional assembly representation after elections in each constitutional type, from table 5.1. The second bars shows the authorized representation in policy making, according to the method used in table 5.4. In both cases we see clearly the downward "stair steps" of effective representation as we move from the proportionate influence designs to the majoritarian designs.

We should notice, however, two important differences between the first and second bars. One is that the second bars are lower, reflecting the fact that in all these systems there were no complete grand coalitions of all legislative parties and that in all of them opposition parties are disadvantaged relative to governing parties. To this extent there are no purely proportional influence systems. A second difference is that as one reads from left to right the steps decline more steeply for the second bars because in the majoritarian systems the opposition voters are more deprived by the decision rules as well as by the electoral systems. This is quite consistent with the idea of concentrated power in the

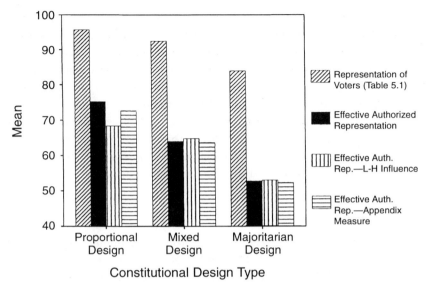

Figure 5.1. Effective Authorized Representation, by Constitutional Design

majoritarian systems. In this way the majoritarian systems are working just as the logic of their designs implies. In this figure we are seeing the price they pay for their good performance in creating the majoritarian linkages discussed in chapters 3 and 4.

The third bars make use of the Laver-Hunt survey of experts, who assessed the influence of the opposition parties in their legislatures in 1989, as discussed above. Regression analysis predicting the Laver-Hunt estimates of opposition influence from the variables in our analysis suggests that perhaps we should weight the components a bit differently. If the experts are right, the regression analysis suggests that the government bargaining variable should be weighted more than (the current) twice as much as the committee structure variable, and perhaps we should take account of lack of party discipline. (In the regression this seems totally dependent on the case of Italy; however, it makes some theoretical sense.) This is done in the third bars in figure 5.1.[27]

The most important point here is that again we see the familiar steeply descending stair steps. The effective representation of the electorate declines sharply as we move from the proportional influence constitutions to the majoritarian ones. Both measures of effective representation are correlated significantly with the constitutional design measure: .79 with our original measure and .78 with the measure using Laver-Hunt's experts. The main difference in the relation between constitutional design and the two representation measures is that the slope is a bit less steep with the Laver-Hunt-based measure.

These two measures, themselves correlated at .90, further suggest the robustness as well as the plausibility of my approach to measuring the conditions for effective representation of all the citizens in policy making.

The final bars in figure 5.1 are based primarily on the original effective representation measure but make an alternative set of assumptions about the bargaining power of opposition parties facing minority government. The details are discussed in the appendix to this chapter. The important point for our purposes here is, again, the familiar relation to the other variables measuring authorized representation in policy making (correlation of .90 with the Laver-Hunt expert-based measure) and to the constitutional design type.

Overview

In this chapter I have developed the proportional influence vision and operationalized a measure of effective authorized representation in the policy-making process that follows from it. I built from the assumption that in voting for a political party the citizens authorize that party to represent them in policy making. I further assumed that if their chosen party becomes part of the government, sharing executive power, those citizens attain not only symbolic, but effective representation by their authorized agents. The effective representation of voters for opposition parties is always less than that of voters for governing parties, but the degree of difference varies, depending on the bargaining resources of those parties. I have estimated those bargaining resources, in turn, on the basis of the needs of the government for political support and the institutional resources in the hands of the opposition. Several methodological variations in estimating opposition influence led to roughly similar rankings of the breadth of authorized representation in policy making.[28]

Insofar as we accept broad and effective authorized representation as in itself desirable, we see consistently better democratic performance in some of our political systems and consistently worse performance in others, especially those based on majoritarian constitutional arrangements. However, democratic theorists favoring the advantages of concentrated political power will hardly accept the desirability of increasing the influence of the opposition party voters. Similarly, the proponents of the proportional vision presumably have little use for the features of clarity of responsibility, preelection identifiability, and majorities that were discussed in the two previous chapters. The next chapter attempts directly to compare responsiveness in choosing policymakers, a virtue presumably desired by each of the alternative visions of representative democracy.

Appendix to Chapter 5. An Alternative
Formulation for Minority Governments

In constructing the bargaining weights for opposition parties facing (pure) minority governments, I assumed in the text that all opposition parties had essentially the same probability of participating in policy making. The government must find support somewhere, as it neither commands a majority itself, nor has a majority with the aid of clearly identified support parties. Therefore, I assumed that the government parties' probability of participating in policy making is 1.0 and that each of the opposition parties has a .5 probability. As noted in the text, in terms of bargaining theory this seems tantamount to assuming some sort of general multidimensionality of the issue space.

Many alternative approaches could be constructed based on various specific assumptions about the goals of both government and opposition parties in bargaining. I want here to consider one alternative which makes only two such assumptions. The first is that we can identify a single policy space, the left-right dimension, and place all the parties on that scale. The second assumption is that government parties will not wish to provide bargaining influence to parties that are very far from them on that scale. While we might adopt specific assumptions about governments preferring to remain on the same ideological side of the continuum or preferring to bargain with adjacent parties or with smaller parties, or the like, each of these seems to fit badly with at least some specific instances. Some governments want to build policies in specific directions; some governments want to maximize their freedom to build different coalitions on different issues; etc. The general assumption that parties will avoid making policy bargains with parties very far from them seems reasonable both for leaders committed to specific policy positions and leaders concerned about their image with committed supporters. This approach seems a clearly defined general alternative to the assumption that all opposition parties receive large and equal bargaining probabilities. We would expect that the assumption in the text and the assumption here would bound the empirical probabilities of the oppositions in our countries.

Of course, this approach commits us to locating the specific positions of the parties and to deciding what it means to be far away. While close studies of parliamentary behavior in each country might give us the answer, we lack such studies on a systematic basis. Here, I used two surveys of country experts (mostly academics) carried out by Francis Castles and Peter Mair in 1982 and John Huber and Ronald Inglehart in 1993 to rank the parties in each legislature along the left-right ideological continuum (Castles and Mair 1984, Huber and Inglehart 1995). (The left-right scale is discussed at more length in chapter 7 below.) I assumed the closer survey was correct and recalculated the Castles-Mair 11-point scale to correspond to the 10-point scale used by Huber and Inglehart and in most citizen surveys, such as the *Eurobarometer* studies. Elections more than five years distant from either survey (in practice, elections before 1973) are excluded from the analysis. I further assumed that a party that was more than 30 percent of the full-scale distance away from the median legislator in the government would be less desirable as a bargaining partner than closer parties, if any existed. That is, I assumed that the minority government tried to find bargaining support from parties within 30 percent of the scale range in each direction from its median.

If the incumbent government did not command a majority (alone or with an announced support party), the opposition parties were classified as having either preferred bargaining power or limited bargaining power. I classified a party as having "limited bargaining power" if it was, according to the average expert placement, more than three points away from the average legislator in the government party or parties on the 10-point left-right scale. The government must also be able to form majorities without including that party; that is, if there were no way to form majorities without including a party, it would have preferred bargaining power, regardless of its left-right position. Parties with limited bargaining power are given a .2 potential bargaining influence weight, just as if they were facing a supported minority government. All other parties are classified as having preferred bargaining power and given a .5 weight, as in the text argument about parties facing a pure minority government.

The empirical implication can be summarized this way: if the government is basically in the center, parties of the extreme left and right will get limited bargaining power, if there are enough other parties to form majorities without them. (For example, a pure center government at 5.5 will prefer if possible to bargain with parties at or between 2.5 and 8.5, but not with parties to the left of 2.5 or the right of 8.5.) If the government itself is substantially to the left or right, then parties on the opposite side of the continuum will have little influence. (For example, a government at 3.0 will seldom bargain with parties to the right of 6.0; a government at 7.0 will seldom bargain with parties to the left of 4.0.) Thus, voters who supported parties that are a long way from the government's position will have less effective representation under minority government than voters who supported parties close to the government's position.

In light of the specific cases, this rough rule seems to capture what we know about the bargaining in practice, judging by the kinds of parties that were on occasion brought into government or allowed to become formal support parties. Scandinavian governments of the left (Social Democrats) relied, on various occasions, on support from far left parties and from center parties but not from Conservative or extreme right parties. The governments dominated by Conservative parties relied on support from the centrist parties and even from the extreme right, at least on occasion, but not on support from Social Democrats or extreme left parties. The rather centrist governments in Belgium, Italy, and the Netherlands built various coalitions of centrist parties and parties of moderate left and right, but did not rely on support from extremist parties at either end of the continuum.

For the twenty-five pure minority governments in appropriate years in the data set, the effective representation scores were then reexamined. All elements were treated as in the general calculations in chapter 5 above, except that the limited bargaining power opposition parties were down-weighted to have bargaining power of .2. Table 5.A shows the revised scores for effective representation in the cases in which pure minority governments were in office for at least part of the period between elections.

As we can see, the differences are in many cases quite small. In Canada, for example, the main opposition party during this period, the Conservative Party, is fairly close to the government, so that the revised scores decrease the opposition probability only slightly. Similarly, in Ireland the main parties are quite close. In Finland the governments were usually large coalitions, even if not commanding the needed 2/3 majority, and, despite the large range of Finnish parties, the major oppositions were often close enough to the coalition to bargain.

The three Scandinavian nations of Denmark, Sweden, and Norway all face

Table 5.A. Alternative Approach to Effective Representation Where Opposition Faces Minority Government

Election	Old Effective Representation: Equal Bargaining Power[1]	New Effective Representation: Differential Bargaining Power[2]
Austria 1970	84	—
Canada 1972	72	—
Canada 1979	68	65
Denmark 1971	72	—
Denmark 1973	76	—
Denmark 1975	81	—
Denmark 1977	84	76
Denmark 1979	82	75
Denmark 1981	82	74
Denmark 1987	82	77
Denmark 1988	81	68
Denmark 1990	72	61
Denmark 1994	83	70
Finland 1970*	77	—
Finland 1972*	79	—
Finland 1975*	73	—
Finland 1979*	71	71
Finland 1983*	84	84
Finland 1991	78	74
France 1988	59	53
Ireland 1981	71	70
Ireland 1982	71	70
Ireland 1987	68	67
Italy 1968	66	—
Italy 1972	67	—
Italy 1976	77	—
Norway 1969	75	—
Norway 1973	77	—
Norway 1977	78	71
Norway 1981	69	63
Norway 1985	76	67
Norway 1989	79	68

Table 5.A. Continued

Election	Old Effective Representation: Equal Bargaining Power[1]	New Effective Representation: Differential Bargaining Power[2]
Norway 1993	79	72
Spain 1979	64	55
Sweden 1970	85	—
Sweden 1973	84	—
Sweden 1976	71	—
Sweden 1979	73	72
Sweden 1982	85	79
Sweden 1985	85	78
Sweden 1991	84	71
United Kingdom 1974	59	—
United Kingdom 1974	51	—

*For Finland, all governments with fewer than 133 seats in the 200-member parliament are counted as minority because of the two-thirds rule in increasing taxes. See text and note.

[1]Calculated as in table 5.4.

[2]In this measure all parties not in the government or announced supporters are classified as either preferred or not preferred in bargaining. Parties 30% or more of the left-right scale away from the mean government position are classified as not preferred and get a bargaining weight of only .2 (as if facing a supported minority), unless a government cannot be sustained without them. Other opposition parties receive a bargaining weight of .5. See text discussion. Party ideology estimates not available before 1977.

marked lowering of the representation scores for some opposition parties under situations of minority government. Moreover, because there are many minority governments, especially in Denmark and Norway, using the recalculated scores lowers the total averages for these countries from 81 to 72 and from 76 to 68, respectively (Sweden falls from 82 to 75.) The reason is roughly the same in each case. The minority governments are toward one side of a relatively polarized situation, with a large number of voters supporting parties quite far from the government. Yet, in those countries closer parties have enough strength to provide the government with majorities. The Conservative-dominated coalition in Denmark in the late 1980s, for example, is quite far to the right (mean around 7.5) and a long way from the largest single party in the legislature, the Social Democrats at 4.2 (even further, of course, from the

Socialist People's Party [SPP] and other parties of the far left). Over 40 percent of the voters supported the leftist parties, which are far from the government. If we assume this distance makes bargaining notably more difficult, the effective representation of this large number of voters is markedly diminished. Yet the government can make policy if it can bargain with the Progress Party on its far right and with other more moderate parties. Problems in bargaining with the extremist and erratic Progress Party on the right and the distance to the Social Democrats on the left made, naturally, for some unstable and short-lived governments in this period.

The main empirical conclusion from this analysis is noted in the text: despite the lowering of effective representation scores in Scandinavia, especially, the advantage of the proportional designs continues to be quite clear. The majoritarian designs have a revised average effective representation score of 51; the mixed designs, 63; the proportional designs, 72 (down from 52, 63, 75, respectively, in the measure used in the text).

The key issue from a theoretical point of view is the single dimensionality of legislative policy making. If all the issues form a single dimension, then it is highly likely that the government will turn to parties close to it on that dimension to form its majorities. If different dimensions appear, then the government can find different allies on those dimensions, and bargaining power cannot be appropriately adjusted by a single left-right scale. Precisely in this time period, the assumption of a single dominant dimension in legislative policy making in these countries, especially in Norway and Denmark, where it makes the most difference, seems somewhat doubtful. Sten Berglund and Ulf Lindstrom (1978, 162–65) report indices of joint voting within and between parties in the Norwegian Storting in 1969–74. These show sharply single-dimension voting in the majority situations before mid-1971, with Labour against the four Conservative parties as a bloc. But in the minority government periods, the Labour Party voted with the Conservatives quite frequently. In 1971–72 and 1972–73, Labour voted with the Conservatives about 40 percent of the time, and only 50–60 percent of the time with the other three parties of the non-Socialist bloc. In discussing the Labour government of the late 1970s, Strom (1990, 225–26) writes, "Labour's ad hoc majorities have included the Left Socialists on many domestic issues of ideological significance, the centrist parties in budgetary matters, and the Conservatives on foreign and defense policy, as well as on industrial and environmental issues."

Similarly, although Berglund and Lindstrom (1978) show that Denmark in the 1960s and early 1970s was quite ideologically polarized, with strong bloc voting, the numerous minority governments in the 1980s have seen many more alignments and shifting policy majorities. Kenneth Miller (1991, 36) writes that "finding the political combinations that can put together a Folket-ing majority has generally been an arduous enterprise." The four parties in the minority government of the early 1980s were able to build stable coalitions on domestic issues but "frequently found themselves outvoted by opposition par-ties in the Folketing" in defense and foreign policy issues (Miller 1991, 36).

These scattered accounts argue for the formulation that treats all the oppo-sition parties as having a substantial probability of policy-making participa-tion under minority governments in Denmark and Norway in the period of our analysis. That is, they support the treatment in the text, which assumes multidimensionality and shifting coalitions on different issues, rather than the alternative assumption of a strongly unidimensional context for minority gov-ernments building policy majorities. Eventually, of course, research on this problem should be able to collect the information needed to measure effective representation more precisely in each legislative session in each country. As shown by John Huber's work on the French minority government of 1988–90 (Huber 1996), even the same legislative configuration of parties can find dif-ferent coalition patterns in different sessions. For our general assessment, it seems safer to assume the rather higher weighting given to oppositions under minority governments in the general text.

6

Testing the Visions: Responsiveness in Selecting Governments and Policymakers

In contemporary democracies elections are supposed to establish connections that compel or greatly encourage the policymakers to do what the citizens want. Throughout part 2, citizens' voting choices are the reference point for assessing whether elections are creating such connections. Elections should lead to the selection of policymakers in a way that clearly follows from the citizens' votes. I refer to this connection as *responsiveness* in choosing policymakers.[1] If the connection is weak, if we can discern little relation between citizens' choices at the election and the makeup of the policy-making coalition in the period between this election and the next one, then responsiveness to elections is poor. If there is a strong connection, then elections have succeeded in creating responsiveness. Both majoritarian and proportional visions of democracy endorse the idea that elections should shape the selection of policymakers, although they offer different strategies for achieving the connection.

Responsiveness in this sense is not, of course, the sole democratic virtue. It may, indeed, conflict with other virtues. At best it captures only part of democracy's broad claim to connect citizen preferences and government policies.[2] In chapters 7–9 I shall use citizens' positions on a left-right scale, rather than their voting choices, as the reference point. But failure of responsiveness, even in this narrow sense, is undoubtedly a matter of concern to citizens and democratic theorists subscribing to either the majoritarian and proportional vision. If the election outcomes are patently irrelevant to selection of policymakers, as in the rigged elections typical of many one-party states, we repudiate the system's claims to be a democracy. Yet more perversely, an election may trigger intervention by the armed forces, who explicitly exclude the citizens' choice, as occurred in Greece in 1967 and Nigeria in 1993.

Even in competitive elections in which all parties adhere to the rules of the constitutional game, the connections between election outcomes and the formation of governing coalitions can be frayed or severed. In New Zealand in 1978, for example, the Labour Party increased its vote share to nearly 40 percent, while support for its archrival, the National Party, declined 8 points, dropping it to second place. Yet thanks to the election rules and the distribution of the votes for these two parties and the third-place Social Credit Party, the "losing" National Party easily achieved a strong absolute majority in the legislature. It formed a majority government with nearly unchecked policy-making power and no place for the Labour vote "winners." The majoritarian system created a controlling majority government — but not one endorsed by even a plurality of voters. This outcome is troubling from both majoritarian and proportional points of view.

If proponents of majoritarian and proportional visions desire responsiveness to the electorate in the selection of policymaker, then the success of the alternative constitutional designs and governing conditions in creating responsiveness can be a kind of test of the performance of the visions in the elections in our twenty democracies in the past quarter-century.

Responsiveness to Elections: Concepts and Hypotheses

Each vision of elections as instruments of democracy implies empirical hypotheses about the democratic connections between elections and the selection of policymakers. The majoritarian vision relies on elections featuring few competitors and identifiable future governments during the election and majority governments that thoroughly control policy making after the election. Such conditions should create tight, almost mechanical connections between election outcomes and the authorization of policymakers. A single party wins a majority of votes, controls the legislature, and makes policy. Governments can claim voter mandates for their election promises[3] and are clearly responsible for their actions. In the selection of policymakers, little needs to be left to the discretion of the elected representatives. The connections between elections and the composition of policymakers should be both strong and highly visible.

The proportional influence vision implies its own hypotheses about responsiveness. This vision stresses the superiority of multiparty electoral competition in taking account of the preferences of all citizens and the need for rules that fairly reflect the choices of citizens in the composition of the legislature. The legislature suffers from neither overweighting of some parties at the expense of others nor forced cohabitation within individual parties or preelection coalitions that can freeze bargaining opportunities. Authorization of policymakers will be dependent on this fairly and equitably reflective body and thus dependent on the expressed preferences of the voters themselves. Parties that have gained substantial voter support will then be indispensable in forming governments or policy-making coalitions or both; those that have done badly will play a lesser role.

The hypotheses of the alternative visions thus counterpoise alternative strengths and weaknesses. The putative strength of the majoritarian vision is a strong, direct connection between votes, legislative seats, and governments. Its potential weaknesses are failure of electoral competition to produce voter majorities or the distortion in legislative representation of voting outcomes. The putative strength of the proportional influence vision is the fair reflection of voter choices in legislative representation; its weakness is the dependence of policymaker coalition formation on elite bargaining among the representatives.

Expressed this way, it would seem a simple, straightforward matter to examine empirically and comparatively the successes and failures of each vision in creating responsiveness connections in our democracies. But such analysis proves a harder task than it might appear. Testing the predictions of the two hypotheses fairly against each other is no easy task because of the differences in their fundamental conceptualizations of to whom policy making should be responsive (see chapters 1 and 2). The majoritarian vision seeks connections between voter choices and concentrated political power, so that voters' choices will provide effective mandates from *the citizen majority* and so that the voting majority can hold incumbents accountable for their performance. The proportional influence vision seeks equitably dispersed political power, so that *the preferences of all citizens,* not just majorities, will be taken into account at the decisive policy-making stage.

Consider a simple, ideal case. Suppose only two political parties, one of which holds office by virtue of having won 55 percent of the vote in the previous election. Suppose the incumbents lose 10 percent, which — because only two parties are involved — implies that the opposition gains 10 percent. After such an election the ideal responsiveness outcome in the majoritarian vision is for policy-making control to shift completely from the former incumbents to the opposition. Both the previous and new situations allow for clear account-ability; the incoming government will represent unmistakably a majority of the voters and be authorized to put into practice the policies promised in the election campaign.

But for the proportional influence vision, the ideal responsiveness outcome in these circumstances would be for the former incumbents to have 45 per-cent of the new policy-making influence and the former opposition, 55 per-cent. These proportions could come about through a grand coalition of both parties in government, with cabinet strength proportional to voting support, or through various devices to enhance the influence of the opposition. In both situations parties representing the choices and presumably the preferences of large minorities of the electorate should be taken into account in making policies. Electoral responsiveness here means to weight the relative impor-tance of the parties in policy making in proportion to their electoral support. It should not be an all-or-nothing proposition unless the voters completely des-ert one party for the other.

This difference in expectations about how the composition of policymakers should respond to the voters' choices is shown in figure 6.1. The horizontal dimension shows the percent of votes the party wins in the election. The vertical dimension shows the share in government that a party would receive as the consequence of voting support. (If parties in government share policy-making power with the opposition, then the vertical dimension on the graph would refer to the party's share of effective authorized representation, as dis-cussed in chapter 5.) The proportional influence outcomes are shown by the dashed 45-degree line—as a party gets more voter support, it should steadily gain in its share of the policy making. The majoritarian control outcomes are shown by the solid line, which is flat at first, indicating that the party has no influence when it has support from less than half the electorate, then rises in a steep slope as its support crosses the 50 percent mark, and is then flat again as it attains complete control of policy making in all cases in which it has the support of a majority of voters.

The expectations engendered by the two visions of democracy are not, of course, completely at odds. We can envision downward sloping lines that would be considered unresponsive according to either vision. (The situation of the increasing probability of military intervention as a party becomes large enough to have real influence exemplifies this kind of negative outcome in extreme form.) Or we can imagine flat lines that indicate irrelevance of voter support to a party's participation in policy making.[4] Nonetheless, the specific expectations of each vision are dissimilar: the proportional vision assumes a steady increase in share of government or policy making as a party wins more

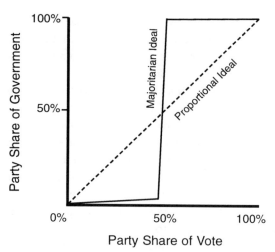

Figure 6.1. Two Ideals of Democratic Responsiveness

voter support; the majoritarian vision assumes an all-or-nothing switch as a party crosses the line of 50 percent backing from the electorate.

The reflection of these normative differences in political science work is nicely illustrated by studies of legislative representation. In the United States such studies usually define greater responsiveness as the steeper slope at the 50 percent crossover point, so that a shift of a few percentage points of the vote will result in a shift of a much greater percentage of seats (see Gelman and King 1995 and the references therein). In Europe, with its strong proportional representation tradition, a one-for-one shift of seats for votes is usually defined as ideal responsiveness, and high American responsiveness would be a form of distortion.

In the face of such divergent expectations as well as different configurations of support, how are we to compare the relative successes and failures of the two visions? There is no easy answer to this question. The primary message of this chapter is that such comparisons are difficult. Therefore, first, I shall consider the responsiveness with which government and policymaker selection corresponds to vote outcomes for each type of system in its own terms. In chapters 2–5 we saw that among our twenty democracies the constitutional arrangements worked fairly clearly, in conjunction with the party systems, to create majoritarian or proportional processes. I shall assess the responsiveness of majoritarian design systems according to majoritarian norms and the responsiveness of proportional influence design systems according to proportional norms. I then compare the fits to the alternative normative models and the trade-off between them.

Government and Policymaker Responsiveness to Elections:
The Majoritarian Vision in Majoritarian Design Systems

The analysis at the end of chapter 2 classified Australia, Canada, France, Greece (except in 1989–93), New Zealand (until 1996), and the United Kingdom as predominately majoritarian systems. Our time period covers about forty-five elections in these countries. Our expectations are reasonably clear about what constitutes good responsiveness to a party's success in winning votes in these elections. To compare these expectations and the electoral experience, I shall (as suggested by figure 6.1) consider the consequences of voter support for the parties winning the most support. In figure 6.2 each circle or triangle represents a political party. The two parties winning the most votes are shown for each election.[5] There are ninety circles and triangles for the forty-five elections in the six majoritarian countries. The larger of the two parties (the plurality or majority vote winner) is represented by a triangle; the smaller of the two parties by a circle. The horizontal dimension (x-axis) shows the percentage of seats the party won in the legislature. The vertical dimension shows the party's share of government after the election. In line with the discussion of government identifiability in chapter 4, the circles and triangles represent single parties unless there was an announced intention of the parties to govern together after the election (as in the Australian Liberal and National Parties) or an electoral arrangement that prevented the voters from choosing between the coalition partners (as in France); in those cases the preelection coalition is treated as a single party.

The top of figure 6.2 indeed shows a nearly perfect, mechanical majoritarian connection between seats won in the legislature and share in government for the parties in the majoritarian systems. In most of these elections a single party or preelection coalition won a legislative majority. In almost all such cases that party took over a 100 percent share of government itself; the main legislative opposition had no share in government at all. (We know from national emergency experiences, such as World War II, that parties need not follow this rule, but they did so perfectly here.) Thus, as we read across the graph, or scattergram, from left to right, we see the flat "no government" line until the party (preelection coalition) reaches 50 percent. After it reaches 50 percent, it gains 100 percent government control. There are a few governing circles and triangles to the left of the 50 percent line, which are the minority government cases, such as Canada 1972 and Britain 1974, but even here the party with the most legislative seats was allowed to form a (short-lived) government by itself. The governing points to the right of the 50 percent line falling below the 100 percent government control level are cases in France in

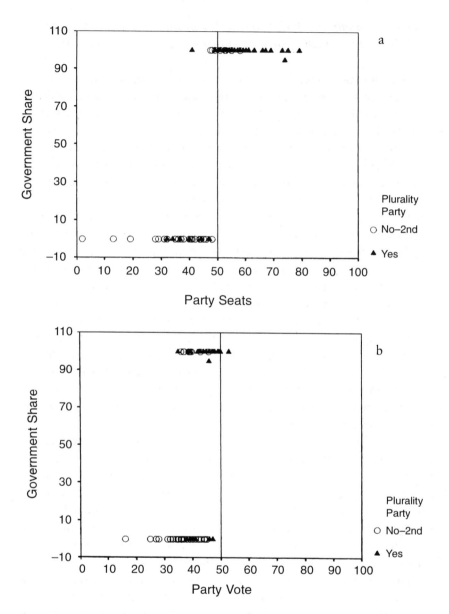

Figure 6.2. Majoritarian Design Systems: Party Seats, Party Votes and Government Share

which small additional parties were added to the government to solidify control or placate presidential constituencies.

Although figure 6.2a illustrates nearly perfect, mechanical responsiveness of
government formation to legislative majorities, it also hints at a problem. If
the legislative seat winners were also the plurality vote winners, all the marks
at the top of the figure would be triangles (majority or plurality *vote*) winners,
while the marks at the bottom of the figure would be circles (parties coming in
second in *vote* percentages). But we see a few exceptions: triangles at the
bottom and circles at the top. These represent vote-seat distortion created by
the interaction of party alternatives, citizens' vote choices, and the election
rules.

The normative expectations of the majoritarian vision assume legislative
majorities based on voter majorities. Whereas figure 6.2a illuminates the actual legislative process of forming governments in the majority systems, figure
6.2b describes the connection between voters and governments following the
normative criterion of the majoritarian vision. It is identical to figure 6.2a
except that the horizontal dimension (x-axis) is the percentage of votes, not
seats, received by the party or preelection coalition.

Figure 6.2b again shows the distinctive all-or-nothing pattern of government participation. But it also shows two problems with the practical realization of the majoritarian vision of responsiveness. One is the persistent refusal
of voters to deliver majority support for a single party or even a preelection
coalition. As we see, there are practically no cases to the right of the 50 percent
voter line — in these forty-five elections only in Australia in 1975 and in France
in 1981 did a party or preelection coalition win a clear voter majority; Canada
1984 and Australia 1972 are very close. The other legislative majorities shown
in figure 6.2b were based on less than a majority of the voters. In some cases
they fall very far short of a majority, New Zealand 1993 being the extreme
(leftmost) case: a single-party government majority based on support of only
35 percent of the voters. In terms of the strict normative assumptions of the
majoritarian model, as discussed generally and as shown in figure 6.1, the
forty-one parties and coalitions falling short of voter majorities should not
have been entrusted with complete control of the government.

Analysts and defenders of the majoritarian vision as a guide to practical
politics are seldom inhibited from replacing expectations about majorities
with expectations about pluralities.[6] In most of the following discussion I shall
follow this practice also. But it is a significant compromise with the underlying
normative premises of the majoritarian model. How significant depends in
part on the differences in preferences between the supporters of the plurality
vote winner and the citizen majority.[7] I shall return to this problem in chapter

8, when I have some direct measures of citizen preferences, and show that on some occasions the problem becomes quite serious, while on other occasions it is not.

The second, less common problem of majoritarian responsiveness in practice that is revealed by figure 6.2b is the vote-seat distortion that in nearly one-fifth of the cases gave a legislative plurality or (usually) majority to the "wrong" party. In Australia[8] in 1969 and 1990 (and probably in the extremely close election of 1987), in France in 1967 and 1973, and in New Zealand in 1978 and 1981 a party or preelection coalition that did not win a plurality of votes won an absolute legislative majority and took government power alone. In Canada in 1979 and in Britain in 1974 the party that won the legislative plurality and in each case was allowed to form a single-party government had finished second among voters. These outcomes are not typical; over 80 percent of the time the majoritarian systems performed appropriately to fit the model of majoritarian (or, more accurately, plurality) expectations. But it is noteworthy that we find at least one such instance of government by the party that lost in voter support in each of the single-member district systems.[9] Because of the all-or-nothing nature of majoritarian government formation, these are clear-cut instances of failed responsiveness.

The majoritarian vision focuses on concentrated governmental power. It is appropriate, therefore, normatively to consider share of government as the expected implication of majoritarian responsiveness. Empirically, however, governments seldom, if ever, have total control over the policy-making process. As I developed most elaborately in chapter 5 but have also discussed in all the chapters, opposition parties may have to be taken into account to some degree in policy making. At a minimum, if they gain legislative representation, they can raise awkward questions, exposing divisions within the government's ranks or at least forcing anticipation of the next election. They often have roles on a few special committees to oversee government agencies. In some countries at some times, the opposition parties may have their influence enhanced either by the weakness of the government's legislative majority (bargaining power, in the language of chapter 5) or by such devices as strong and dispersed committee chairs (structural power, in the language of chapter 5). An empirically more accurate test of the working of the majoritarian vision, then, is to replace the party's share of the government with its share of the authorized effective representation. Figure 6.3 shows a scattergram with votes on the horizontal axis and the proportion the party contributes to the effective authorized representation (from chapter 5) measure on the vertical axis.

Figure 6.3 presents a rather compressed version of the familiar S-shaped figure expected from the majority control vision. As in the case of government

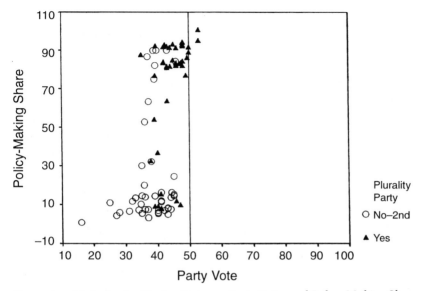

Figure 6.3. Majoritarian Design Systems: Party Votes and Policy Making Share

share (see fig. 6.2), the figure would be somewhat clearer and nicely centered at about 50 percent if we looked at the relation between seat percentages and policy-making share. The voter graph 6.3 shows again the failure of parties to win vote majorities and their reliance on the election rules and party competition to push the largest party across the threshold of legislative control. The predominance of triangles (plurality parties) at the top and circles (runners-up) at the bottom demonstrates again the success of plurality responsiveness in somewhat over 80 percent of the elections. Triangles below the vertical 50 percent level show the responsiveness failures induced by vote-seat distortion.

The one notable difference between this graph and the two previous ones is the scattering of cases between 20 and 80 percent, which indicates some sharing of power between government and opposition, in contradiction to the majoritarian vision. These cases primarily reflect minority government situations in which the governing party's power is reduced and the opposition's increased relative to majority situations. Opposition control of the Senate in Australia and of the presidency in France also pulls their respective parties toward the middle in some elections. Assuming that the legislative opposition has some small influence, pulls the bottom up and the top down in all elections, but does not change the shape of the graph much. In these forty-five elections in six countries, the average plurality party (preelection coalition) won 45 percent of the vote, 55 percent of the seats in the legislature, and 74 percent of the government shares and contributed 72 percent to the effective representation in policy making. The last two averages reflect very close approximations to the plurality ideal in about 80 percent of the cases and very poor approximations in the rest. The failures are scattered across five of the six countries and a wide time span.

Bargaining and structural influence refinements give a more accurate picture of the responsiveness of the distribution of policy-making influence to voting outcomes. The "halfway" quality of the minority governments is especially interesting. But figure 6.3 primarily confirms the largely effective working of plurality dominance in these countries.

Government and Policymaker Responsiveness to Elections: The Proportional Vision in Proportional Influence Designs

The critical normative standard of the proportional influence vision, of course, is that all the voters should be fairly represented in policy making. For governments, the implication is that the ideal government would be the government of all political parties, a true grand coalition, and that these should be included in proportion to their voting strength.[10] Such sharing of power is the implication of the dotted line in figure 6.1. Full grand coalitions are rare, which is why the various arrangements that give substantial policy-making influence to opposition parties play a role of great normative, as well as empirical, importance in the proportional influence systems.

We already know from chapters 2 and 5 as well as from a large body of political science research that vote-seat correspondence is much greater in these PR systems than in the majoritarian ones. In fact, the relation between votes and legislative seats is a beautiful fit to the proportional norm. The upper scattergram in figure 6.4 shows the vote-seat relation, again for the two largest parties, after seventy-four elections in the nine countries whose rules closely approximate the proportional influence vision.[11] (Switzerland, although a proportional design system, is excluded from analysis in this chapter because its rules for choosing the executive and the nature of its coalition government are so different that their inclusion might be thought to bias the results.) Consistent with the rest of the analysis in this chapter, when several parties announced before the election their intention to govern together, they are counted as a single party.[12] We can see that election outcomes for both large parties correspond very closely to the expectation of a 45-degree slope; the plurality winners, the triangles, win only a small percentage more seats than their votes would predict (on average 39 percent of the vote and 42 percent of the seats).

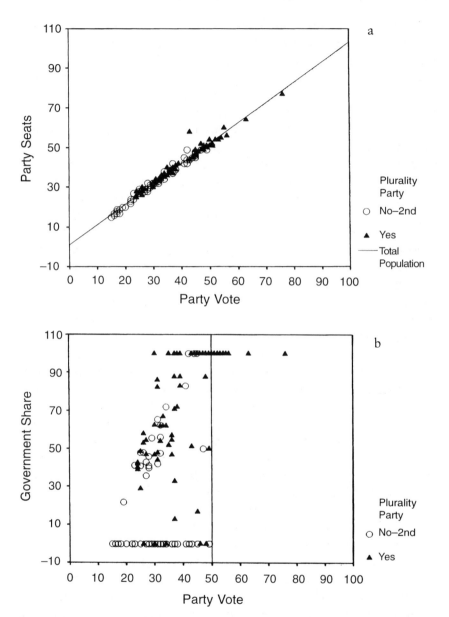

Figure 6.4. Proportional Design Systems: Party Votes, Party Seats, Government Share

The lower of the two figures (6.4b), however, shows the relation between percentage of votes won by the largest party (triangles) and second largest party (circles) and the share of government each obtained after the election. Figure 6.4b looks more like the proportional norm than did its counterpart in majoritarian elections in figure 6.2b. There are many more intermediate cases of shared government power in the proportional influence systems, lowering the seat share of plurality parties and raising the share for their runner-ups. Most of these literally involve multiple parties in the government; a few (for example, in Germany 1980 and Norway 1985) involve governmental turn-over between elections. (Governments are weighted according to their relative time in office between elections.) Both of these features are strongly at variance with the majoritarian vision, a more comfortable fit to proportional influence. (Government changes between elections are discussed in more detail below.)

Nonetheless, in comparison to the proportional norm and to the vote-seat relation shown in figure 6.4a, the vote-government share relation still has a strong majoritarian flavor. About 60 percent of the parties/preelection coalitions are either out of government entirely in the period between elections (42 percent receive no share, as shown in the line of circles at the bottom) or control government alone through the entire interelection period (18 percent enjoy unshared government power, as shown in the line of triangles at the top). There is no mystery in this outcome. On the contrary, it follows naturally from a familiar fact: most of the proportional design systems still use simple majority rule in most legislative voting, including the confidence votes that sustain or overthrow governments. Just as the majoritarian vision usually accepts plurality support as sufficient justification for concentrating policy-making power in the hands of a minority, so the proportional vision usually shrinks from the full implications of sharing governmental power. Requiring a more inclusive decision rule for choosing governments is seen, I think, as unworkable. When we come to grips with the empirical realizations of the two great visions of democracy, it is important to notice the compromises each routinely makes in the name of practicality.

Figure 6.4b also shows that, as in the plurality ideal and practice, plurality vote winners are much more likely to have a share in government than are the runners-up: the triangles predominate at the top of the graph. In contrast to the ideal from figure 6.1, there is not much sharing of power after the plurality winner gets close to 50 percent of the vote. Moreover, plenty of parties, including quite a few with over a quarter of the vote, received no share of government at all. Indeed, there is little relation between vote proportion won by the runner-up and its probability of joining in the government. Strong extremist parties like the Communists in Italy, the National Coalition in Finland, and

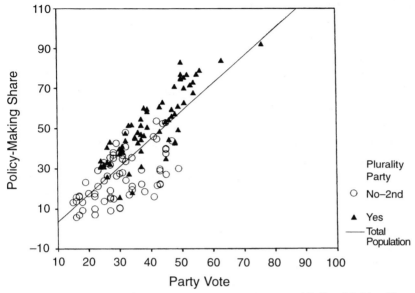

Figure 6.5. Proportional Design Systems: Party Votes and Policy-Making Share

Progress in Denmark were routinely excluded from government when they were the second-largest party.[13] The outcomes of government formation, although building from a relatively reflective party base in the legislature, show a mixture of proportional and majoritarian practices. (If we included Switzerland here, its parties would fit the proportional ideal much better than most of the other proportional influence systems.)

But it is especially important in the proportional systems, with their influence-sharing institutions at the policy-making level and their frequent minority governments, to go beyond a fixation on government alone. We know that these systems are designed, in part, to provide influence to opposition parties. Limiting ourselves to governments is likely to be much more misleading here than in the majoritarian systems. For this reason, figure 6.5, showing the relation between votes received by the parties and their share of effective representation in policy making, as calculated in chapter 5, is the critical test of proportional responsiveness in the proportional influence design systems. This scattergram corresponds to the graph of the relation in the majoritarian systems in figure 6.3.

Figure 6.5 is striking for its more successful approximation to the proportional norm. In the majoritarian systems it made little difference whether we considered share in government or domination of effective policy making. But in the proportional influence designs the bargaining and institutional features contribute significantly to improved proportionality of influence. The slope still goes up a bit too steeply, but a 10 percent increase in votes predicts only a 13 percent increase in policy-making share, whereas in the majoritarian systems the slope is nearly three times as great (and has many more errors of fit because of the nonlinear relation). The predominance of the large plurality parties is more constrained; the influence of parties outside of government is boosted. Of course, concentrated majoritarian practices in government formation leave their traces. We see the triangles (plurality winners) are mostly above the best fit line and the circles (runners-up) are below it. We know from the previous figure and the basis of the influence calculations in chapter 5 that this pattern is largely a result of the enhanced influence that any governing party is likely to enjoy. But just as figures 6.2 and 6.3 demonstrated that the majoritarian systems were performing, with a few large errors, responsively according to the plurality norm, so figure 6.5 demonstrates that the proportional systems were generally performing (with some majoritarian bias) responsively according to the proportional influence norm.

Comparing Responsiveness by Visions and Systems

THE PARTY LEVEL

The two ideals of responsiveness to elections presented in figure 6.1 offer two normative baselines against which to compare empirical election outcomes. For a given percentage of the vote, we know what percentage of government or of policy-making authority a party should receive according to the majoritarian or proportional influence visions. The difference between the actual share and the ideal share is the degree to which responsiveness to the party's voting success fails, according to each standard. That difference can range from 0, in the case where the standard is met perfectly, to 100, where a party that is supposed to gain total control has no impact at all. Comparing of our real election outcomes against the ideals in figure 6.1 provides a common metric for describing responsiveness and failure in any empirical system. There remain, however, two ideal standards.

One problem must be confronted immediately: majorities versus pluralities in the majoritarian model. The majoritarian model in figure 6.1 assumes only two parties and thus the crossover to plurality and majority status are both at 50 percent of the vote. But almost none of our parties, or even preelection coalitions, win vote majorities. Practice in the majoritarian systems typically builds on pluralities. With a few explicitly noted exceptions, I shall follow that rule in deriving our normative expectations for the majoritarian model: the largest party should win 100 percent control of government and policy making.[14]

As figure 6.1 and the discussion thus far focus on parties, let us first analyze responsiveness with the party as the unit, then turn to characterizing the election as a whole. It is also useful to consider results for both share of government and share of·policy-making authority. In the majoritarian ideal, of course, these are the same. But in practice they are different, although the differences are, on average, even greater in the proportional influence systems. It would be desirable to use share of policy-making authority as the final baseline because it is based on realistic considerations of factors shaping policy making. It can be misleading to assume governments are all-powerful, especially minority governments in systems with strong institutional roles for the opposition. It is, though, easier, more reliable, and less controversial to measure government share than policy-making share. I shall present both, but I consider policy-making share, despite whatever doubts we may have about the specific weights used in chapter 5, the more valid description of the election outcomes. Most of the inferences are largely unaffected by somewhat different weight assumptions.

Table 6.1 compares the average failures of responsiveness — distances between ideal and practice — for plurality winners and other parties in the majoritarian and proportional influence systems. The first two lines under each type of system show the parties we have considered thus far in the chapter: the plurality vote winner and the runner-up. The third line adds all the other parties' figures into a single "third+ party." Reading across the table, we see first the average votes, seats, government shares, and policy maker shares obtained by each type of party in the given type of system. The last four columns show the differences between ideal and realized responsiveness — first for government share, then for policymaker share. The differences are shown directionally, such that positive numbers mean that the given type of party has received too much governmental or policy-making authority and negative numbers that the type of party has received too little influence. Including directionality also means that over- and underresponsiveness are allowed to cancel out, a problem to which I shall return in a moment.

Table 6.1 shows clearly the differences in meeting the normative ideals across parties and across systems. Consider first the plurality parties. In the majoritarian systems the plurality parties won 45 percent of the vote, on average, which converted into 55 percent of the seats, 80 percent of the government shares, and 72 percent of the policy making. How do the last two numbers compare to the ideals of the respective visions? They are too low for

Table 6.1. *Voter Support and Election Outcomes: Party Difference from Normative Ideal by Party Type and System Type*[1]

System Type	Party Rank	Average Election Outcome				Difference from Government Share		Difference from Policymaker Share	
		Vote %	Seat %	Government Share	Policymaker Share	Plural Ideal[2]	Proportional Ideal	Plural Ideal	Proportional Ideal
Majoritarian									
	Plurality	45	55	80	72	−20	+35	−28	+27
	2d	38	39	20	25	+20	−18	+25	−12
	3d+	18	7	0	3	0	−18	+3	−15
Proportional influence									
	Plurality	39	41	66	49	−34	+27	−51	+10
	2d	30	32	18	26	+18	−12	+26	−4
	3d+	31	28	17	25	+17	−15	+25	−6

[1]Scores for majoritarian systems are based on forty-five elections in six countries; scores for PI systems are based on eighty elections in nine countries. Systems classified as in chapter 2. Mixed systems of Ireland, Japan, Spain, and United States are not shown. Switzerland is also excluded.

[2]Difference numbers are signed so that "+" means too much influence according to the relevant norm and "−" means too little.

the majoritarian vision, which posits that both should be 100 percent, but too high for the proportional vision, which posits that they should correspond to the (45 percent) vote share. The differences are thus −20 and +35 for the government share, and −28 and +27 for the policy-making share. In the proportional systems, we see the same pattern, in that the plurality parties are underrewarded according to the majoritarian vision and overrewarded according to the proportional vision. In the proportional systems the plurality vote winner received on average 39 percent of the votes, 41 percent of the seats, 66 percent of the government shares, and 49 percent of the policymaker shares. Hence its distances are −34 and +27 (majoritarian and proportional standards, respectively) for government share and −51 and +10 for policy-making share.

Comparing the differences from the normative ideals, we see that the best fits to the ideal are just where we might expect them: in the majoritarian systems the plurality party is only 20 percent short of the majoritarian ideal of 100 percent government shares; in the proportional influence systems the plurality party is only 10 percent above its ideal of 39 percent of the policy-making shares. The most clear-cut clash of normative standards comes in trying to assess the responsiveness of the policy share to plurality party votes in proportional systems: the 39 percent vote to 49 percent policy-making share is very good (although a shade too majoritarian) by proportional vision standards; it is terribly far from the majoritarian ideal of total plurality party control.

The runners-up and third+ parties generally show a pattern opposite to that of the plurality parties. They are overrewarded in terms of government and policymaker shares by majoritarian standards, which assert they should receive nothing; but they are underrewarded by proportional standards, which assert they should receive government and policymaker shares according to their votes. In the majoritarian systems the runners-up received on average 38 percent of the votes, while the third+ parties received only 18 percent, reflecting the greater concentration of voter support (closer approximation to two-party systems). In the proportional systems the runners-up received 30 percent of the vote and the collective third parties won 31 percent. Interestingly, the government and policy shares given to the runners-up were similar in the two systems, as were the normative evaluations. The third parties did extremely badly in the majoritarian systems: 18 percent of the vote garnered only 7 percent of the seats, no government shares, and practically no policy influence share. This result was in accordance with the majoritarian ideal but disappointing in proportional terms.

The results in table 6.1 are interesting, but they are misleading in one re-

Table 6.1a. Distance from the Proportional Normative Ideal — Average Absolute Difference

Majoritarian System	Government Share	Policy Share
Plurality party	52	38
2nd party	42	28
3+ party	18	15
Proportional System		
Plurality party	36	12
2nd party	27	9
3+ party	17	8

spect. The averages can conceal some cases of overrewarding and some of underrewarding which cancel out, thereby understating the distances from the ideal as considered case by case. This is not true of the majoritarian norms. Because the expectations were always for 100 and 0, the averages do not mix overshooting and undershooting for a given type of party. But the distances from the proportional norms do contain this mixture. All the distances from the proportional norms understate the average absolute difference. Table 6.1 is useful because the directions show that in all the systems the plurality parties are advantaged and the other parties disadvantaged. But it does not give a true picture of distances from the proportional ideals. These are larger than shown in table 6.1, except for the third+ parties in the majoritarian systems. Not surprisingly, the changes are greater in the majoritarian systems, which show more extreme patterns of overrepresentation and underrepresentation. However, there is also a good deal of fluctuation for the second parties in the proportional systems, where parties like the Italian Communists are always excluded while others are virtually always included. Table 6.1a shows these differences, which lead, however, to the same general conclusions about the relative fits across systems and parties.

THE ELECTION LEVEL

Although tables 6.1 and 6.1a show us differences between ideal and realization by party type in the two systems, we cannot easily compare performance of the elections as a whole. We can see that parties relate in different ways to the normative standards. But how are we to compare the successes and failures of the elections in which they compete? The answer forces us again to consider carefully the divergence between the normative ideals of the two visions. The majoritarian vision, even accepting the plurality party substitute, focuses responsiveness success only on the largest group of voters, whose privileged position should dominate government and policy making. In this vision the other party groups are really irrelevant. Success or failure of responsiveness depends on the government and policy-making shares of the largest group of voters. In the proportional vision, on the other hand, responsiveness depends on treatment of all groups of voters. In Lijphart's words, when the citizens disagree, policymakers should be responsive to "as many people as possible" (1984, 4). Because the vision stresses proportionality, it is appropriate to consider the fate of each party in proportion to the support it won from the voters. Net responsiveness success or failure in the election depends on the proportional responsiveness (difference between ideal and realization) received by each party, averaged across parties by the voting strength of the party. The rules for aggregating responsiveness success across parties must themselves be different for the two visions, depending only on the plurality party in the majoritarian vision and proportionally on all the parties in its counterpart.

Table 6.2 shows these average differences by both system and normative standard. It also provides an opportunity to remind ourselves of the very stringent requirements of the true majoritarian norm: governments should be composed only of party or preelection coalitions (known to the voters before the election) who succeed in obtaining the support of a majority of voters. If we have no such party/coalition or if we have one and it does not share government, the responsiveness is zero. If we have such a thing and it shares power, responsiveness corresponds to the share of power or policy making it obtains.

The first point to observe about table 6.2 is that neither system scores well by purely majoritarian criteria. Both are very far (90 percent or greater distance) from the ideal of a governing party/preelection coalition based on a voter majority. The problem, as we have seen many times, is that too few majorities for single parties or even preelection coalitions appear in either system. The proportional influence systems actually do better by government share criterion. There are single-party majority victories for the Socialists in Austria in 1971, 1975, and 1979 and for the Social Democrats in Sweden in 1968, as well as the string of preelection coalition victories in Germany 1972–90 (not continued in 1994 and 1998). I count individual preelection coalition majority victories in Austria in 1990 and 1994, Belgium in 1985, the Netherlands in 1986, and Sweden in 1976. (This last government collapsed before the end of the term, although it is included here.) Switzerland would add all of its governments to this set if we considered its unique arrangements as a true preelection coalition. In all these cases the party/preelection coalition winning

Table 6.2. *Electoral Responsiveness Failures According to Alternative Visions: Government Formation and Policymaker Authorization*[1]

	Distance from Ideal Responsiveness According to								
	Majoritarian Norm (Government Party)		Plurality Norm (Plurality Party)		Proportional Influence Norm (All Parties)	
Type of System	Government Share	Policymaker Share	Government Share	Policymaker Share	Government Share	Policymaker Share
Majoritarian	91	91	20	28	43	31
Proportional influence	81	99	34	51	30	11

[1]Countries and elections as in table 6.1.

a majority took 100 percent of the government without adding additional parties. The problem is that these cases constitute only about a fifth of the elections. In the majoritarian systems we find no clear single-party majority victories; Australia in 1972 and Canada in 1984 come extremely close and are counted here as satisfying the majoritarian criterion; there are preelection coalition majorities in Australia in 1975 and France in 1981 (although the Communists, needed to bring the coalition voter total over 50 percent, did not remain in government throughout the postelection period). Considering the authorized policymakers, the situation becomes worse as following all but one election in the PR systems the various power-sharing arrangements pull the governing party's share below 80 percent. In the majoritarian systems the few majority-based governments that do appear hold government power alone. But however one looks at it, pure majoritarianism is very seldom achieved by the configurations of party offerings and voter choices in the elections of most of these countries.

If we concede the plurality criteria as appropriate for majoritarians, then the table shows above all that each system type does pretty well by its own criteria and, as we might expect, rather badly by the criteria of the alternative vision. Despite the spectacular failures in nearly a fifth of the cases, the majoritarian systems are much closer to the ideal of giving unshared government and policy-making power to the plurality party than are the proportional systems. On the other hand, the proportional influence systems are on average much closer to proportional shares for all parties than are the majoritarian ones. This is relatively true even when it comes to government share and markedly true once we consider policymaker share. Thus we are left with a conclusion that is cheering for democracy — each type of system is fairly successful at delivering the promised type of responsiveness — but does not deliver clear-cut victory to one side over the other.[15]

Responsiveness Failures as Trade-offs or Design Flaws

Each type of constitutional design is responsive to elections on its own terms only. Chapter 1 argued that there was potentially a deep incompatibility between the majoritarian vision's requirement of concentrated political power that citizens could control and the proportional vision's requirement of dispersed political power that offered some influence to everyone. As soon as citizens' preferences diverge, the contradiction between concentrating power and dispersing it becomes apparent. We have seen repeatedly that citizens' preferences are dispersed enough that it is unusual for a single party or even preelection coalition to win even a vote majority, let alone near unanimity.

Moreover, we saw in chapter 2 that there was generally a close fit between the majoritarian or proportional tilt of the election rules and the corresponding properties of policy-making rules. I have taken advantage of that fit to identify constitutional designs as predominately majoritarian or proportional and to focus this chapter on the designs that were consistent. It is to be expected, then, that when government formation after an election conforms closely to the ideal associated with its constitutional arrangements, it will very often have to diverge sharply from the alternative ideal. A positive aspect of this trade-off is that when an election slips away from the ideals of its own normative design, that very failure may move toward improvement by the alternative standards. The deviation from one ideal can be counterbalanced, intentionally or inadvertently, by better correspondence to the other ideal. Elections could move along a kind of ideal trade-off curve between the alternative norms.

But not all failures may receive such compensation. Some may fail on their own terms and actually become worse — or at least no better — according to the other vision as well. Such elections are unmistakable indications of poor democratic responsiveness. As we have seen, both kinds of designs do occasionally diverge from their ideal. Are such divergences primarily trade-offs or unmitigated failures? Are some types of failure more likely to be offset than others?

The all-or-nothing property of the majoritarian (plurality) ideal makes its failures easy to identify and explain. They fall primarily into two types. When the elections do not manufacture a majority for the plurality winner, one is seldom created by legislative bargaining. Rather, the party with the legislative plurality forms a minority government. Such governments depart from the majoritarian ideal because they can easily be blocked from carrying out their campaign promises, and their vulnerability makes it difficult to assess their responsibility for policy outcomes during their time in office. Yet these very features tend to be associated with greater dispersal of policy-making influence among additional political parties at the expense of the overrewarded plurality winner. Majoritarian failure of this type is to some degree counterbalanced by improvement according to proportional ideal standards.

On the other hand, vote-seat distortion that delivers a legislative majority to a plurality vote loser is an unmitigated failure. It is a disaster from the majoritarian point of view, subjecting the larger number of voters to unchecked domination by the representatives of the smaller group. But it is also worse, not better, according to proportional standards. (However, if the "wrong" winner's margin is slight, the divergence will be small.) If representatives of some group are to be given unchecked power, it is always better, even according to the proportional vision, to give it to the largest group.

The differences in the two types of majoritarian failure show up clearly in figure 6.6a, which shows the distances from the two policymaker ideals on the two dimensions of the graph. The horizontal dimension (x-axis) shows the distance from the plurality ideal (majoritarianism in practice). Elections on the far left of the graph, little distance from zero, are close to the plurality ideal. The vertical dimension (y-axis) shows the distance from the proportional ideal. Elections at the bottom of the graph, close to its zero, are close to the proportional ideal. Note that, consistent with the trade-off concept, few elections appear in the lower lefthand corner, which would be close to ideal on both dimensions.

The symbols in figure 6.6a show different fates of the plurality vote winner. The elections shown by circles fit the majoritarian model — the plurality vote winner forms a majority government. Not surprisingly, these cases are mostly in the upper left of the graph, showing close correspondence to the majoritarian ideal but substantial distance from the proportional ideal. The other symbols show various forms of failure: plurality vote winner forms a minority government (open square); plurality vote loser forms a minority government (solid square); plurality vote loser forms a majority government (triangle). What stands out in the figure is the very different configuration when the plurality vote winner loses the election and is excluded from government. The triangles are clearly unmitigated failures in the sense described above — they not only move across the graph from far left to far right (plurality failure, of course), but they are no closer to the proportional ideal — improvement according to proportional norms offers no compensation for this kind of failure. We might think of them as indicating not the inevitable tensions between conflicting ideals, but a design flaw in the majoritarian systems.

We can see that the minority governments, on the other hand, shown by the squares, are an improvement by proportional standards (closer to the bottom of the graph,) even as they diverge by majoritarian ones. If the wrong party wins the legislative plurality, we can even see that it is helpful for it to be a minority government (solid square) according to both visions. The same compensation occurs in the Australian and French cases, in which opposition control of the Senate or presidency accounts for the circles at the lower right end of the string of plurality winner majority governments. The minority governments of plurality winners roughly extend that line. Indeed, if we look only at the circles and open squares in the graph we see quite a strong trade-off relation, fitting a negative sloped line, between the two types of distances.

Figure 6.6b shows the distances from the two policymaker ideals in the proportional influence designs, using the same axes. This graph shows the trade-off between the two ideals much more consistently. The symbols form a gentle

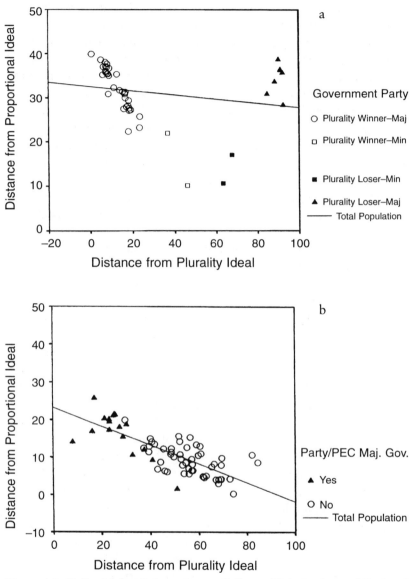

Figure 6.6. Policy Maker Responsiveness Failures: Majoritarian and Proportional Designs

slope down from left to right, most of the elections fitting the trade-off line fairly well. There is no counterpart to the group of unmitigated failure outliers in the majoritarian design graph. The elections corresponding most closely are the two elections somewhat above the best-fit line on the right of the graph. These are two elections (the Netherlands 1977 and 1981) in which postelection negotiation resulted in a strong majority government which nonetheless did not include a rather large plurality vote winner (Labour). That party was quite a long way from its majoritarian ideal, and the party reward configuration was some ways from the proportional ideal also, although the size of the government, fair legislative representation, and an encouraging committee system kept these elections closer to it than we find in majoritarian elections. In this graph the symbols distinguish between elections in which a single party or preelection coalition won legislative majority control (triangles) and elections in which there was a minority government or postelection coalition (circles). While elected majorities are unusual in proportional design systems, as we see from the smaller number of triangles, they fit along the trade-off line, at its top left.

The triangle furthest above the line is the Social Democratic majority win in Sweden in 1968; the one on the far left below the line is a preelection coalition between the large parties that won in Austria. Both are good fits to majoritarian standards; the much larger Austrian coalition fits proportional standards fairly well also. The cases on the bottom right are generally small minority governments.

Figure 6.7 gives an inclusive view of the two design types on the same graph. The majoritarian design elections are indicated by the triangle, the proportional by the circle. The graph invites two inferences. First, we see that most elections in both types of systems fit fairly well with a single trade-off line. As we expect, the majoritarian design systems are at the upper left of that line, while the proportional design ones, with a few exceptions, string out down the slope to the right. The majoritarian systems are bunched fairly closely together, as befits their all-or-nothing ideal and practice, with only a few minority governments and the opposition control of outside institutions pulling a few of them down off the trade-off line. The proportional systems all fit the proportional ideal fairly well (almost all are closer to the bottom of the graph than the vast bulk of the majoritarian systems) but show quite a diversity in plurality fit. This diversity, we know from the previous figure, largely reflects the fact that sometimes they do turn up legislative majorities for parties or preelection coalition. In such cases the coalition is rarely expanded. Moreover, postelection bargaining turns up majorities and minorities of various sizes but typically overrewards the plurality winner.

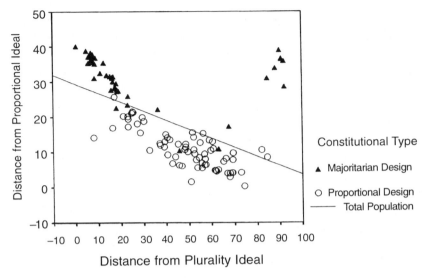

Figure 6.7. Policy Maker Responsiveness Failures: Two Ideals and Two Types of Designs

The second inference is that the elections in which a party that finishes second in the vote actually wins unchecked legislative majority control not only are unusual, but comprise the unique cluster of unmitigated failures. They stand alone as a group at the top right of the graph, distinctive in their double distance from both majoritarian and proportional standards. In this sense they appear quite obviously as a design flaw in majoritarian systems.

Proximity of Election and Government Formation: A Disputed Criterion of Responsiveness

The successful "mechanical" connections that deliver undisputed control of policy making to the plurality vote winner in the majoritarian vision depend on another feature that we have not yet considered: the new government should endure unchanged until the voters are consulted in another election. The breakup or other alteration of such a government, whether because of intraparty dissent (New Zealand 1993) or a quarrel between coalition partners (France 1981), is certainly a departure from the majoritarian (pluralitarian) vision of citizen control. In practice such government changes in the majoritarian design systems are quite rare. Only France with its complex multiparty system and the complications of a separately elected president (as well as second round runoffs in both presidential and legislative district elections) offers multiple examples. The most obvious case is the breakup of the Socialist-Communist coalition between the 1981 and 1986 legislative elections. Forming a majority in themselves, the Socialists did not need their electoral allies in the legislature, and the commitments to govern together were never fully developed in the 1981 campaign. But the voters who saw their candidates withdraw in favor of the other party on the second round had a right to be disturbed. There were also parties added to the government after the initial governments following the 1968 and 1973 French legislative elections (and a party change of prime minister as well in the latter case). Britain saw the loss of the Labour government's (thin) legislative majority and a pact with the Liberals (who were consulted but not brought into the government) between the October 1974 and 1979 elections. New Zealand saw the breakup of the National Party's majority after the 1993 election, although the anticipation of proportional representation elections in 1996 no doubt played a role there. Still, in the other three majoritarian countries there were no cases of government change between elections, and, counting even the French cases, the average first government endured 93 percent of the period between elections in the majoritarian design countries.

In the proportional design systems, on the other hand, the average government formed after the election endured only 81 percent of the time until another election. In Italy, despite the durable government after 1983, the average was only 38 percent and in Belgium, Finland, and Norway the average government lasted less than 80 percent of the time until the next election was called. There is a large theoretical and empirical literature explaining the tendency of governments to be less durable in the multiparty systems encouraged by proportional representation designs.[16] Minority and "oversize" governments are more common in these systems and tend to be less durable than their minimal majority counterparts. The presence of extremist parties in the legislature can create particularly serious problems for the formation of stable coalition governments. Governments in these systems are also somewhat less likely to consult citizens to resolve governing disputes, because the outcome of such consultation is less likely to be decisive.

The question for the proportional vision of democratic responsiveness, however, is not durability as such. It is whether a change of government between elections should be regarded as diminishing democratic responsiveness. On one hand, changes in the parties in government — or at least new bargains over government formation and thus over policy-making influence — are taking place with no consultation of the voters. This seems suspiciously unresponsive. On the other hand, the legislative resources such parties bring to the bargaining are still derived from the previous election outcomes. Furthermore, changes in government participation might serve even to increase the proportional participation of all parties in policy making in the total period between elections. That is, there could be virtually a grand coalition in series, rather than simultaneously.

Germany between 1980 and 1983 is a nice example. In 1980 the Social Democrats (SPD) and the Free Democrats (FDP), who had governed together since 1969, announced before the election that they would continue in government together if they won a joint legislative majority, which they did. But in late summer of 1982 increasing budgetary pressures induced by international economic conditions led to a sharp dispute over potential welfare cuts and related issues. The coalition broke up, and in October 1982 the FDP joined the Christian Democrats (CDU/CSU) to elect the CDU's Helmut Kohl as the new chancellor, regaining the Foreign Ministry and two other cabinet positions in the new government. Considered from the majoritarian perspective, this interelection change was normatively undesirable. The SPD and FDP had explicitly offered the voters a choice of alternative governments in the 1980 election, and the voters' collective choice was abrogated without consulting them. The speed with which the new coalition government decided to arrange an early election (in the spring of 1983) suggests that the parties were distinctly uneasy about it. In the election the voters ratified the change by giving the CDU/CSU and FDP a new collective majority. From the perspective of the proportional vision, this change of government has attractive features. In the period between 1980 and 1983 the vast majority of German voters at some point found their chosen party in office and, thus, wielding authoritative influence over policy making. Norway offers several similar examples: after both 1985 and 1989, a minority three-party (Conservative, Agrarian, Christian) coalition government was replaced by a minority Social Democratic government part way through the fixed four-year legislative term. The interelection government changes ensured that voters on both sides of the political spectrum had powerful representation in policy making at least part of the time.

The possibility that interelection government changes could expand the diversity of voters represented in the government is so appealing from the proportional point of view that it is worth more systematic exploration. There were 116 elections from 1968 through 1994 in the nine proportional influence design countries we have been considering. (I am excluding the Italian election of 1994 for a variety of special reasons.) In Austria and the Netherlands all of the sixteen governments in this period endured until a new election was called. In the other seven countries the first government failed to endure the full interelection period following 24 of the 100 elections. What is the record of government change in these 24 cases? As shown in table 6.3, it is supportive of

*Table 6.3. Multiple Governments Between Elections in Proportional Design
Systems: Party Representation in Governments and Policy Making*

Country	Election Year	Effect of Additional Governments on	
		Diversity of Parties in Government[1]	Weighted Average Effective Authorized Representation[2]
Belgium	1971	Increase	Increase
	1974	Increase	Less
	1978	Increase	Similar
Denmark	1977	Increase	Increase
	1981	Increase	Similar
	1990	Increase	Less
Finland	1970	Cut	Similar
	1972	Increase	Increase
	1975	Cut	Less
	1979	Cut	Similar
	1987	Cut	Similar
Germany	1981	Increase	Similar
Italy	1968	Increase	Increase
	1972	Increase	Increase
	1976	Increase[3]	Increase
	1979	Increase	Similar
	1987	Cut	Similar
	1992	Indeterminate	Unclear
Norway	1969	Increase	Increase
	1981	Increase	Less
	1985	Increase	Increase
	1989	Increase	Similar
Sweden	1976	Cut	Increase
	1979	Cut	Increase

[1]Increase in diversity means that subsequent governments involved parties in addition to those in the first government, even if the original parties were no longer there. Diversity cut means that the subsequent governments involved fewer parties than the original without adding new ones.
[2]Similar effective representation means first government is within 2 points of the weighted average effective representation score (from chapter 5).
[3]Parties outside the government were given increased consultative role as support parties.

the idea that interelection changes are on average helpful in encouraging diversity of voter representation in government.

If we compare the parties represented in the first government formed after the election to the subsequent governments, we see that in 16 cases (two-thirds of the total), the subsequent government changes allowed additional parties to share in cabinet government between the elections (see table 6.3). This does not mean that these all shared government at the same time but reflects the idea of a sequential approach to grand coalitions. Subsequent government formation increased the diversity of parties participating in government between elections after all the Belgian, Danish, German, and Norwegian cases and most of the Italian ones. Several of the complex reshufflings in Belgium and Italy did not expand diversity, but at least one subsequent government improved diversity compared to the original. In one case (Italy 1992) the interelection changes were somewhat indeterminate. In seven cases, on the other hand, the subsequent governments involved government breakups that resulted in less inclusive versions of the original coalitions. Smaller governments replaced larger ones at some point after four of the five elections in Finland, one in Italy, and two in Sweden. (These are referred to as cuts in the table.) Interelection changes were about twice as likely to improve diversity of party representation in government as to diminish it.

Consequences of government change for effective authorized representation are harder to compute and visualize because this concept, as developed in chapter 5, involves the relative sizes of the parties and the majority or minority status of the governments. Thus, the deletion of the Conservatives from the three-party governing coalitions in Sweden formed immediately after the elections of 1976 and 1979 actually improved the effective representation level. The much greater influence of the (now much larger) opposition facing the new minority governments more than compensated for the smaller numbers of voters whose parties remained in the government. Comparing effective representation under the first government with weighted average effective representation for the full election period takes account of the percentage of the term each government was in office. But it does not accumulate over-time diversity; a number of government changes that brought new parties into government had little net effect on average representation (as in Germany in 1980). Thus, this measure is a harder standard than sequential diversity. Still, postelection government changes were more than twice as likely to increase effective representation as to diminish it (ten elections to four), as shown in the last column of table 6.3.

I shall return to the issue of changes of government between elections from a substantive point of view, using the left-right scale, in chapter 9. But here it is sufficient to have shown that such changes are more often than not (although not always) helpful in increasing diversity of party representation in government and higher levels of postelection effective representation in policy making. One should not accept without reservation the majoritarian view that interelection government changes are clear failures of democratic responsiveness. The proximity criterion remains largely a matter of dispute between the normative criteria of the visions, rather than a standard for choosing between them.

Concluding Comments

WHERE HAVE WE BEEN?

The concept of responsiveness to citizens' choices in elections is attractive as a summary measure of democratic performance. Elections should shape the formation of governments and policymakers in a way that is directly responsive to citizens' votes. But its apparent simplicity conceals subtle problems:

1. Careful consideration of the nature of the relationship between voters and policymakers assumed by the majoritarian and proportional influence approaches to democracy suggests substantial divergence in their ideals of responsiveness. Majoritarian democracy assumes an all-or-nothing relation, while the proportional influence approach rejects it (see fig. 6.1).
2. No matter what the constitutional design, it is rare for a clear majority of voters to back a single political party or an announced preelection coalition of several parties. Therefore, it is problematic to rely on majority vote support as a guide to responsiveness in government or policymaker formation.
3. In order to validate their vision and to make it empirically relevant, proponents of the majoritarian vision find themselves arguing that responsiveness requires providing unchecked policy-making control to the party (or announced preelection coalition) that wins more votes than any other: that is, the plurality vote winner. Responsiveness in this sense is, indeed, the typical outcome of elections in the majoritarian design systems. Proponents of these systems should not, however, deceive themselves that there is responsiveness to majorities; the 45 percent plurality vote winner lost 55 percent of the votes to the other parties.
4. The proportional influence vision implies that all parties should share in policy making to a degree proportional to their voter support. In practice, however, most proportional influence design systems combine PR legislative election rules with simple majority rules in choosing or sustaining

governments and in passing most legislation. Grand coalitions are very rare. Such rules and practices tend to strengthen the influence of some parties, especially the largest party, while limiting the influence of others. This disproportional role is mitigated to some extent by strong committees and other structural features.

5. We can examine the degree to which responsiveness in each type of constitutional design meets the criteria established by the associated vision of democratic politics. In doing so, we find that each type of design is relatively successful on the terms established by its own vision, much less so by the alternative criterion. This outcome is encouraging for the meaningfulness of democracy in either form (accepting pluralities as a substitute for majorities in the majority vision). Each system design type has also some failures, most notably the wrong party victories in 15–20 percent of the majoritarian elections and the overrepresentation of the plurality winners in proportional design governments.

6. Because of the tension between the two ideals of democratic responsiveness we can distinguish two kinds of responsiveness failures: (i) those in which failing to meet one ideal draws the election outcome closer to the alternative ideal and (ii) unmitigated failures, in which distance from one ideal does not draw the outcome toward the alternative. In the majoritarian design systems the lack of plurality party control implied in the formation of minority governments is mitigated by improving the opposition influence, acting as a trade-off type of failure. Similarly, in proportional design systems too much influence for the plurality vote winner is mitigated in the sense that it brings the outcome closer to the majoritarian ideal. On the other hand, the provision of legislative majorities (and government control) to parties that finish second in the vote is an unmitigated failure, very troubling for the majoritarian norm and actually worsening (less severely) performance relative to the proportional norm also. The unmitigated nature of its occasional failures may be seen as a design flaw of majoritarian systems relying on single-member district election rules.

7. The propensity of the first government formed after the election to endure until the voters are consulted again is a disputed criterion of democratic responsiveness. It seems essential to the majoritarian vision. The first government was indeed significantly more likely to endure until a new election was called in majoritarian designs than in their proportional counterparts. (Again, encouraging for democracy.) However, many proponents of the proportional vision may be rightfully unwilling to accept proximity of government formation to elections as a meaningful criterion. In the proportional design systems the postelection government changes did result about

two-thirds of the time in increased diversity of party participation in government between elections. Average levels of effective representation also improved. There is good reason, then, to regard the durability of the first government as primarily a majoritarian criterion, not a neutral one.

The main point of this chapter, exemplified in its many graphs, is to argue the difficulty of comparing democratic responsiveness to voters' choices across the two great visions of democracy. The visions offer different ideals of responsiveness when voters disagree, ideals that cannot be reconciled empirically. At best we can see whether the empirical forms of each vision succeed in their own terms, which they generally do; whether they succeed in the opposition's terms, which they generally do not; and whether the respective failures are mitigated (advantage to the proportional designs).

WHERE NEXT?

Because the vote is so essential to the democratic election and so conveniently recorded, it is easy to assume that the essence of democratic responsiveness is some kind of correspondence between votes and policymakers. I have done so throughout this chapter. But if we return to the fundamental principles articulated in chapters 1 and 2, we recall that the promise of liberal democracy is that the preferences of citizens, not their votes, will prevail in policy making. Elections are not democracy itself but an instrument of democracy.

Citizens' voting choices are shaped by their preferences, but they are also shaped by the available choices and by citizens' expectations about the choices of others. Parties may fail to offer alternatives close to the citizens' own desires, or too many parties may do so, splitting the vote between them and electing a more distant alternative. By beginning our responsiveness analysis with the vote distributions we may have already biased the results.

To put it another way, it is something of an illusion to think that the mechanical processes of vote-seat-government connections in majoritarian systems are shaped more by citizens and less by party leaders than are the bargaining processes of vote-seat-policymaker connections in proportional systems. It is the party leaders, typically, who choose what policy positions to offer and where and how to compete at the election stage. Citizens largely rely on parties to solve their coordination problems. In single-member district systems, especially, the coordination needs are very great and the implications of coordination failure may be very large (see Cox 1997, chapter 12). These decisions before the election can largely determine citizens' vote choices.

In the next three chapters, therefore, I turn to a set of tools that will allow us to begin with the preferences of citizens, not their votes, in examining the connections of democratic responsiveness. We shall have to confront again the somewhat differing ideals of the majoritarian and proportional visions. But the various types of vote connections can now be examined as alternative processes that are hypothesized to connect preferences and policymakers, not as embodiments of the ideals themselves.

PART **III**

Congruent Representation: Connecting Citizens'
Preferences, Governments, and Policymakers

7

Citizen Preferences and Party Positions

Careful analysis of the role of voting choices of citizens in shaping policy making is essential to our understanding of democratic connections. Chapters 3 to 6 have offered this kind of analysis, describing the working of alternative visions of democracy in such terms. Two lines of thought suggest that this is enough. One argues the conceptual impossibility of comparing what the people want and what policymakers do. The other argues that votes are adequate indicators of what the people want. While each builds from an element of truth, the first argument is too pessimistic and the second too optimistic. We can do more and in so doing remain closer to the traditional understanding of democracy. Moreover, it is important to try because votes alone can be misleading as indicators of citizen preferences. An analysis of the role of elections that relies only on the way citizens vote may be a useful beginning, but it is both normatively and empirically insufficient. This chapter introduces tools for going beyond it, and the next two chapters employ those tools.

WHY PROCESS ALONE IS INSUFFICIENT:
DEMOCRACY IMPLIES THAT CITIZENS MATTER

Through the overwhelming mass of historical and contemporary argument about democracy runs the belief that a democratic system implies that the preferences, or wishes, or (treacherous term) interests of the people should to some degree prevail. In her careful review of the concept of representation, Hannah Pitkin finds substantive policies, not merely procedures, essential: "We require functioning institutions that are designed to, and really do, secure a government responsive to public interest and opinion"[1] (Pitkin 1967, 234). For this reason even when we accept the presence of competitive elections as a rough indicator of national democracy in practice, we require that citizens be able to form new parties and offer new policy alternatives. Few proponents of liberal democracy would accept as meaningful elections in which (as in Nigeria in 1993) a ruling military council imposes two candidates to compete for votes in a presidential election.

Some, most famously Joseph Schumpeter (1942, chap. 22), have attempted to define democracy purely in terms of the processes of participation and competition.[2] They urge us to conceptualize democracy, government by the people, in terms of citizens' participation in the choice of policymakers without regard to substantive content. The justification is that the configurations of the preferences of the citizens are, or may be, too complex to permit meaningful comparison of those preferences with the views and actions of policymakers. While the power of this argument demands careful consideration, its counsel of despair runs contrary both to traditional ideals and common understanding. Even thoughtful proponents are left uneasy that so little remains of ordinary democratic usage. If we can find meaningful ways to ascertain the general directions of citizen preference, we should employ them.

In titling this book, I have already come down firmly on the side that public opinion should matter. Elections, even free, competitive elections with universal suffrage, are the instruments of democracy, not democracy itself. Citizen participation in a democracy should influence policy making, pressing it closer to the citizens' preferences than it otherwise might be. Electoral participation should not suffice in its own right. Various forms of competitive elections and representative government are, in part, hypotheses about how to bring citizens' preferences to bear on public policies. Testing these hypotheses requires beginning with citizens' preferences,[3] not with the process through which they are expressed.

WHY BEGINNING WITH VOTES IS INSUFFICIENT

The second justification for relying on votes in analyzing the role of elections assumes that citizens' voting choices reveal their preferences, or all we need to know about them, or perhaps all we can reliably know about them. This is a serious argument because in a democracy votes do give all citizens an opportunity to express their preferences on a meaningful occasion. The discussion in part 2 assumes that citizens' preferences are important, but that they are revealed in the election through voting choices. The task of elections as instruments of democracy, as analyzed in the previous four chapters, was to connect the voting choices to the policymakers.

The problem is that election choices are not simply reflections of preferences. Even setting aside citizens' tendencies to be swayed by emotional symbols, attractive candidates, and irrelevant side issues, election choices are constrained and shaped by the alternatives offered by the party system. The alternatives offered by the party system include candidates, immediate issue promises, long-term party-issue or party-group commitments, and so forth. Citizens may vote for a party because it is the best of several unpalatable alternatives or as a nearly random pick among equally desirable parties. Moreover, citizen voting decisions may be strategic, taking account of voters' expectations about the choices of others, the rules of representation, and the future bargaining between parties in policy making.

The vote does not ordinarily tell us how the voter relates to other party choices — whether she or he is relatively indifferent toward several parties or closely committed to one of them.[4] The absence of this information should make even majoritarians somewhat uneasy about using victory for the plurality party (winner of more votes than any other party) as a sufficient criterion of electoral responsiveness. What if many voters are nearly indifferent toward several parties with relatively similar positions on the spectrum — but feel quite estranged from a large party far away from them? The latter might win a plurality if the similar parties split the vote; yet we feel intuitively that it would be wrong to include such a party in government, while excluding the slightly smaller parties that are substantively close to lots of voters.

If we are to escape limitations of relying on voter choices to compare how elections function (and fail) as instruments of democracy, we need a more direct measure of citizens' preferences. All the concerns about multiple similar parties or distant parties require some information about citizens' preferences. Having a direct measure of citizen preferences, we could relate the preferences to the commitments (and, eventually, to the actions) of the governments and influential policymakers that emerge after the elections. The processes of electoral competition and citizen choice are still relevant in creating linkages between what citizens want and the commitments of policymakers. Accidental correspondence is not, in itself, a demonstration of democracy. Neither is the studied benevolence of a dictator. It is when we see the conjunction of representative correspondence and explicable electoral and policy-making processes creating such correspondence that we can assess the performance of elections as instruments of democracy.[5] We have been investigating the processes; if possible, we need to investigate the substantive correspondence they are supposed to create.

Congruence of the Preferences of Citizens and the Positions of Representatives: The Left-Right Scale

Measuring the relation between citizens' preferences and governments' positions and policies in countries is conceptually and empirically exacting. Public policy in modern society covers an enormous range of possible activities. Preferences about defense policy, for example, will be shaped by assessments of foreign threat and loom far larger in some countries and at some times than in others. The same holds for preferences about economic policy, the environment, education, and so forth. Even within a single country citizens care about numerous issues. Many citizens will be uninformed about the details of policy issues and the reasonableness of alternatives. Which issues and which formulations shall we choose to compare?

Except for the sheer scale of modern polities, there is nothing new about this situation. For more than two thousand years political philosophers have worried about the ignorance of the average citizen on specialized policy issues. The general answer they propose is that citizens are not expected to know the details of specific issues and programs. Rather, they are supposed to give general direction to policy, to steer, not run, the ship of state.[6] This line of thought transforms the problem of identifying citizens' detailed policy preferences into identifying their stance toward a general policy direction in the discourse of his or her society. Ideally, we should like the citizen himself or herself to identify this general policy stance, taking account of all the various issues in which he or she is interested. We need, however, a comparable language of policy discourse.

The instrument that I shall use for directly assessing a citizen's preferences is his or her self-placement on the left-right ideological continuum. Fortunately, in most of the modern democracies in my analysis in this period the language of left and right reflects (and perhaps helps create) a unidimensional discourse familiar to citizens and elites. It is not only the most widely available single measure of the preferences of citizens in different countries but seems to meet reasonably well our need to capture comparably the general stances of citizens and the general policy orientations of the parties that compete for policy-making positions.

Originally, *left* and *right* reflected the physical seating of deputies opposing or supporting the monarchy in the Assembly during the French Revolution. Over the years, the left-right terminology has assimilated various issues and alternatives that became important to the voters and the parties who appeal to them in West European countries. In the 1960s and 1970s the degree of government intervention in the economy was perhaps its most common referent, but it also generally included views on defense policy. In some countries left and right included views on the role of the church in politics. Later the left-right dialogue came to incorporate the "new politics" issues of the environment and citizen participation.[7] Studies of mass publics and political elites in many of our countries show that they are able to think about public policy issues in the language of left and right.[8] (In the United States, the terms *liberal* and *conservative* have similar meaning in this discourse.) Existing studies also show that when surveyed, most citizens in these countries can place themselves meaningfully when asked about their positions on a left-right scale.[9]

The left-right scale seems to be fairly effective, at a general level, in assimilating issues and reducing them to a single dimension. Students of legislative voting can describe voting patterns over long periods by this single dimension.[10] Students of elections in many countries have also been able to describe party competition in these terms.[11] (But the degree to which a single dimension assimilates all the issues in competition probably does vary across party systems.)

For our purposes we need not assume that the meaning of a 5 on a 10-point left-right scale implies the same substantive policy preferences to citizens of different countries. It almost certainly does not. A middle-of-the-road position on health policy in the United States is quite different from a middle position on health policy in Britain. The countries have diverse state institutions, policies, and needs. But it is not necessary to compare the preferences of the citizens in one country to those of the citizens in another country. Rather, we want to compare the citizens in a country with the positions of the political parties competing in elections in that same country. When the parties in the government or policy-making coalition are close to the citizens on the left-right scale, elections are performing well as instruments of democracy. The further away from the citizens, the less successful the performance of elections in creating *representational congruence* between voters and policymakers.[12] The availability of a language of discourse identifying comparably the similarities and dissimilarities in general policy-making orientation within each political system makes it possible to move behind the vote and begin with the preferences of the citizens.

A Normatively Privileged Position: The Median Voter and the Two Visions of Democracy

A strong body of theoretical literature demonstrates that on a single issue or a single dimension of issues, if we assume that the preferences of voters are single-peaked, the position of *the median voter* is the only policy that would be preferred to all others by a majority of voters.[13] This is a theoretical point, not an empirical one. I introduce it here to justify my emphasis on the position of the median voter on the left-right scale as a critical normative criterion. A government at the position of the median voter is as close to its electorate as it can possibly be.

I assume that in a democracy all citizens are empowered to vote. Thus, the appropriate normative standard for the congruence of citizens and policy-makers is the position of the median citizen, not the median position among those voters who turned out to vote in a particular election. In the subsequent discussion, I use the terms *median citizen* and *median voter* more or less interchangeably. All empirical analysis, however, refers to the position of the median citizen, as measured by public opinion surveys.[14]

The position of the median voter has no absolute substantive meaning. The median voter may support different policies in different electorates. That position may favor change or continuity, government intervention or government disengagement. The meaning of the position of the median voter is simply that it is the position that finds exactly half of the electorate on either side of it.

To see the normative significance of the median voter's position, imagine that the voters did not elect representatives, but rather voted directly on the left-right continuum positions as policy alternatives. We should expect these voters to adopt (eventually) a policy position that corresponds to the policy position of the median voter because the median voter's position is the only one that cannot be defeated by a majority. If some position other than the median is adopted, then a minority has prevailed over a possible majority. Indeed, as the adopted policy position moves farther away from the median voter, the size of the majority that prefers some other policy grows larger and the size of the winning minority grows smaller. The concept of democracy in all visions — but especially in the majoritarian — surely depends on minorities not positively prevailing over majorities: so the position of the median voter has notable normative consequence.

To put it yet another way, which is logically equivalent but conceptually closer to the proportional influence vision, choosing the position of the median voter minimizes the number of voters opposed to the chosen position. This is one way of interpreting Lijphart's observation (1984, 4) that the alternative to majoritarianism proposes that when citizens disagree governments should be responsive to as many people as possible. Staying at purely the normative level, the position of the median voter thus seems privileged over any other position in both majoritarian and proportional visions. It is the position that can defeat any other position in a simple majority vote; that minimizes the number of opposing voters.

Yet there are some difficulties. For the majoritarians, the difficulty seems to lie in the assumption of a continuum—a continuous distribution of issue positions. Majoritarians often seem to assume a discontinuous, "lumpy," or even dual distribution of possibilities. The median voter position will always fall, however, in the larger chunk of a dual distribution. It is only, I think, the imagery that seems slightly unsettling. Congruence with the citizen median seems the best possible standard from the majoritarian perspective.

The position of the median voter is less satisfactory as the sole criterion for the proportional influence vision. There are at least two reasons. First, I pointed out in chapter 1 that one justification of the proportional influence vision is that it allows more easily for the possibility of different majorities forming on different issues. It explicitly rejects the freezing of a single majority at the point of the election because such alternative majority coalitions may be prematurely excluded. The idea of the left-right continuum, which reduces all issues and issue dimensions to this one super dimension, does away with the multiple dimension problem by its very conceptualization. To this extent, my adoption of the single left-right scale is more consistent with assumptions of the majoritarian than of the proportional vision. Put another way, the majoritarian vision assumes that the concept of the citizen majority is a meaningful one; in a unidimensional space the concept is always meaningful—in a multidimensional space it may not be.[15] Of course, the dimensionality of the issue space of citizen preferences is an empirical question in any election, but one with implications for the appropriate normative standards.

Second, the normatively privileged position of the median voter depends on that position defeating any other in a majority vote. If we require something greater than a majority or if we accept something other than one person–one vote as appropriate political resource distribution to approve any policy, the situation is less clear. Arguments for proportional or, especially, consensual decision rules sometimes rest on protecting minorities by allowing them to block change.[16] We might then privilege the status quo, as minorities can block change, rather than the median voter position. The dominating normative status of the median voter in the proportional vision depends on our accepting the principle that in the final decision majorities should have more influence than minorities, although the latter should have full opportunity to participate. Not all democrats accept this.

We saw in chapter 6 that the normative differences between the ideals of the two visions of elections and democracy made it difficult, perhaps impossible, to construct a single satisfactory standard for comparing responsiveness to citizens' voting choices. Some of the same problems emerge in comparing congruent representation. In a space appropriately described by a single left-right scale, no other single position, except perhaps the status quo, can be more normatively appropriate than the citizen median. But the proportional influence vision suggests that the government ideal should not only be centered at the citizen median, but extend around it to reflect proportionally the full distribution of citizen preferences. A fit to the citizen median is part, but only part, of the proportional ideal, even assuming a single political dimension in political discourse. In chapters 8 and 9 I shall accept the median voter position as a normative policy standard in testing the empirical success of each vision. But a full evaluation from the proportional perspective would require additional consideration of the full distribution of policymaker positions and its correspondence to the citizen distribution.[17] If the empirical systems were to prove equally effective in achieving congruence between median voter position and influential policymaker position, majoritarians might be satisfied. Advocates of the proportional vision would appropriately demand further analysis of the fate of minorities. We cannot fully escape the differences in the normative ideals, although the position of the citizen median is an essential first step because of its importance to both visions.

One other normative concern can be more easily deflected, on empirical grounds. If we were to wish to minimize the distances from the chosen policy, rather than the numbers of voters not supporting it, the privileged point would be the citizen mean, not the citizen median (as pointed out by Achen 1978). In a situation in which many voters were fairly close to the median on one side and fewer voters a long way away on the other side, the mean would be pulled toward the latter, in order to minimize the distances. Empirical studies of representation have usually used the citizen mean.[18] Whether we would wish normatively to minimize the distances (or the square of the distances, which has nice statistical properties) might depend on what assumptions we would make about intensities and distances and how these should be taken into account. The classic utilitarians assumed that we could indeed measure the intensities of citizen preferences and weight their desirable influence by that intensity. The claim of the mean to weight the electorate by intensity of preference is potentially a serious concern, as those who would limit pure majority rule have often been worried about the fate of intense minorities.[19] Their concern recognizes that modern elections do not take intensity into account — all votes (are supposed to) count the same, regardless of the intensity (or wisdom or wealth or ethnic status) of the voter.

A major objection to using the mean on the left-right scale for this purpose, of course, is that we have no solid evidence that voters far from the mean hold their positions more intensely. It would be more satisfying to measure intensity directly or at least to buttress the distance/intensity assumption in the societies being studied with some direct data. Development of reliable measures of preference intensity that can be compared across systems (or even within them) is an extremely difficult problem.

I cannot solve the intensity question in general at either the normative or empirical levels; it remains a fascinating and vital problem in the study of democracy. However, in the countries studied here, there is little difference in the current data set between the means and medians of the citizens. Table 7.1 shows the distribution of voter self-placements in each of the countries close to the time of an election in the early 1980s. (When possible these are the same elections as those in our example in chapter 5.)

In each country the general shape of the distributions of citizens on the left-right scale is similar. The point with the largest number of voters (shown in bold numbers) is around the center at position 5 or 6. The points with the next largest numbers are usually adjacent to the center, with declining numbers of citizens as we move away from the center, as in the classic bell curve. In almost all cases the means and modes are very close to each other, usually within .1 of a scale point, never more than .3 of a scale point, as we would expect with these kinds of distributions. None of the substantive results reported in the next few chapters would be altered by using the citizen mean rather than the citizen median.

In some countries the distributions are slightly asymmetric in favoring the left or right side (although we cannot be sure what this means substantively). In the early 1980s the voters in France, Italy, and Spain were more leftist in their self-identifications, while those in Australia, Austria, Ireland, Japan, and Switzerland were more rightist, as can be seen in the means and modes or by looking at the distributions in detail.

Inspection of the country distributions or comparison of their standard deviations, shown in the last column, also shows that the distributions are more centrist in some countries, more evenly spread across the continuum in others. In Denmark 31 percent of the citizens placed themselves at 5, with another 17 percent at 6, and the next largest groups at 7 and 4. Only 14 percent placed themselves at the four most extreme positions 1, 2, 9, and 10. In Greece, by contrast, 29 percent of the voters placed themselves at the four most extreme positions—with roughly equivalent numbers on right and left. One implication is that a government at the median (or mean) would be further from more voters in Greece than in Denmark. The median is the best position for a government to minimize the number of opposing voters; the mean would be slightly better to minimize the distances. But in either case a more polarized electorate, as in Greece, will probably be more difficult to

Table 7.1. Voter Self-Placement on Left-Right Scale: Early 1980s or Closest Election Survey[1]

Country	Year	Percentage of Citizens at Each Scale Point[1]										Median	Mean	Standard Deviation
		1	2	3	4	5	6	7	8	9	10			
Australia	1981	2	1	6	9	36	14	12	10	4	5	5.5	5.8	1.9
Austria	1975	3	3	10	10	16	19	13	14	6	7	6.0	6.0	n.a.
Belgium	1981	3	4	9	8	21	22	11	9	4	9	5.7	5.8	2.2
Canada	1981	2	1	4	6	37	20	12	11	4	4	5.7	5.9	1.8
Denmark	1981	3	3	7	10	31	17	13	9	5	3	5.5	5.6	1.9
Finland	1981	2	3	7	11	26	14	13	15	6	3	5.7	5.9	2.0
France	1981	7	5	15	13	31	11	9	5	1	3	4.8	4.8	2.0
Germany	1983	1	3	10	15	28	14	14	9	4	3	5.4	5.5	1.9
Greece	1981	8	7	12	14	26	9	4	7	4	10	4.9	5.2	2.4
Ireland	1982	2	1	5	8	19	23	17	14	6	5	6.2	6.2	2.0
Italy	1983	6	8	16	14	29	13	5	4	2	3	4.6	4.6	2.1
Japan	1981	2	2	7	9	22	20	13	13	4	7	6.0	6.0	1.8
Netherlands	1982	4	5	12	13	19	12	12	12	4	6	5.4	5.5	2.4
New Zealand	1981*	2		24		49		22		2		5.5	5.5	n.a.
Norway	1981	2	2	9	10	27	13	14	13	4	6	5.7	5.8	2.1
Spain	1981	4	7	16	16	25	13	9	7	2	2	4.8	4.9	2.0
Sweden	1981	3	6	14	12	22	12	11	11	5	5	5.3	5.4	2.3
Switzerland	1976	2	1	9	11	25	18	13	12	4	4	5.7	5.8	n.a.
United Kingdom	1983	3	2	7	10	27	16	14	14	4	4	5.7	5.8	2.0
United States	1981	2	4	6	7	26	18	14	12	5	6	5.8	5.9	2.1

*Survey in New Zealand (Bean et al. 1981) used 1–5 scale; however, mean and median were recomputed as if based on 10-point scale.

[1]Most 1981 distributions and scores are from the 1981 World Values Study. Greece was not in the 1981 World Values Study; uses Eurobarometer Oct. 1981; others in the early 1980s, but not 1981, are from closest Eurobarometer surveys. Mid-1970s scores in Austria and Switzerland from the Barnes and Kaase eight-nation study, as these are not included in the 1981 World Values Study. They are included in the 1990 World Values Study, however, and subsequent analysis uses those data.

represent than a more homogeneous one, as in Denmark. Representing the distribution is, of course, a problem for proportional influence theorists; strict majoritarians would be unconcerned about it.

Placing the Parties on the Left-Right Continuum

Having located the positions of the citizens on the left-right scale, we still have to compare them to the positions of the policymakers. I shall use positions of political parties to estimate the positions of governments and influential policymakers. To place the parties, we are fortunate to be able to use the assessment of expert observers in each country,[20] who have placed the parties on the same left-right scale on which citizens are placing themselves. Thus, to compare the citizen and expert positions, it is only necessary that, for example, a 5 and a 7 mean the same thing to citizens and to experts within the same country. On this point it is reassuring that, despite the usual problem that citizens can vote only for available parties and that strategic considerations may enter, the citizens who vote for a party usually place themselves at roughly the same positions as the experts place the party. To compare the distances across countries, we must assume that the distance between scale points reflects in different countries roughly similar differences in stances toward important issues. There is some, admittedly limited, evidence for this assumption.[21]

My analysis of the representative congruence between voters and their governments and policymakers uses, then, the left-right scale. We have measures of the position of the median (and mean) voter from opinion surveys that have asked citizens in many countries to place themselves on a left-right continuum (usually ranging from 1 to 10, but which I have adjusted accordingly if it does not). Measures of the position of political parties are based on two surveys (in 1982 and in 1993) of scholarly experts that asked the respondents to place the parties on a left-right scale. Representative congruence is the distance between the position of the policy-making party and the position of the median citizen on the left-right scale. The larger the distance, the less the congruence; the smaller the distance, the greater the congruence.[22]

Empirical Predictions from the Two Visions

The general arguments that connect citizens, governments, and policymakers in the two visions are by now familiar. However, the rather well articulated bodies of empirical theory involving the median voter make it possible to lay out more precisely the empirical linkages that (theoretically) lead to congruence in the two visions. Setting out the linkages explicitly draws

Table 7.2. Visions of Democracy and Processes That Create Congruence Between the Median Citizen and the Policymakers

Process Stages	Majority Control Vision	Proportional Influence Vision
Electoral stages		
Election competition	Identifiable alternative governments, one a responsible incumbent; one or both close to the median citizen	Wide range of party choices; absence of explicit coalition commitments
Election outcomes	Party close to median citizen wins majority: Median legislator close to median citizen	Proportional legislative representation of all parties: Median legislator close to median citizen
Postelection stages		
Government formation	Election winner forms majority government	Bargaining: government coalition includes party of median legislator
Policy making between elections	Government dominates all policy making	Coalitions may change but still include median; negotiation with opposition parties may help balance government parties right or left of median party
Congruence predictions	Government is the policymaker and is close to the median citizen	Government includes the median legislator, but weighted position of all policymakers will be closer to the median citizen

Note: Both visions assume that the median voter will be at the same position on the left-right scale as the median citizen.

attention to points where linkage may fail and the connection weaken. I examine these in the next two chapters. Table 7.2 (adapted slightly from Huber and Powell 1994) summarizes the processes that create congruence between voters and policymakers in the two visions of democracy.

In the majority control vision the decisive stage is the election: party alternatives, voter choices, and the aggregation of the votes by the election rules. For election outcomes to create congruence, the voters must be provided with identifiable alternative governments. Elections must also produce majority government control over policy making for the party preferred by the citizens. If these defining characteristics of majority control are achieved, then close correspondence between voters and policymakers will depend on another feature of the election: the presence of at least one party or candidate located at or very near the median voter. If all parties are close to the median (as would be predicted in the well-known strategic two-party competition model of Anthony Downs) then a victory for either will result in a government close to the median voter. If only one party is at the median and the other is not, that party must win the election to create congruence. Even with perfectly behaving voters, this might be a problem if more than two parties compete and several parties close to the median split the voter support.

Given all the conditions, the majoritarian model predicts good congruence. The defining conditions of the majoritarian model, identifiable alternative governments and clear policy control, are more closely approximated in some countries and after some elections than in others. Moreover, it is rare for a single party anywhere to win a majority of the votes. I noted in chapter 6 some cases in which election law distortion prevented the party receiving the most votes from winning government control. In the next chapter, I shall also have to consider whether or not the election offers at least one party choice that is close to the median voter and whether the voters indeed choose that party.

The proportional influence vision also predicts empirical connections between the median voter and the policymakers, but they are reached by an alternate route. This is, of course, a multistage model. At the electoral level, the defining conditions provide for multiple parties offering a variety of alternatives, so that all citizens can find compatible choices. The parties need not converge to the center unless virtually all the voters are located very close to it. Such lack of convergence is roughly what the strategic competition literature predicts from multiparty competition (as discussed at more length in the next two chapters). At the time of the election, the choices of voters and the working of proportionate election laws result in a legislature composed of parties representing all these groups in their proportional strength. The critical implication of these defining conditions is that the position of the median legislator (or median party, if parties are in fact the relevant units) should be very close to that of the median voter.[23]

The second stage of the proportional influence vision concerns coalition bargaining. Given a diverse electorate and, hence, legislature, the governing or policy-making coalitions might stray from the position of the median voter. But coalition theory predicts that in one-dimensional situations the median party will play a dominant role in government formation;[24] that is, all coalitions should include the median party, although any coalition may incorporate other parties that fall to one side or the other (or both).

Existing theory does not, however, predict unambiguously whether the median legislative party will dominate policy making, even in the one-dimensional situation. Laver and Schofield (1990) and de Swaan (1973) argue that the policy position of the median legislator will prevail, but Austen-Smith and Banks (1988), in a model that integrates electoral competition and government formation, find that in equilibrium final policy outcomes never correspond to the preferences of the median legislator. More generally, in situations in which a single party or coalition of parties forms a government and must maintain tight party discipline, which empirically is the case in almost all parliamentary systems, the government might be expected to make policies that correspond not to the legislative median but to its own internal distribution.

Thus, a potential for connection exists—through the inclusion of the median party in the coalition—but with less than ideal congruence. The processes that connect legislative bargaining to government policy may also lead to policies somewhat off the median. We know from earlier chapters that the defining conditions of the proportional influence processes—party choices and proportional outcomes—are more closely approximated in some countries and elections than in others. We have now to see whether, even if those conditions are met, the choice of governments indeed includes the median legislator's party.

A final theoretical point concerns the degree of opposition influence in policy making. The majoritarian model assumes that the majority government will control policy making. If that government is at the median, all is well for congruence, and, in fact, giving weight to the opposition will pull the policy-making coalition further from the median voter. The proportional influence model, however, assumes that parties outside the government may well have influence and that this influence is generally desirable because it gives authorized participation in policy making to all parties. Increasing the influence of the opposition may also help pull governments whose internal weight is off the median back toward it. Thus, contrary to the expectations of the ideal majority control model, giving opposition parties weight in policy making may improve congruence between what citizens want and what policies result. But whether in fact this happens depends on the specific positions of the government and other parties.

Positions of Multiparty Governments and Influential Policymakers

If a single political party forms a government and totally controls policy making, then we can use the expert placement of that party on the left-right scale to locate the position of the government. But a number of democratic governments involve party coalitions, rather than a single political party. Moreover, as I discussed in chapter 5, the government, whatever its makeup, is to some degree influenced by other political parties as it makes policy. How estimate, then, the position of multiparty governments and policymaker coalitions, given the positions of the individual parties?

Little direct evidence tells us how to make these estimates. Theory might direct our attention to the median legislator inside the government coalition;[25] or, as noted above, to the median legislator in the entire legislature. But governments apportion their cabinet portfolios to parties in simple proportion to the relative percentage of seats held by each in the lower house of the legislature. Such proportionality of distribution of portfolios is one of the strongest empirical regularities in the study of cabinet governments.[26] In a two-party government coalition, for example, the larger party does not keep all the cabinet positions for itself, or ordinarily control all the party policies. In estimating the government policy position on the general left-right scale, then, it seems safest to assume that the chosen position will be an average of the position of the government parties, weighted by the percent of seats they hold in the lower house of the legislature.

Similarly, I shall estimate the position of the influential policymakers by weighting the average position of all the legislative parties. Having spent considerable effort in chapter 5 estimating the relative policy-making influence of the opposition parties under various conditions — there called structural and political — we can use the same weights here. Thus, we estimate the position of government, support parties, and opposition parties by using the average position of the parties in each category weighted by their relative proportion of legislative seats. We have also the percentage of seats in the legislature held by each type of party. Those percentages are multiplied by the weights from chapter 5: 1.0 for the government, .75 for the support parties, and the sum of structural influence and political influence for the opposition parties. (See chapter 5, especially tables 5.3 and 5.4, and the discussion of deriving and validating the weights.) The overall policymaker left-right position is computed from the government position multiplied by its percentage of seats; plus the support party average, multiplied by its percentage of seats times .75; plus the opposition party average, multiplied by its percentage of seats times the influence weights; this sum is divided by the sum of the weighted seats.

While the computation seems complex, the implications are straightforward. According to its share of legislative seats and probability of bargaining effectiveness, every party in the legislature has some influence on the policymaker position. If the government commands a large seat share with unchecked majority control of the legislature, the policymaker position will be close to the government position. If the government has relatively fewer seats or the opposition has important bargaining resources or both, then the policymaker position will be more heavily shaped by the opposition position. Of course, how much difference it makes for the government and opposition to have varying influence will also depend on how far apart they are in the first place. If all the parties cluster close to the median of the legislature, then it does not make much difference how we add influence of various parties. Similarly, if the opposition parties are spread symmetrically away from the government, they will cancel each other out and the government position will prevail. On the other hand, if the government is at one extreme and the opposition at the other, then the degree of influence of the opposition (from the number of seats and its bargaining power) will affect estimated positions of the policymakers.

As we shall see in the next chapter, the positions of the government and the influential policymakers are likely to be especially different in the case of minority governments, which are typically small, sometimes located off the center, and always forced to bargain seriously with other parties to stay in power. We know from earlier chapters that minority governments constitute a sizable chunk of postelection government formation, particularly in some countries. Thus, we shall need to take careful account of differences between governments and policymakers in our analysis of congruence with the citizen median.

8

The Majoritarian Policy Vision: Decisive Elections, Governments, and the Median Citizen

The majoritarian vision includes both a normative foundation and an empirical hypothesis. In the previous chapter I argued the case for policies at the position of the median voter as the appropriate normative standard from the majoritarian perspective. In a single-dimensional distribution, the policy at the position of the median voter can always defeat any alternative in a majority vote. Insofar as the left-right continuum reduces all dimensions to one superdimension, the median position on this continuum should have a powerful normative claim on majoritarian theory.

In this chapter I shall assume the meaningfulness of the left-right continuum and the normative desirability of left-right policy at the position of the median voter without further discussion. The chapter investigates the empirical success of majoritarian designs and processes in producing governments at that position.

As discussed in the previous chapter, I measure the position of the citizen median by the surveys of citizen self-placements on the left-right scale. With the distribution in these countries, the medians and means are at very similar positions. I measure the position of the governments and influential policymakers by the expert placements of the parties in the legislature and the share of seats commanded by them. I shall assume that governments and policymakers will make policy corresponding to their own (weighted average) position on the left-right continuum. Thus, for majoritarian processes to succeed in making elections function as instruments of democracy, they must produce a party government close to the position of the median voter on the left-right scale.[1]

Majoritarian Empirical Theory: Predictions

The empirical hypotheses in the majority control vision argue that political power should be concentrated in the hands of identifiable majority governments chosen by the electorate and responsible to it. Such identifiable and responsible governments will be forced by the voters to hold positions close to the median voter.

Majoritarian elections involve competition between incumbent governments and a major challenger. Voters evaluate the past performance and the future promises of each and choose the contender whose policies they expect to be closer to their preferences. That contender wins electoral and legislative majorities and comes to office committed to a set of policies favored by a citizen majority. While in office, the new government carries out those policies under the eye of the electorate, which can evict it in the next election if it fails to keep its promises.

The decisive stage in the majoritarian vision is the election: party alternatives, voter choices, the aggregation of the two. Elections must provide voters with identifiable future governments; they also must produce unambiguous control over policy making for the election winner. These features, as discussed in chapter 4, identify majoritarian processes in practice. If these defining characteristics obtain, then whether there is a close congruence between the median citizen and the government policymakers will depend on another feature of the election: victory of a party located at or near the median. If neither identifiable alternative government is close to the median citizen, then by our definition the majoritarian democratic process cannot result in a government that is committed to what the voters want. If both alternatives are close to the median, then victory for either will lead to satisfactory results. If one party is close and the other far away, the closer one must win in order to create congruent representation of the voters by the government.

Scholars have offered a variety of specific models of positive (non-normative) theory to explain how the dynamics of competition in majoritarian systems might lead one or both contenders to take positions close to the median voter. Most famously, in the two-party competition model proposed by Anthony Downs (1957), the desire to win elections drives both parties toward the position of the median voter. With a single dimension of party competition and voters voting for the closer party, a party that fails to converge to the median can always be defeated by a party that does move to the median.[2] If the parties want to win the election, they should seek the median position. If the theory of center-driven two-party competition were empirically true, it would strongly underpin the majoritarian vision's claim to create congruent representation. There is, however, much controversy about the correspondence between Downs's theory and the empirical facts of party competition.[3]

Because only the winning party needs to be near the citizen median to create congruence, the majoritarian vision need not depend on Downs's strategic parties. It can encompass other two-party models in which incumbents face challengers who over time offer a large array of possible alternatives.[4] The parties may not be anticipating voter preferences or even be able to estimate them, at least initially. With the voters always choosing the more preferred alternative, eventually the election winners will be at or near the median voter. This is what traditional mandate versions of majoritarian theory seemed to expect, as discussed in chapter 4. We can even imagine a version of this in which true party positions are not revealed to the voters until the party has held office. So voters begin by "randomly" choosing a government, keeping it if it turns out to be close to their preferences, discarding it if it does not. Again, eventually the voters find and hold on to governments close to the median.

In these less strategic versions, if the system were starting from scratch as a democracy, it might take some time for random offerings of party policies, especially if only retrospectively discovered by voters, to converge on the median. As all the democracies in this study except Spain and Greece had been operating as democracies for some time even at the earliest points here considered, we would expect from these theories, too, to find at least one party near the median, unless there were radical changes in the position of the electorate. Given the continuity we see over time in the location of the citizen median and the parties, as well as what we know about public opinion configurations, such major changes seem to be rare.

All the majoritarian models assume that the election winner will subsequently dominate the policy process and implement the promised policies. The election should be the decisive stage in setting the course of policy. Moreover, clearly responsible incumbents in office at the time of the election should be helpful: single-party majority governments that bear obvious responsibility for their actions will be pressed to anticipate the citizen majority as they face reelection; voters will find it easier to evaluate the credibility of promises and to choose the party whose true position is closest to their preferences.

One potential problem, of course, is that various empirical studies and also some theoretical work suggest the failure of party competition consistently to produce a party at the median.[5] Another potential problem, discussed in chapters 4 and 6 above, is the occasional failure of elections in majoritarian systems to provide legislative control to the vote winner; or, even worse, to give it to the vote loser. In the latter cases, congruent representation will be created only when party competition has driven both contenders to the median.

Alternative Future Governments and the Median Voter

We can now merge chapters 4 and 7 and see what the alternative governments are offering the electorate. Our best data for examining this question are based on the two surveys of experts who placed the parties on the left-right scale in 1982 and 1993, respectively, and the citizen self-placements from the *Eurobarometer* surveys (available twice each year from the mid-1970s through the 1990s for countries in the European Community) and the two *World Values Studies*, carried out about 1981 and 1990. Some data from national election surveys in Australia and New Zealand also contain appropriate measures of citizens' positions at these times. Table 8.1 shows the left-right positions of the alternative future governments and of the median citizen for specific elections in the early 1980s in the sixteen countries for which we have both citizen self-placements and elite party placements. (The 1982 expert survey did not cover Greece, Japan, or Switzerland; I have not been able to locate citizen left-right self-placement data for Austria in this time period.) The position of the winning contender, that is, the contender forming a government immediately after the election,[6] is indicated in bold. In the far right column is the distance between the new government and the citizen median.

The majoritarian vision, with its emphasis on the decisiveness of the election itself in creating congruence, depends on future governments (connected to the election outcome) identifiable to voters and on the policy choices offered by these governments. To examine when and whether these conditions hold, I have divided the elections in the early 1980s into four major groups (see table 8.1). In the three countries at the bottom of the table—Italy, Finland, and Belgium—the party system did not offer defined government alternatives to the voters. Government formation was a matter of postelection bargaining; the electoral stage was not decisive. These elections in no way fit the assumptions of the majoritarian model, so I shall defer analyzing them until the next chapter. They do, however, offer a relative standard for comparison; the governments formed after the election in these countries were on average slightly less than one scale point from the median citizen.

The other thirteen elections did offer the voters possibly decisive elections: either two major-party alternatives, competing formal coalitions, or at least widely held expectations about how voters' choices between two groups of contenders would determine the future government. (See chapter 4 for identifiability as a characteristic of elections.) These thirteen cases should support the empirical hypotheses of the majoritarian vision.

On the basis of party competition the thirteen elections with substantial future government identifiability in the early 1980s fall into three roughly equal groups. In the first group are elections in four countries that look most like Downs's "convergence to the median voter" prediction about two-party competition. I have had to be rather generous about the degree of convergence that qualifies. If we expect both contenders to be within a single scale point of the median voter on the ten-point scale, we are disappointed. None of the elections in these years quite fulfills this expectation. As the average government in the systems at the bottom of the table, produced by legislative bargaining, fell within a point of the median, that seems an appropriate standard — but one that is not achieved. The absence of highly convergent systems is a point to which I shall return later.

If we use 1½ scale points as our criterion, then the elections in Canada, New Zealand, Ireland, and the United States do show both parties (party versus two-party coalition in Ireland) achieving this standard. The bold number shows the actual winner of the election, but with both parties being fairly close to the center good representative congruence between median citizen and government will be assured regardless of the actual winner. In fact, the average government is within a point of the median voter. The larger government distance in the United States reflects Republican control of the presidency; the Democrats, quite close to the median in that year, continued to control the House of Representatives.

The second group of high identifiability cases in table 8.1 includes elections in which one party or coalition is fairly close to the median voter, but the other is not. Although this does not accord with Downs's predictions about convergent two-party competition, it does offer good opportunities for congruent representation. The voters must endorse the closer party, whether that party is strategically driven or just has the good luck to be in the right place at the right time. In three cases (Spain, Denmark, and the Netherlands) they did so, although the minority Danish government proved rather short-lived. (Multiple governments are explored in more detail in the next chapter.) Unfortunately, in the other two cases they did not. (The position of the party or coalition that formed the government is shown in boldface type.) German voters in 1983 backed an FDP/CDU-CSU coalition that was somewhat further from the median voter than the SPD alternative. In Sweden the Social Democrats, helped by the election rules,[7] won nearly 48 percent of the seats in the legislature and were able to form a minority government with the implicit support of the

Table 8.1. *Ideological Distance Between the Two Alternative Governments in Sixteen Democracies, Early 1980s*

| Country | Year | Alternative Governments Identified | Left-Right Positions | | | Distance Between New Government[1] and Median Citizen |
			Left Contender	Median Citizen	Right Contender	
Both contenders within 1 1/2 scale points of median citizen						
Canada	1980	LIBERAL v. PC	5.8[3]	5.7	6.9	.1
Ireland	1981	FG/LAB v. FF	6.6	6.2	6.6	.4
New Zealand	1981	LABOUR v. NATIONAL	4.4	5.5	6.4	.9
United States	1980	DEM v. REP	5.3	5.8	7.1	1.3
Only one contender within 1 1/2 scale points of median citizen						
Spain	1982	SOC v. AP	4.2	4.4	8.6	.1
Denmark	1981	S.DEM v. CD/CH/LIB/CON	4.4	5.5	7.2	1.1
Netherlands	1982	LABOUR v. CDA/LIB	3.3	5.4	6.8	1.4
Germany	1983	SPD v. CDU/FDP	4.0	5.4	7.1	1.7
Sweden	1982	S. DEM v. AG/LIB/CON	3.6	5.3	6.6	1.7

Neither contender within 1 1/2 scale points of median citizen

France	1981	COMM/SOC v. UDF/RPR	**3.2**	4.8	7.8	1.6
Norway	1981	LABOUR v. AG/CH/CON	3.7	5.7	7.9	2.3
United Kingdom	1983	LABOUR v. CONS	3.1	5.7	8.0	2.3
Australia	1980	LABOUR v. LIB/CTY	3.8	5.5	7.8	2.3

Alternative future governments not identified in election[2]

Italy	1983	COMM v. DC	2.4	4.6	**5.9**	.8
Finland	1983	SOC v. NAT	**3.7**	5.7	7.5	.8
Belgium	1981	SOC v. CH/LIB	3.4	5.7	7.0	1.3

Missing data countries

Austria	1983	SPOe v. OeVP		n.a.		—
Greece	1981	SOC v. NEW DEM	n.a.	5.4	n.a.	—
Switzerland	1983	SOC* v. CATH-CON*	n.a.	n.a.	n.a.	—
Japan	1983	SOC* v. LIB DEM	n.a.	5.2	n.a.	—

[1]Average placement of parties in government, weighted by their size, by experts in 1982 survey (Castles and Mair 1984). Scale (0–10) converted to correspond to 1–10 citizen scale.

[2]Party alternatives are illustrative only; see discussion of preelection identifiability of future governments in chapter 4 above.

[3]Boldface type identifies the position of the party or coalition that in fact formed the governemnt after the election.

Communists, although the conservative coalition was closer to the median voter. The vote outcome, nearly a dead heat between the two contenders, may have reflected voter distress with the severe disagreements within the bourgeois coalition that had led several times to its collapse while in government during the previous six years. The five cases in this category provide only mixed support for majoritarian theory.

The third group of elections is much more disconcerting for majoritarian empirical theory and for achievement of the normative standard of congruent representation. In the four elections in France, Norway, Britain, and Australia, both of the major alternative parties/coalitions were at a substantial distance from the median voter. Thus, even when the closer of these won a decisive election, as in France and Britain, the winner was quite far from the median voter. In Norway the two groups were equally distant (2 full points) from the median, and in Australia the further alternative actually won, although the difference between them in their (substantial) distance from the median voter was not too great.

The overall record of the early 1980s, then, is disappointing for the empirical processes of majoritarian theory. There are no cases of complete convergence of both contenders to the median voter. Only a third of the cases meet the looser standard of both contenders being within 1½ scale points of the median. The median government in the thirteen cases with identifiable alternative governments is about 1½ points from the median voter. In a third of the countries the government is about 2 scale points from the median, double the distance of the clearly nonmajoritarian cases.

Because we are dealing with so few cases, possibly some unique events of the early 1980s were responsible for the poor showing of empirical majoritarian theory in creating representative congruence between the electorate and the government. For this reason, it is interesting and (for consistency, if not for majoritarian theory) reassuring to examine the elections of the early 1990s shown in table 8.2. We now have data for citizens and parties from elections in all of our twenty countries except Greece.

It is especially good fortune to be able to consider the situation after 1990 because vast changes had taken place in world politics since the previous expert survey of party positions. Some of these changes obviously affected the discourse of left and right in the European countries that make up the bulk of these democracies. The collapse of international Communism in 1989 and the associated discrediting of command control economies led to major transformations in most of the European Communist parties and were associated as well with shifts toward market-oriented economic policies in Socialist and Labour parties that had not previously accepted a "social democratic" approach. A comparison of the scale positions of the leftist contenders in tables 8.1 and 8.2 shows this shift quite unmistakably in the left contenders in Australia and New Zealand; the Netherlands and Belgium; Norway, Sweden, and Finland; France and Britain.[8] (The German SPD has moved left.) There is some tendency for the parties on the right to move a bit further to the right, but there are plenty of exceptions. Controversy over the European Union obviously affects a number of these party systems, resulting in various changes in specific countries. Most striking is the breakup in a number of conservative coalitions.

Table 8.2 shows at the bottom the countries in which elections did not offer identifiable alternative future governments to be chosen in decisive elections. As in the previous table, elections in Italy (still before the constitutional revisions and party system upheavals of 1993–94), Finland, and Belgium are primarily a prelude to postelection bargaining. Majoritarians would not expect these to result in good correspondence. But, in fact, they do better on average than the majoritarian cases. We also have data for Switzerland, which is obviously in this category. Moreover, in Ireland, the Netherlands, and Norway the preelection coalition alternatives that we saw offered in the early 1980s had broken up. Elections in these countries in the early 1990s were also a prelude to bargaining, not decisive in their own right. The representative congruence that does (and does not) come about in these countries will be discussed in the next chapter. But, again, most of the governments that are eventually negotiated are around 1 scale point or less from the median voter.

Of the twelve majoritarian elections offering fairly identifiable future governments to the electorate, only the United States might still be characterized in the early 1990s as somewhat Downsian (that is, both parties within 1 ½ scale points of the median). The theoretically reassuring point here might be that the United States is the only true two-party system. In addition, the two major-party presidential candidates in 1992 (George Bush and Bill Clinton) were almost certainly closer together than the averages of their respective parties. It would be foolish to write off in general the powerful center-seeking incentives that do operate in clearly two-candidate situations. Yet, as suggested even by the stubborn refusal of U.S. parties to ignore their activists and fully seek the center, the simple Downsian model does not take us very far toward understanding the world of democratic politics, even in two-party situations. Note that the U.S. parties are farther apart in the early 1990s (2 ½ points) than they had been in the 1980s (1.8 points).[9] Even in a two-party system, the role of party activists and multiple stages in the selection of leaders and policies may work against the consistent convergence to the median so plausibly portrayed in Downs's model.

By far the largest number of majoritarian elections in table 8.2 finds one

Table 8.2. *Ideological Distance Between the Two Alternative Governments in Twenty Democracies, Early 1990s*

Country	Year	Alternative Governments Identified	Left-Right Positions			Distance Between New Government[1] and Median Citizen
			Left Contender	Median Citizen	Right Contender	
Both contenders within 1 1/2 scale points of median citizen						
United States	1988	DEM v. REP	4.2	5.6	6.3	1.3
Only one contender within 1 1/2 scale points of median citizen						
Spain	1993	SOC v. PP	4.0	4.4	7.5	.4
Germany	1990	SPD v. CDU/FDP	3.8	5.5	6.4	.9
Austria	1990	SPOe v. OeVP	4.8	6.4	6.3	1.0
Australia	1990	LABOUR v. LIB/CTY	4.8	5.8	7.4	1.0
New Zealand	1993	LABOUR v. NATIONAL	5.8	5.6	7.3	1.7
Canada	1988	LIBERAL v. PC	5.1	5.5	7.3	1.8
United Kingdom	1992	LABOUR v. CONS	4.4	5.3	7.7	2.4
France	1993	COMM/SOC v. UDF/RPR	3.6	4.8	7.3	2.5

Neither contender within 1 1/2 scale points of median citizen

Sweden	1991	S. DEM v. LIB/CON	4.1	5.6	**7.6**	1.6
Denmark	1990	S.DEM v. LIB/CON	4.2	5.5	**7.8**	2.3
Japan	1990	SOC* v. LIB DEM	3.8	5.9	**8.4**	2.5

Alternative future governments not identified in election[2]

Ireland	1992	FF v. FG	**5.8**	5.5	7.0	.2
Netherlands	1989	LABOUR v. CDA	4.2	**5.1**	6.3	.2
Belgium	1991	PS/SP v. FDF/PRL	**4.1**	**5.4**	7.1	.4
Switzerland	1987	SOC v. CATH-RAD	2.6	**5.5**	5.3	.8
Norway	1993	LABOUR v. CON	4.1	5.1	**8.0**	1.0
Italy	1992	PDS v. DC	2.5	4.8	**6.3**	1.2
Finland	1991	SOC v. NAT	4.4	6.0	**7.4**	1.2

Missing data countries

Greece	1993	SOC v. NEW DEM	n.a.	5.4	n.a.	—

[1]Average placement of parties in government, weighted by their size by experts in 1993 survey (Huber and Inglehart 1995).
[2]Party alternatives are illustrative only; see discussion of preelection identifiability of future governments in chapter 4 above.
[3]Boldface type identifies the position of party or coalition that formed the government after the election.

party quite close to the median and the other well away from it, shown in the second group in the table. Spain and Germany remain in this category, although the CDU is now closer to the center, while the SPD (troubled by the emergent Greens on their left as well as their hesitation over the reunification issue) has moved further away. In Canada and New Zealand, which were in the convergent category in the early 1980s, the rightist parties have drifted further from the median voter, creating asymmetrical contests.[10] The move toward the center by the left parties in Australia, Britain, and France brought them to about 1 scale point from the median, but their rightist competitors remained substantially further away. Thus, they move from the nonconvergent to the asymmetrical category. In Austria, for which we now have World Values data, both major parties show up to the left of the (very conservative) median voter, although the OeVP (People's Party) is only slightly so. After the election they were faced with a strong extremist third party on the far right, the FPOe (Freedom Party), and negotiated, with substantial difficulties, a grand coalition with each other, as many had expected.

In the pattern of asymmetric party competition, good correspondence with the citizen median depends on the closer party winning the election. Victories for the Spanish Socialists, the German CDU/FDP coalition, and the now-more-centrist Australian Labour Party, as well as the implicit Austrian coalition, speak of good majoritarian performance (with quite a stretch in the Austrian case). The other half of the group, however, is quite troubling.

In Canada, New Zealand, Britain, and France, the closer party (coalition in France) was within the 1½ scale point boundary — but the more distant opposition won the election! As often happens in these systems, the single-member district election rules converted pluralities of around 40 percent of the vote into absolute majorities of seats in the legislature. In Canada the split between the Liberals and the moderately leftist NDP (New Democratic Party) gave the Conservatives a legislative majority with 43 percent of the vote. The New Zealand Labour Party, which had moved sharply to the right while in power in the 1980s, faced challenges from breakaway movements on its left. In 1993 the single-member district election rules and a badly splintered vote delivered a (bare) legislative majority to a National Party that won only 35 percent of the vote. In Britain the electorate gave about 18 percent of the vote to the Liberal Democrats, who were almost exactly at the median, certainly contributing to Labour's failure despite their movement toward the median after the disasters of the early and mid-1980s. However, the Conservative victory certainly surprised election forecasters at the time. The replacement of Margaret Thatcher with John Major may have been taken by the voters, more than the experts, as a sign of Conservative movement toward the median. In

France the incumbent Socialist government and its Communist electoral allies were crushingly defeated by the conservative party coalition, providing little confidence that the left-right scale distances dominated in shaping voter choices in that election. Negative evaluations of incumbent performance in office seemed, in the accounts of the election, to loom much larger and not to have been captured in the left-right images.

Finally, we have in the 1990s, as in the 1980s, a group of three countries (now Denmark, Sweden, and Japan) in which both party groupings were quite a way from the electoral center. (I have included Denmark here because the Danish situation is quite similar to that in Sweden, although the Social Democrats are not quite so far from the median.) In Denmark and Sweden the relation between the voting outcome and the government formation was quite complex because neither contender/coalition won a majority. In both cases the Social Democrats won more votes than their two-party coalition opponents. Moreover, their efforts to form a government could probably count on informal backing from small parties to their left. But bargaining involving other centrist and conservative parties dominated the government formation process. In both cases the outcome was a rightist, multiparty, minority coalition government that still had to rely on support from or negotiations with parties outside the government. The substantial identifiability of would-be governments in the election campaign seems to have shaped and constrained the government formation process, but the elections were not decisive in choosing the government. The result was that the somewhat more distant contender took office, although without having full legislative control. In Japan the Liberal Democrats were assisted by both the election rules and deep divisions (and distance from the median) within the opposition in converting 46.1 percent of the vote into an absolute majority in the legislature, despite their very substantial distance from the median voter.

The results from both tables can be summarized easily enough. Some elections with majoritarian conditions (of future government identifiability) work more or less as they should. In about half of them either both parties converged to within 1 ½ scale points of the median voter (five cases) or the closer party was pretty close and won the election (seven cases, although the 1981 minority Danish government did not endure). Both circumstances give somewhat congruent representation, although it is not notably superior on average to that of the postelection bargaining. Substantial convergence of both parties to the median is, admittedly, rare; the majoritarian alternatives usually stand on the two sides of the median, one of them substantially further than the other.[11] Good correspondence then depends on the closer party winning the election and forming a government.

But in the other half of the cases (thirteen of the twenty-five in tables 8.1 and 8.2) either both major alternatives began quite far from the median voter (seven cases), or the wrong (further) alternative won the election (six cases). For either of these reasons, the elected government ended up substantially — around 2 scale points of the 5 usually available between the median and the extreme in either direction — to the left or right of the median voter. In these cases, majoritarian elections seem to function poorly as instruments of democracy.

Majoritarianism and Congruent Representation

We can reassure ourselves about the robustness of our interpretation from tables 8.1 and 8.2 by looking across a wider range of our election experiences and by considering systematically the measures of government identifiability, mandate and combined majoritarian conditions from chapter 4.

We can expand the number of cases by assuming that the party placements used in tables 8.1 and 8.2 are roughly valid measurements of the party positions within five years of the time of the study — which means we can investigate with reasonable confidence the relation between citizen median and government position from about 1977 through 1998. The 1982 survey covers 1977 through 1987 and the 1993 survey covers 1988 through 1998. (A few elections must be excluded because of the appearance of new, unrated parties.) Everything we know about parties suggests that we shall not make too many mistakes in using these assumptions. Also accurate as measures of the citizens' positions are surveys done within two years of the election. (Calculations based on the closer and slightly further surveys yield nearly identical results.) While we still lose quite a few cases from the 150 elections of our original sample, we have about 80 elections, covering all of our countries except Greece, for which we can compare the citizen median and the government and policymaker positions.

Let us first consider preelection identifiability of future governments, which is critical if decisive elections are to link citizen preferences with future governments. Recall that this measure, from chapter 4, identifies the degree to which voters seem to expect that the outcome of the election will be decisive as to which alternative will form a government. It does not address whether voters associate particular policies with those governments, a point on which we have no direct comparative information. Such identifiability is pretty clear in about 60 percent of the elections in this study; in another 10 percent there was some expectation that the election would determine the government, usually of a left versus right alternative, even if the parties had no explicit agreements. (These proportions remain roughly the same in the subset of cases for which we have the data on citizen and party placements.)

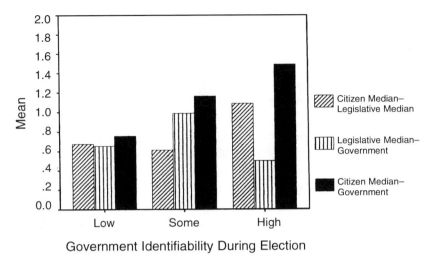

Figure 8.1. Left-Right Distances: Citizens, Legislatures and Governments by Level of Government Identifiability

The three bars for each group in figure 8.1 show, first, the distance between citizen median and legislative median; second, the distance between legislative median and government; and finally, the congruence measure itself: the absolute distance between citizen median and the government's position. Considering the first bar in each group, we see that both low and median identifiability elections tend to have legislatures centered around the citizen median. There is a much greater distance between citizen and legislative median in the high identifiability systems, a point to which I shall return below. But in the moderately identifiable elections the eventual governments are much further from the legislative median than in low identifiability, purely postelection bargaining situations, resulting in governments further from the citizen median. The Danish election of 1990 in table 8.2 is an example of this situation. On the far right of the figure we see that elections with high identifiability are often based on distorted legislative representation (often necessary to create the identifiability). The average government is about the average distance from the legislative median, but this mean is composed of governments with a legislative majority (thus including the legislative median by definition) and distant minority governments. The combination results in an average government nearly twice as far from the median citizen as in the low identifiability cases: 1.4 versus .8.

Figure 8.1 shows that as identifiability is clearer, the distance between the median voter and the government increases. The increasing stairsteps of the third, solid bar are just the *opposite* of what we would expect from major-

itarian views of the desirability of elections as the decisive site linking voter
and government. This pattern is consistent, of course, with data in tables 8.1
and 8.2. The low identifiability elections, which rely on postelection bargaining to form governments, negotiate governments that are the closest to the
median voter, on average less than .8 of a scale point. Higher identifiability
elections produce average governments significantly further away (at the .01
level with 79 elections).

Consideration of the additional elements in the majoritarian processes discussed in chapter 4 simply reinforces these findings. We can, for example, add
a second touchstone of majority government: the production of majorities. We
can group the elections by the mandate conditions measure from chapter 4.
This measure multiplied the government identifiability score by the nonforma-
tion (0.0) or formation (1.0) of a majority government after the election. Thus,
elections receive the minimum score either by having low identifiability or by
failing to result in formation of a majority government afterward. We can
further subtract points for conditions that limit the ability of the new government to carry out its promises (blocking conditions or party disunity). This
analysis isolates elected governments that should reflect the mandate model
especially well because they have been identified to the voters as a future
government before the election, they have received a legislative majority, and
they are able to control policy making after the election. But these governments are even further from the median voter. Similarly, if we add consideration of clarity of responsibility of the government before the election (see
table 3.4) we isolate elections that ever more closely approximate the majoritarian model. Yet these twenty-one governments are on average 1.6 points
from the median voter. The contrast between these majoritarian elections and
the average of .8 from the median in the systems without preelection identifiability is deeply distressing for majoritarian theory.[12]

If we try to disentangle the effects of government identifiability and the
production of majorities, we find that each is of some importance, and, interestingly, they are slightly negatively related to each other across our full set of
elections. That is, 80 percent of the low identifiability elections (16/20) eventually resulted in the negotiation of majority governments. This was true of
only 53 percent of the moderate identifiability elections and 73 percent (32/
44) of the high identifiability elections. Minority government seems to have
been more frequently a consequence of high identifiability settings that did not
produce legislative majorities (for a single party or preelection majority) than
of bargaining failures in low identifiability situations. (This pattern is discussed further in the next chapter.)

Looking at the various combinations in table 8.3, we see, reading down the

Table 8.3. *Mandate Processes and Congruent Governments*

Preelection Identifiability Level of Alternative Governments	Postelection Majority Status	Left-Right Distance Between Government and Median Citizen		
		Mean	Standard Deviation	N
Low identifiability	All	.8	(.5)	20
	Minority	.9	(.4)	4
	Negotiated majority	.7	(.5)	15
	PEC seat majority[1]	—	—	—
	Single-party seat majority	—	—	—
	PEC vote majority	.8	—	1
	Single-party vote majority	—	—	—
Some expected identifiability	All	1.3	(.7)	15
	Minority	1.5	(.7)	7
	Negotiated majority	.8	(.5)	5
	PEC seat majority	1.0	—	1
	Single-party seat majority	2.6	—	1
	PEC vote majority	1.2	—	1
	Single-party vote majority	—	—	—
High expected identifiability	All	1.5	(.7)	44
	Minority	1.4	(.6)	12
	Negotiated majority	—	—	—
	PEC seat majority	2.2	(.5)	6
	Single-party seat majority	1.4	(.9)	17
	PEC vote majority	1.4	(.3)	6
	Single-party vote majority	1.0	(.5)	3
Totals		1.2	(.7)	79

[1]PEC = Preelection coalition. See chapter 4 for definition and estimation of preelection identifiability of alternative future governments.

majority status outcomes within each identifiability situation, that minority governments tend to be farther from the median voter, whether the product of negotiations or (in higher identifiability situations) a legislative "plurality winner." As noted, nearly a third of the high identifiability elections produced these outcomes. Negotiated majorities do very well, as we shall see in more detail in the next chapter, but are not found in the high identifiability settings.

Comparing similar identifiability situations in different majority situations, we see that for almost all the majority situations building from a low identifiability election seems to work better. The especially sharp contrasts in the table are between majority governments in low and high identifiability situations — the latter are far from the median voter, except for the handful built on single-party vote majorities. This handful, of course, represents the full working of the majoritarian model. One interpretation of these results is the following: The problem with the majoritarian model is that voters rarely create majorities without various artificial aids that undermine the connections needed for good congruence.

Election Rules: Disproportionality and Distance Between Median Citizen and Median Legislator

The election rules are one of the sources of distortion in the democracies that in fact experience elections that are decisive for government formation. In the majoritarian vision the election itself must be decisive for the creation or rejection of majority governments. The election rules can in principle play a triple role here:

1. Long-Term Effects: Election rules can encourage the consolidation of the party system. Duverger's Law proposed that single-member district plurality systems would tend to be two-party systems. Gary Cox (1990, 1997) has generalized this into an "M + 1 Rule" that proposed there will be no more than one party more than the number that can be elected from a district. This limit would be sustained by the mutual anticipations of both voters and politicians about the futility of supporting additional parties. Fewer parties should make majorities more likely. (See chapter 2 above, especially table 2.1.)

2. Short-Term Effects: Preelection Coalitions. Election rules can encourage or help sustain multiparty coalitions before and during the election. (See chapter 4.)

3. Short-Term Effects: Vote-Seat Disproportionality. Election rules can reduce

the number of vote-receiving parties that actually gain legislative representation (see table 2.1). As we have seen in earlier chapters, voters in our twenty democracies rarely delivered majorities for single political parties. Rather, such majorities usually depended on the election rules to create majorities in the translation of votes into seats. Such majorities depend, then, on disproportionality of representation.

In previous chapters we have seen evidence that election rules do, indeed, contribute in all three ways to majority government. But need this be at the expense of good congruence between the median citizen (voter) and the government?[13] In principle, no. We can imagine models in which raising the electoral threshold contributed neither to disproportionality nor to poor congruence. We can also suggest models in which disproportionality in vote-seat translation would be nonetheless associated with good congruence. Suppose, for example, we begin with a normal distribution of opinion, as we saw in table 7.1, and ten parties, appealing to voters at each position on the left-right scale. If we hold an election under these conditions we expect ten parties in the legislature, representing the proportion of votes at each position. Suppose we then raise the threshold for entry into the legislature, keeping the number and positions of parties fixed and assuming each voter votes sincerely for the closest party. As the threshold rose from 1 percent to 10 percent, parties at the extremes would be deprived of representation; greater proportions of seats go to the more centrist parties, whose left-right positions are favored by more voters. Disproportionality would increase as extremist voters lost representation and centrist voters gained it, but congruence of medians would be unaffected. If we allow voters and parties to anticipate the exclusion of smaller parties, they should coordinate their vote on fewer parties, but if this happens symmetrically, the median correspondence should still be preserved.

In practice, though, competition and representation under high threshold election rules do not seem to work this way. Majorities are often created by dual processes of reducing the number of serious competitors and increasing disproportionality in representation. But the process frequently fails to preserve the correspondence of citizen and legislative medians. As a party with a legislative majority contains, by definition, the median legislator, the correspondence of citizen and legislative median is essential for good congruence in majoritarian systems.

Although long-term and short-term elements are tangled together as strategic citizens and voters anticipate effects of the rules, we can to some degree separate them by considering the party medians before and after the votes are converted into seats. Let us look at the lineup of parties on the left-right scale and consider the vote percentage won by each party. Adding the vote percentages as we read across the scale, we can find the voted median at the party in the 50th percentile position. If votes were converted into seats perfectly, this would be the position of the median legislator. Perhaps it is helpful to think of this as the outcome of a simulated legislature based on perfect proportionality of vote-seat conversion.

We can then calculate for each election in each country the distance between the preferred median (preference of median citizen) and the voted median (position of the median party in the simulated perfect legislature). If there is a substantial distance between the two, that distance reflects interaction of the alternatives offered by the parties and the choices made by voters. In France in 1981, for example, there simply was no substantial party very close to the median citizen. If there are only a few parties and large gaps in their placement, small shifts of the vote or even in voter turnout might swing the parties from one side of the citizen median to the other. In the absence of Downsian convergence to the median, whose limitations we have already noted in tables 8.1 and 8.2, we would expect these gaps between preferred and voted medians to be more common in systems with only a few parties, a configuration encouraged, in turn, by electoral rules with higher threshold. The cross-hatched set of bars in figure 8.2 shows the distance between citizens' preferred and voted medians under different election rules. That is, these would be the legislatures if there was perfect proportionality of seat distributions. As we can see in reading from right to left across the figure, the distance from the median citizen to the voted median does not seem to increase as the threshold increases.

We can compare this voted median distance to the distance between preferred median and the median legislator after the votes are aggregated into seats by the real election rules. The solid bar in figure 8.2 shows this distance. The additional distance added by vote-seat disproportionality will be shown by the difference between the two bars. As we have already noted, it is very unusual for voters to give a majority to a single political party. It is usually the working of the election rules that creates the legislative party majorities. It is possible for this disproportionality to give a legislative majority to the voted median party, as in Canada in 1980, Spain in 1982, and Australia in 1980. It is even possible for vote-seat distortion to be helpful, as in France in 1988, where the UDF had the voted median but the same disproportionality that shut out the National Front resulted in a legislative median to the Socialists, who were actually closer to the median citizen than the UDF.

But, as is clear from figure 8.2, it is more likely that if vote-seat disproportionality has an effect, it will move the legislative median away from the voted median. In the PR systems the solid bar is low and similar in height to the

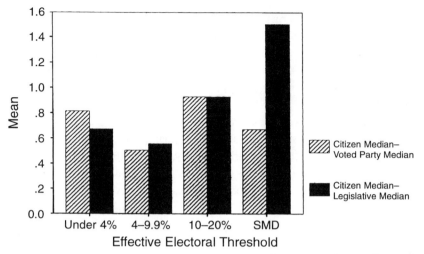

Figure 8.2. Left-Right Distances: Citizens, Voted Party Median and Legislative Median by Election Laws

cross-hatched bar, showing little effect of vote-seat disproportionality on median congruence. But in the single-member district systems the solid bar is about twice as high as the cross-hatched bar, showing the net problem for congruence associated with legislative disproportionality in these systems. Britain in this period exemplifies the problem. Proportionality of representation would have created a legislature in which the Liberal Democrats (or their Alliance predecessors) had the median legislator. They were the voted median party. But the working of the election rules severely distorted the outcome and gave a solid legislative majority to the Conservatives, who were a long way from the citizen median.

A common problem occurs when several parties compete for a similar policy space, leading one or both to fall below a national or district threshold. This kind of "coordination failure" may allow the opposition to win the election even if it does not include the voted median. A number of the cases in which the wrong party won the election in table 8.2 look like this. New Zealand in 1993 is a spectacular example. The Labour Party is close to the citizen median and is, in fact, the voted median. But the Alliance Party to its left took enough of the national vote to give the rightist National Party a legislative majority (and thus the legislative median) with only 35 percent of the vote, while being much further from the citizen median. Canada in 1988 looks similar. Vote-seat distortion may also work through underrepresentation of small center parties, as in the British cases between 1983 and 1992 and Australia in 1980. The price paid in these systems for direct election of majorities is a substantial one. The average legislature is nearly a full scale point further from the citizen median than in the PR systems.[14] In the majoritarian systems, of course, these legislative majorities become unchecked government majorities.

Why Do Majoritarian Processes So Often Fail?

The empirical analyses of correspondence between the median citizen and the government are discouraging for the majoritarian vision of democracy. Both in its own terms and, as we shall see shortly, in comparison to the proportional vision, majoritarian processes frequently fail to deliver governments at desirable policy positions. The proximate cause, obviously, is that winning parties and preelection coalitions are often too far from the median. But why, given the plausible theories about the electoral connections in majoritarian systems, should this be so? One answer is that despite the apparent robustness of the theoretical connections, correspondence depends in fact on achieving some very specific conditions and, importantly, that it is the nature of the majoritarian processes that fairly small deviations from these lead to large, undesirable consequences. A second answer is that it frequently is asking too much of elections that in a complex world they bear the full, decisive burden of connecting voters and policymakers as the majoritarian vision presumes.

Consider first what is assumed in the systems with majoritarian processes: the identifiability of future governments at the election stage. If we recall the preference distributions shown in chapter 7, we see in these countries relatively normal curves centered around the median. There are no cases of bipolar opinion distribution on the left-right scale among the general publics of these modern democracies. How does identifiability of alternative governments emerge from this continuous, center-weighted preference distribution? The analysis in chapter 4 suggested three paths to preelection identifiability of future governments:

1. Two political parties dominate the system of electoral competition, in the sense that parties and voters alike assume that most votes will go to these two parties, one of which will win a majority;
2. Two political parties dominate the expected government formation because the working of the electoral rules of aggregation is expected to convert votes into seats in a way that will sharply reduce the presence of some parties and create legislative majorities for one party;
3. Preelection agreements between parties determine the expected postelection process of government formation, so the voters expect one of the preelection coalitions to win a majority.

Empirically, a huge problem for the fit between the empirical theories and the practice of majoritarian democracy is that the theories assume the first (simple two-party) path. The theoretical models that predict large parties consistently at the median assume only two political parties. But in practice, purely two-party politics is a rare phenomenon and often not robust when it appears. Simply, there is only one consistently two-party system (the United States) in this first sense in which only two parties (are expected to) win most of the votes. Even in the United States in the presidential elections of 1980 and 1992 a third-party candidate deprived the winner of a voting majority and limited the two main parties to around 85 percent of the votes. Britain and New Zealand had a number of elections in the 1950s and 1960s in which the two major parties won over 90 percent. But beginning in the mid-1970s, 80–85 percent became more typical. In Canada it was rare for the two large parties to win much over 80 percent at any time. Australia is two party only if one counts the National-Country alliance as a single party.

We saw in table 2.1 that the effective number of parties winning votes in the countries with single-member district election rules was slightly under three. Except for the United States, legislative majorities in these countries were almost always created by the aggregation of votes into seats. Higher election law thresholds do seem to reduce the number of competing parties.[15] But the election rules in the democracies examined here do not reduce the number of competing parties all the way to two. While there is truth in Duverger's Law that single-member district election laws tend toward two-party systems, the effects are more striking in converting votes to seats than in the anticipation of such effects that might reduce the number of parties in the first place (see table 2.1). In the language of Cox (1997), the single-member district systems face persistent "coordination failures" in that the anticipation of defeat does not sufficiently encourage third-party candidates and voters to join forces with one of the two larger parties. Failures by a party or its supporters to estimate correctly their election chances can occur in many circumstances. But in systems with high electoral thresholds and only a few parties, the consequences of coordination failure for legislative representation may be greater than in a system with low thresholds and many parties.[16]

The failure of election rules and political history to reduce the number of parties to two serious competitors cuts majoritarian practices loose from comforting moorings of center-oriented party competition theories (Downsian two-party strategies or even the randomized convergence over time). With more than two seriously competing political parties or even the anticipation of more than two parties, the theories of party competition do not give strong predictions of robust equilibria (Cox 1997). We might, therefore, expect to find a variety of different party placements in different countries and different times. Tables 8.1 and 8.2 seem to show something like this variety.

Cox (1990, 1997) suggests that if there were equilibrium positions in multiparty competition, they would likely involve parties distributed along the political spectrum at intervals that leave roughly the same number of (prospective) voters between each of their positions: thus, after the election, a string of parties of roughly the same size. If there were two parties constrained from convergence to the center by anticipation of the entry of two more on their extreme wings, such an equilibrium would presumably find them equidistant from the median, about a quarter of the electorate away on each side. Given an odd number of parties (such as three anticipating entry of more on each side), one of them should be at the median, but it will be about the same size as the other two. Although formal theory does not at this point have much to say about preelection coalitions, easy entry of more parties is a familiar feature of the PR systems with preelection coalitions, and this possibility, again, would limit the degree to which the coalitions can be expected to converge consistently to the median.

The expectation that the election rules will create an artificial majority for one of the larger parties (the second pathway to majority government) would not in itself seem to encourage convergence to the median. As multiple parties are seeking votes, a party could be expected to converge to the median only if it could ignore the possible vote losses to a party at its extreme. Having election rules that create majorities through overrepresentation of some parties and underrepresentation of others is no guarantee that a party could do this. Elections become more of an all-or-nothing contest, but the search for a voter plurality does not necessarily mean moving to the center. In some circumstances it may and in others it may not.

We can easily see how creating majorities through vote-seat distortion is fraught with peril for good correspondence between the governing party and the median voter. Suppose we have three parties spaced evenly (equal numbers of voters between them) along the left-right continuum. If the election rules cause enough distortion to result in a legislative majority for one of them, it is two chances out of three that it will not be the party at the median. And in terms of the most likely equilibrium, if any, a third of the electorate will lie between that party and the median voter. In terms of the kinds of preference distributions we saw in table 7.1, that would put the party around 2 to 2½ scale positions from the median.

Another way to think about this problem is to consider in the abstract how we might create governing majorities in the absence of voting majorities for a single party. If we want accountability and mandates, we need such majorities.

If we want congruence of voters and governments, we want them to go to parties close to the median voter. In most democracies there are simply too many parties to get majorities directly from the vote, even with single-member districts or high threshold PR. The party leaders do not seem sufficiently encouraged by such rules to coalesce into fewer parties. If we want to keep elections as the decisive stage, we need artificially to inflate the legislative representation of the some of the parties at the expense of others. This can happen with single-member districts and high threshold PR, but with multi-party competition even the plurality winner is often quite far from the median voter. In almost all the cases in tables 8.1 and 8.2, the plurality vote winner did form the postelection government. (If the aggregation of votes results in a party other than the plurality vote winner gaining a legislative plurality or majority, the government can be even further from the median, like the Con-servatives in Canada in 1979, who were 2.2 points from the median.) The governments with poor correspondence in tables 8.1 and 8.2 are the result of the plurality party (or preelection coalition) being quite a way from the me-dian. These outcomes did not mean that either voters or parties behaved in a nonstrategic, let alone irrational, fashion. On the contrary, they can be per-fectly understandable results of multiparty competition.

I do not mean to imply that these outcomes were in fact simply the conse-quence of strategic multiparty competition interacting with the election rules. In fact, I think that an examination of how parties choose policies and leaders in the majoritarian countries shows that internal party processes and tradi-tions and the need to respond to political activists (often mobilized by intense, noncentrist preferences) play a role in pulling parties away from the center.[17] Parties may be captured by true believers whose desire to carry out their preferred policies may outweigh their desire to find a simple winning position. Or they may need to respond to such activists in their party or face a party split that will guarantee a victory for the opposition.

Given these difficulties at the level of theory and complexities at the level of practice, once we recognize more than two parties and policy concerns of activists, even in the countries with majoritarian constitutions, it is perhaps remarkable that we get as many cases with good correspondence as we do. The United States seemed to behave pretty much like a convergent two-party system, although the degree of Downsian convergence to the center is less than one might theoretically expect. Further, despite a few examples of the smaller party being advantaged by the vote-seat conversion, that degree of distortion rarely happened in these systems. In some cases, as in Spain and in Canada 1980, the plurality winners were close to the median and the vote-seat conver-sion created governments close to the median. Australia in the early 1990s shows that a "doubly divergent" situation in the early 1980s could be transformed into asymmetric competition won by the closer party. The point to stress is not that majoritarian processes must result in governments well off the median, but that there is great variability in their electoral competition and outcomes. About half the majoritarian conditions produced good congruence; about half did not. The relatively small number of parties and exaggeration of vote swings in the legislative results magnify strategic mistakes, short-term swings due to issues and personalities of the day, and implications of intraparty struggles.

Majoritarian situations also sometimes create for their voters choices involving multiple issue dimensions (which these systems are ill-equipped to reconcile) or between the differing time perspectives of accountability and mandates. We see especially in France in 1993 the huge victory of the rightist (Gaullist/UDF) coalition, despite the much greater proximity of the Socialists (and even Socialist/Communist coalition) to the median voter. While the difference in votes was not as great as that in seats (the winning coalition had a little less than 40 percent of the vote), the RPR/UDF coalition definitely routed the incumbent Socialists and their allies. An important reason seems to have been the strong rejection of the performance of the incumbent Socialist government, including a series of large scandals. A two-party or two-group alignment can definitely put voters in a hard place if they wish to show their disapproval of an ideologically compatible but incompetent or unlucky incumbent.

These results emphasize the tenuousness of one of the underlying assumptions of the majoritarian vision. That vision, as sketched in the first few chapters and articulated more explicitly in chapter 7 (see especially table 7.2), posits elections as the decisive stage in policy making and imagines that decisive elections show direct domination by citizen majorities. Majoritarians seem suspicious of the role of political elites in negotiating governments and policies and are desirous of restraining their postelection independence. But it appears to be an illusion that in representative democracy citizens can prevail without depending on elite coordination. Making elections the decisive stage just pushes the dependence on elites back to the decisions made by present (and possible) political parties as to what promises to make and what candidates to offer. This is obviously true when preelection coalitions are required to make the elections decisive, as in most of the elections under PR election rules. But under the variations of single-member district rules used in most of the majoritarian systems studied here, the decisions made by parties are also of very great importance in determining which policy position will achieve legislative domination. Either no parties or too many parties at the citizen median can lead to the election of government majorities far away from it.

9

The Proportional Influence Vision: Representing the Median Citizen Through a Multistage Process

The proportional influence vision, too, includes both a normative foundation and an empirical hypothesis. Chapter 7 discussed the position of the median citizen as a valuable normative standard from the proportional as well as the majoritarian perspective. If the preferences of the citizens can be understood as lying on a single superdimension, choosing the position of the median citizen minimizes the number of voters who would prefer the most popular alternative position. This is one way to interpret the idea that, when citizens disagree, governments should be responsive to as many people as possible.

There are some difficulties with this normative standard, as discussed in chapter 7.[1] In this chapter, however, I shall set these aside and assume both the meaningfulness of the left-right continuum and the normative desirability of left-right policy at the position of the median citizen. The chapter investigates the empirical success of proportional influence designs and processes in producing governments at that position. The analysis in chapter 8 indicated that majoritarian processes were not very successful in creating congruent representation between government and median citizen. The results hinted that proportional influence approaches could do better. Here I shall explore both their successes and their failures.

Proportional Influence Empirical Theory: Predictions

Like the majoritarian vision, the proportional influence vision predicts empirical connections between the median citizen and the policymakers, but by a very different route. As we saw in chapters 5 and 7, this is a multistage model. At the electoral level, the defining conditions provide for multiple, diverse party options and for election rules allowing highly proportional representation. Multiple parties are needed so that all groups of citizens on the left-right scale can choose compatible representative agents. These parties need not — normatively must not — converge toward the center unless virtually all the voters are located very close to it.

Theories of party formation and competition lead us to expect that election rules with multimember districts, low thresholds, and a proportional representation formula encourage easy formation and representation of multiple political parties. Cox's generalization of Duverger's Law predicts no more than M + 1 political parties, where M is the number of representatives per district (Cox 1997, chaps. 5, 7). As only M parties can win seats in the most equal distribution, parties beyond M + 1 should have little chance and be avoided by strategic politicians and voters. That is, single-member districts should usually offer only two parties (Duverger's Law), whereas eight-member districts, like those in Sweden, could in principle carry up to nine parties.[2]

As noted in chapter 8, formal theories of party competition give us less clear predictions about party strategies in multiparty than in two-party competition. There may be no stable equilibria. Cox (1990, 1997) suggests that if there were an equilibrium, party positions would be spread along the continuum, roughly as the voters are.[3] If each voter supports the party closest to his position (again, a less sure theoretical result because of the many strategic possibilities at work in multiparty situations), the working of proportional election laws should result in a legislature with parties representing all the left-right groups in their proportionate strength.[4] The critical implication of this outcome is that the position of the median legislator (or of his or her party, if parties are in fact the relevant units) should be very close to that of the median citizen.

The second stage of the proportional influence vision concerns coalition bargaining. In this vision, the election is not the single decisive stage imagined in the majoritarian approach. Unless a majority of voters is grouped near a single ideological position, the election will result in a legislature with no single party majority. Given a diverse electorate and, hence, legislature, many governing or policy-making coalitions are possible. These could stray from the position of the median citizen. The freedom of elite bargainers to depart from the voters' choice is one of majoritarians' concerns and criticisms of this vision.

As discussed in chapter 7, however, we have strong predictions from formal coalition theory: in one-dimensional situations the median party will play a dominant role in government formation.[5] That is, all policy coalitions should include the median party, although any coalition may incorporate other parties that fall to one side or the other (or both.) Empirical research on coalition formation suggests that inclusion of the party with the median legislator is likely, but not inevitable. Existing formal theory does not, however, provide clear predictions about whether the median legislative party will dominate policy making.[6] When a single party or coalition of parties forms a government and must maintain tight party discipline, which empirically is the case in almost all parliamentary systems, the government might be expected to make policies that correspond more closely to its own *internal* configuration than to the legislative median. The fact that governments usually distribute the cabinet portfolios among their member parties in proportion to the size of the parties, not in proportion to closeness to the legislative median, suggests that after the government is formed its internal ideological distribution, not the distribution of the whole legislature, tends to dominate policy.

A final point concerns the degree of opposition influence in policy making. The majoritarian model assumes that the majority government will control policy making. Chapter 8 considered, therefore, only the relation between the citizen median and the government. If that government was at the median, all was well for congruence; in fact, to give weight to the opposition might pull the policy-making coalition further from the median citizen. The proportional influence model, however, assumes that parties outside the government may well have influence and that this influence is generally desirable because it gives authorized participation in policy making to all parties (see chapter 5). Increasing the influence of the opposition may also pull governments whose internal weight is off the median back toward it. Thus, contrary to the expectations of the ideal majoritarian model, giving opposition parties significant — but not equal — weight in policy making may improve congruence between what citizens want and what policies result. Whether in fact this happens will depend on the specific positions of the government and the other parties.

The proportional influence vision, then, directs our attention to the role of opposition parties in policy making. Normatively, they should have a substantial role to play, even if that role is deprecated by majoritarians. In addition, given the various opportunities for opposition influence (through minority governments, the committee system, and so forth) in the proportional influence constitutional designs, our empirical analysis may well misinterpret the true situation if we focus only on the government. For both reasons it is essential that we take account of the effect of opposition parties in policy making as part of the analysis of this chapter.

The Median Citizen and the Median Legislator

The first stage in proportional influence theory is the election of a legislature that reflects, as closely as possible, the distribution of preferences of the citizens. I discussed in chapter 2 the bodies of theory that lead us to expect that elections based on proportional representation and low thresholds for representation will reflect the preferences of the voters more precisely. There are generally three elements in this reflection:

1. The presence of multiple party choices available to voters, which is a product of the historical development of the system of political parties and the current strategies and goals of the party leaders. The party strategies are themselves presumed to be shaped by the election rules and the number of parties expected to achieve legislative representation. The proportional influence approach assumes many parties, offering a wide range of left-right policy alternatives. Such party systems are expected to be found primarily in systems in which the election rules are based on proportional representation with low thresholds of representation. (See also the above discussion of Cox's M + 1 rule.)

2. The choices made by the voters themselves from among these party alternatives. The proportional influence approach assumes that each voter will choose the party whose announced policy position is closest to him or her. Assuming that the party policy packages reduce to the left-right scale, then voters should choose the party closest on that scale to create party policy connections. Of course, if voters are more influenced by candidate personalities, previous performance, or strategic calculation of bargaining outcomes, they may deviate from this expectation.

3. The accurate reflection of the voters' electoral choices in legislative representation. Again, election law theory leads us to expect that party representation will be most precise in the proportional representation, low threshold systems. We have seen in previous analysis that this expectation is generally well founded.

The election rules, then, could have major effects on the accuracy of reflection of the voters' preferences in the legislature. These effects are expected in part because of the long-term relations between the rules and the number of competing parties, which shape the strategic possibilities for the parties and voters, and in part because of the short-term effects on the outcome of voters' choices. In the previous chapter I tried to some extent to separate these two effects by calculating a voted party median that simulated a pure PR legislative median along with the realized legislative median in the specific country. Figure 8.2 showed the distance between the median citizen and each type of party median. The cross-hatched bar in each category of election rules showed average distance between the citizens and the pure PR legislative median; the solid bar showed the average distance between the citizens and the actual legislative median.

The results in figure 8.2 accorded quite nicely with the expectations from proportional theory. In the PR systems the median in both simulated and real legislatures is quite close to the median citizen (about .6 of a point, on average). There is some variance from country to country: elections in Italy, the Netherlands, and Sweden resulted in legislative medians nearly a full point from the citizen median, while in many other countries the two are very close. The difference seems to be purely a function of the positions of the parties and the citizens' choices of those parties, not of the (relatively low) distortion in the aggregation of votes into seats in the real legislature. Interestingly, the distances do not increase much as we read across the categories of election rules until we hit the single-member district systems on the far right of the chart. Although we saw in chapter 5 that there was some increase in vote-seat distortion as the thresholds increased, there was no relation between vote-seat distortion and distance between the medians in the systems with thresholds under 20. As the degree of preference distortion in the PR systems is generally low, it is not here investigated further in detail.[7]

In the single-member district systems, the average voted party median (legislative median in a hypothetical legislature with perfectly proportional representation of votes) was still only about .8 from the median citizen, but the actual legislative median was twice as far away. The bases of this distortion were discussed in the previous chapter. (For a more extensive discussion, see Powell and Vanberg forthcoming.) From the proportional influence point of view, figure 8.2 confirms the successful reflection of the citizen preference medians in the legislature under PR election rules. This generally good correspondence of citizen and legislative medians provides a basis for the formation of governments through bargaining between parties in the legislature. Coalition theory tells us that the median legislator will be critical in coalition formation.

Forming Governments: Median Legislator and Government

The second stage in proportional influence theory is the formation of governments after the election of the legislature. It is precisely this stage that majoritarians view with suspicion. The election has not been decisive. The voters have not given control of the legislature to a single party or preelection coalition. It is up to the representatives to negotiate the formation of a government. Can they be trusted to create a government close to the citizen median?

One answer from general coalition theory is that it is not necessary to assume that the parties act in the general citizen interest. Rather, because the parties seek to achieve their own policy commitments the negotiations to form a government will revolve around the party at the legislative median — which, as we have just seen, is itself usually close to the citizen median in the PR systems.

Tables 9.1 and 9.2 show the parties in the legislatures formed after elections in the early 1980s and early 1990s, respectively, the elections for which we have the most accurate opinion and party data (and which were discussed from the majoritarian point of view in tables 8.1 and 8.2). These tables are complex, but the rich information they convey repays examination:

1. The countries and their elections are grouped in each table by the degree to which the election has largely predetermined the government bargaining. At the top are the cases in which a single party has won a legislative majority. In the middle are the cases in which preelection identifiability was high — subdivided into cases in which a specifically announced preelection coalition won a majority and cases in which the election outcomes were less decisive. In most of the latter, neither the election nor the postelection bargaining resulted in a majority for the coalition. (This failure occurs because the preelection coalitions still may not include all the parties; parties at the extreme left or right, for example, may be excluded from both coalitions.) At the bottom of each table are the cases in which electoral competition left the government formation process largely unconstrained. The last grouping in each table is identical, respectively, to the bottom category in tables 8.1 and 8.2.
2. In each legislature we see abbreviations for the parties placed at approximately the party position on the left-right scale, according to the expert placements. We can thus see in general the span of left-right positions represented in the legislature. Because of the small size of the table, distances are rough approximations.
3. The parties in the government — actually sharing cabinet seats — are shown

in bold. Thus, we can see at a glance the rough left-right position and the span of left-right distance of the government itself. The position of the median citizen is not shown, but one can refer back to tables 8.1 and 8.2 to locate it. The citizen medians are usually around 5.5, but to the left of that in Spain, France, and Italy in both tables and to the right in Austria, Japan, 1981 Ireland, and 1993 Finland.

4. Following the placements of the parties in each country are two numbers: the first is the distance between the weighted average of the government on the left-right scale and the median legislator and the second is the distance between the government and the median citizen. The latter numbers are the same, of course, as those in tables 8.1 and 8.2.

The tables show above all that the results accord well with expectations from proportional influence theory. Because the patterns are so similar I shall discuss the tables together. The cases at the bottom of the tables have the two-stage government formation process and are, therefore, the critical test of the proportional influence approach. Notice first that they generally have quite a few parties, and those parties cover a wide range of the political spectrum, especially in contrast to the systems at the top of the tables, which usually produce single-party majorities. Their median legislator is quite close to the citizen median (as we know from figures 8.1 and 8.2). Therefore the party and electoral processes here approximate the expectations of the proportional model quite well.

The open question has been the degree to which postelection bargaining would result in governments close to the median legislator. The results here generally support empirical expectations from coalition theory and the normative expectations of the proportional model. If the postelection bargaining resulted in a majority coalition government, as happened in nine of the ten cases shown in tables 9.1 and 9.2, it usually included the party with the median legislator. In some number of cases, for example, Italy, Switzerland, and 1983 Finland, governments that straddled the median, including parties on both sides of it, were formed. It is not surprising that their internal mean is close to the median of the legislature as a whole and thus, given the proportional election results, to the median citizen.

As anticipated theoretically, a number of governments extended to one or the other side of the median. The consequence depends on the relative sizes of the government parties as well as the distances. In Ireland the large party in the coalition is virtually at the median, keeping the coalition close to the citizens. Where the nonmedian party is larger, as in the Netherlands and 1991 Belgium, its presence does pull the government away from the legislative median. But on

Table 9.1. *Legislative Bargaining Situation After the Election: Majorities, Election Commitments, Left-Right Positions in Early 1980s*[1]

Country	Year	1	2	3	4	5	6	7	8	9	10	Legislator	Citizen
					Party Positions on Left-Right Scale (Approximate) — New Governing Parties Shown in Bold							Distance Between New Government and Median:	
A single party has a legislative majority													
Canada	1980			NDP		**LIB**	PC		PCS			0	.1
Spain	1982			COM	**SOC**		GiU		AP			0	.1
New Zealand	1981			LAB		SC	**NAT**					0	.9
United States	1980				DEM			**REP**				1.8	1.3
United Kingdom	1983		LAB			SDP/LIB			**CON**			0	2.3
An announced preelection coalition has a legislative majority													
Ireland	1981				**LAB**		FF	FG				.1	.4
Netherlands	1982*		COM RD	LAB		D66	**CDA**	**VVD**		GVPSGP		.7	1.4
France	1981		**COM**		**SOC**		UDF	RPR				.2	1.6**
Germany	1983			GRN	SPD	**FDP**	**CDU/CSU**					1.5	1.7
Australia	1980			ALP		AD			LPA NCP			.1	2.3

Preelection situation had substantial identifiability — but no formally announced coalitions and no majorities

Denmark	1981	VS	SF	SD	RD	CD	CH	L	CON	PROG	.9	1.1**
Sweden	1982	VPK	SD		LIB	AG		MOD		PROG	0	1.7
Norway	1981	SV	LAB	LIB	AG	CH		CON		PROG	1.7	2.3**

Alternative future governments not identified in election

		1	2	3	4	5	6	7	8	9	10		
Italy	1983	COM		SOC		R	SD	DC	PLI	MSI		.1	.8
Finland	1983	COM		SD		CEN	LIB	SW	R	NAT		.8	.8
Belgium	1981	COM	SOC	RW		FDF	CHR	V	PVV		VB	.9	1.3

*There was substantial identifiability but not a formal preelection coalition; the expected partners won a majority and formed a government.

**A second government was formed later in the legislative term.

[1]Preelection coalitions and future government identifiability from chapter 4. Missing data countries as in table 8.1.

Table 9.2. *Legislative Bargaining Situation After the Election: Majorities, Election Commitments, Left-Right Positions in Early 1990s*[1]

Country	Year	1	2	3	4	5	6	7	8	9	10	Distance Between New Government and Median: Legislator	Citizen
							Party Positions on Left-Right Scale (Approximate) — New Governing Parties Shown in Bold							
A single party has a legislative majority													
Spain	1993			COM	**SOC**		CiU			AP		0	.4
Australia	1990			AD		**LAB**		LIB	NPA			0	1.0
United States	1988				**DEM**		REP					2.7	1.3
New Zealand	1993				AL		LAB	**NAT**				0	1.7*
Canada	1988			NDP		LIB		**PC**				0	1.8
United Kingdom	1992			LAB		SDP/LIB			**CON**			0	2.4
Japan	1990		JCP		JSP		KOM		**LDP**			0	2.5
An announced preelection coalition has a legislative majority													
France	1993			COM	SOC		**UDF**	**RPR**				.6	2.5
Germany	1990			GRN	SDP	**FDP**	**CDU/CSU**					.7	.9

Preelection situation had substantial identifiability — but no formally announced coalitions and no majorities

		1	2	3	4	5	6	7	8	9	10		
Austria	1990			GRN	**SPO**	OVP			FPO			.9	1.0
Sweden	1991			VP	**SDEM**	AG LB	CH		MOD ND			1.3	1.6
Denmark	1990		RG	SF	**SDEM** RV		CD CH	CON L		PROG		2.1	2.3*

Alternative future governments not identified in election*

		1	2	3	4	5	6	7	8	9	10		
Ireland	1992			DL	**LAB**	FF	FG		PDP			.5	.2*
Netherlands	1989		GRN		**LAB**	D66	CDA VVD	GVP	SGP			1.0	.2
Belgium	1991			GRN	**SOC**	CH		VU LIB				1.0	.4
Switzerland	1987			**SOC**	CH	RAD	PEO	LB	AU			1.3	.8
Norway	1993			LS	**LAB**	AG	LIB	CH	CON	PROG		1.2	1.0
Italy	1992	RC		PDS		**PS**	RP DC	PL	LG	MSI		.4	1.2*
Finland	1991			LA	**SDEM**	LB	SW AG	KOK	CH			.2	1.2

* A second government with (at least some) different parties formed later in the term. In France the status of government changed owing to elections, but the same parties continued in government.

¹ Preelection coalitions and future government identifiability from chapter 4. Missing data countries as in table 8.2.

average the negotiated majority coalition governments are quite close to both legislative and citizen medians. Six of the ten are .8 or less from the median citizen.

The exceptions show that, of course, this close congruence need not be the case; it is an empirical probability, not a determined result. In 1992 Italy and 1991 Finland the governments are close to the legislative median, but those legislatures were about an additional point from the citizens. Even more important is the 1993 Norway election. This is the only minority government among the low identifiability elections in the table. Table 8.3 showed that about a fifth of the governments formed in low identifiability situations in the 1980s and 1990s were minority governments. As in the Norwegian case shown here, those governments are typically quite some distance from the median citizen. (Table 8.3 shows them an average of .9 scale units, 30 percent further than the majority governments negotiated under similar circumstances.) But while these problems can occur, the overall picture is one of close correspondence to proportional influence theory and its prediction of high congruence between government and median citizen — in cases in which the elections left the bargaining unconstrained by majorities and preelection commitments.

In contrast, the elections at the top of the table, with their single-party majorities, all have governments which by definition include the median legislator. (The exception is the United States in 1980, where the Republican president appointed the cabinet, facing a House of Representatives controlled by the Democrats.) In some elections in some countries (1980 Canada, 1981 New Zealand, 1990 Australia, Spain in both elections) this legislator was close to the citizen median. But in Britain, Japan, 1988 Canada, and 1993 New Zealand the winning party and thus the median legislator were quite far from the median citizen, resulting in governments at least twice as far from the median citizen as the average postelection bargained government (the range is 1.7 to 2.5 points). Even in the United States, the majority party is about as far from the median as the worst postelection bargaining cases.[8]

For the most part, distances from the medians in the countries with announced preelection coalitions winning majorities look more like the single-party majorities than like the postelection bargaining countries. Australia and France, of course, have single-member district election rules, and their strong electoral coalitions and substantial vote-seat distortion look very much like the problems of majority government: dominated legislative medians frequently far from the citizen median. Germany in 1990 and especially Ireland in 1982 look like more successful majoritarianism. The small size of the center party in Germany implies governments some distance from the median, although without the vote-seat distortion of the single-party majority situation adding to the distance. The identified preelection coalitions tended definitely to be on one or the other side of the median, not across it. Austria's grand coalition is the exception and in 1990 was only vaguely identified as a preelection coalition.

Perhaps most interesting are the cases in the third group in tables 9.1 and 9.2, which show at least moderate preelection identifiability but no majorities for the identified contender. Additional small parties, not a part of one of the contenders, prevented either side from winning direct control of the legislature. The postelection bargainers could have negotiated centrist majority governments of the sort seen in Finland or 1992 Netherlands. But they did not. The subsequently formed minority governments in Denmark, Sweden, and Norway still reflected the preelection alignments. Having minority governments off the median, the three countries not surprisingly show substantial distance between government and the median citizen.[9]

On one hand, we could say that a problem for proportional influence theory is the possibility that political elites will constrain the postelection bargaining by preelection agreements. Some political systems with proportional rules and many parties, most notably Denmark, consistently offer such agreements. Such preelection coalitions, whose dynamics have been too little studied, are undoubtedly an important feature of policy making in these countries. They usually seem to increase distance between average postelection government and the median citizen. The agreements weaken the connection between proportional constitutional and party conditions and close correspondence between the median citizen and the government.

On the other hand, this fact is small comfort to the majoritarian vision. These elite actions are making the elections more directly decisive and thus impressing majoritarianism upon the basic constitutional and party situation, apparently to the detriment of congruence between citizens and governments as cross-median majorities are eschewed.

Minority governments are potentially a second problem for the proportional influence approach's congruence hypothesis. Postelection negotiations that resulted in minority government usually created governments farther from the median citizen. (This outcome might be somewhat surprising to those who expect minority governments to be formed by the median legislative party.[10] However, we do not have many cases.) But empirically the minority governments in these countries seem more frequently to be the outcome not of failed postelection bargaining in open situations but of failed majoritarianism, especially preelection agreements that did not result in majorities for the coalition.

The results shown in tables 9.1 and 9.2 can be summarized and extended by

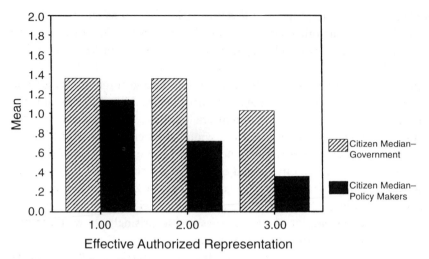

Figure 9.1. Left-Right Distances: Citizens, Governments and Policymakers: By Level of Effective Authorized Representation

including other elections within two years of our citizen median estimates and by adding more cases from the yearly *Eurobarometer* results in the European systems. Figure 9.1 does this by comparing the distance from median citizen to governments and policymakers in elections resulting in low, medium, and high levels of authorized effective representation. The authorized effective representation measure, from chapter 5, gave full representation to voters for governing parties, but only representation of the lower of votes or seats — multiplied by their putative bargaining influence — to voters for the opposition parties. Authorized effective representation was the critical intervening condition for the proportional influence vision discussed in part 2. Here, the (weighted) average effective representation scores for the governments forming after the election are divided into three roughly equal groups for visual purposes.

The cross-hatched bars in each group of elections show the average distance between the government and the median citizen. As we would expect from the previous analysis, the average distance declines somewhat by about .3 scale points, as we move from the low to high levels of effective representation. The countries with higher levels of effective representation are generally those with representative election rules, multiple parties, and the postelection bargaining that more often results in governments straddling or being close to the legislative (and thus citizen) median. However, the frequent minority governments among the high effective representation elections diminish the effect.

Proportional Influence and Congruent Representation: Policymakers

As originally suggested in chapter 1 and developed in chapter 5, the proportional influence model favors giving some continuing influence to all groups in policy making, rather than putting control in the hands of a single majority. To this degree the proportional influence model is appropriately viewed as not merely a two-stage, but a multistage, process. To be sure, the government in a parliamentary system will have the most influence, but parties outside the government can expect to have some voice also. Figure 9.1 offers even more striking support for the proportional vision in the solid bar in each set, which is the distance between the median citizen and the policymakers.[11]

To calculate the impact of represented left-right positions on policy making I assumed that each party began with a left-right position (estimated from the expert surveys) and with an amount of influence proportionate to its percentage of seats in the legislature. I then weighted these proportions by the same logic of policymaker influence that was introduced in chapter 5: government parties are assumed to have full impact on policy making; formal support parties are assumed to have 75 percent of the influence of government parties; opposition parties' influence depends on their bargaining and structural opportunities. Opposition parties facing minority, or even supported minority, governments have enhanced bargaining power. They can also benefit from control of an outside institution or from a strong committee system that shares leadership positions with all parties (see chapter 5, especially table 5.4).

Having the policy-making bargaining begin with a legislature centered about the citizen median, which is typical of these systems, helps reduce the citizen-policymaker distance. Fair representation of all groups will generally also be helpful. Giving more weight to the representatives of opposition voters in policy making, which increases the effective representation scores, in practice usually results in governments pulled toward the median citizen. The oppositions in the high authorized representation group benefited both from fairer legislative representation and from structural policy-making factors, especially the committee system, which increased their influence. While it was better, of course, to be in government than in opposition, the opposition voters had much more influence under minority governments than when facing disciplined majorities. Their strong influence helped pull minority governments markedly toward the median in almost all cases.

Figure 9.2 shows these effects with a scattergram in which each point is a separate government. The horizontal dimension is the distance of the govern-

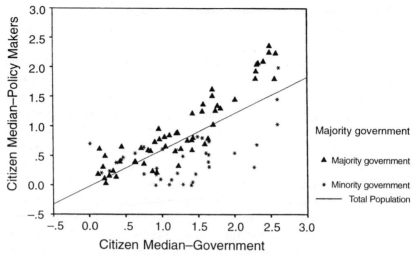

Figure 9.2. Government and Policymaker Distances from Median Citizen: Majority and Minority Governments

ment from the median citizen; the vertical dimension is the distance of the influential policymakers from the median citizen. Minority governments are shown as stars, majority governments as triangles. The upward sloping line is the best-fit regression line between the two distances.

The upward sloping line shows that the two distances are related to each other-the government receives, after all, the heaviest weight in estimating the policymaker position, so having a government close to the median is a powerful start to having policy making close to the median. The slope of the line is less than 1.0 (45-degree line), as the policymaker position is nearly always closer to the citizen median than is the government.[12] The general regression prediction would be that the policymakers would be .6 of the government distance. Points below the line have policymakers even closer to the citizens than we would expect from the distance of their governments. It is clear in the figure that minority governments are generally below the line, pulled sharply toward the citizens by taking account of the nongovernment parties in making policies.

This need not be the case, as is shown by the sharp outlier in the middle left, which is the (supported) minority government in Spain 1989. In that case the Socialist government was nearly exactly at the citizen median; the influence lost to more conservative parties pulled the government over half a point to the right of the citizens. Nonetheless, the overwhelmingly predominant pattern for minority governments is to be advantaged by giving influence to the other legislative parties. On average minority and majority governments start out about the same distance from the citizens. Under minority governments, however, the policymakers are .75 of a scale point closer to the citizens than the governments; under majorities the policymakers are only .3 of a scale point closer than the governments.

Two clusters of cases in figure 9.2 merit attention. First, at the top right is a set of ten governments in which governments and policymakers alike are about 2 points from the citizen median. Nine of these are in countries with majoritarian constitutional designs; one is a mixed design (Japan). Second is the cluster of minority governments below and to the right of the line. These are virtually all proportional design countries. The United States, with "divided governments" between the president and at least part of the Congress, is at the edge of this group. These distributions further confirm the superior performance of the proportional designs in comparison to the majoritarian ones, especially in creating good congruence between citizens and policymakers.

I noted above in the discussion of government formation that two problems weaken the connections predicted by the proportional influence model. One of these is the formation of preelection coalitions that tended to freeze the postelection bargaining and result in government coalitions substantially to the left or right of center. The second, often related problem is the formation of postelection minority governments rather than negotiated majorities; such minority governments are often a substantial distance from the citizen median. Both problems are partially overcome by giving bargaining power to representatives of opposition parties even after the formation of the government itself. Thus, the provision of bargaining influence to the opposition parties not only gives them procedural consultation in the governing process, but also results in policy-making coalitions that are closer to the citizen median.

Government Congruence and Government Proximity

The analysis of responsiveness to elections in chapter 6 discussed the failure of governments to endure for the full period between elections as a disputed criterion. In the majoritarian vision, elections are supposed to be the decisive stage in government formation, so changing the party makeup of the government between elections is undesirable. In fact in the majoritarian design systems the government formed after the election usually lasted until the next election. Single-party governments and preelection majority coalitions often lasted their full electoral term. Where identifiability was high, regardless of the design, minority governments often called early elections if they had the authority to do so, rather than changing the composition of governments without consulting the voters. In the proportional influence designs, however, it was fairly common to change governments between elections. Table 6.3 showed that these changes were more likely to increase than decrease the diversity of representation in government between elections and that they generally tended to increase, rather than decrease, the average level of effective representation between elections. Thus, these changes often had desirable features from the proportional influence point of view, undesirable from the majoritarian. It remains to be seen whether this lack of proximity between the election and the new governments is harmful to the generally high level of congruence between the citizens and the negotiated governments.

We can imagine various possibilities. It might be that government coalitions and minority governments further from the electorate are more likely to fall and be replaced by governments closer to it. In this case, lack of proximity could help average congruence. Conceivably, governments might fall as parties respond to changing citizen preferences, perhaps anticipating the next election, in which case the new governments might be further from their electorate but closer to preferences measured at the time of the new government's formation.[13] Alternatively, governments might fall because of elite negotiations (or manipulations of agenda and issue space) unrelated to citizen preferences, moving the later governments away from the citizen medians. In general, majoritarian theorists are suspicious of elite negotiation, which removes government formation from connections to the election, while proportional theorists often suggest the advantages of being able to respond to considerations not emphasized in the election. As far as I know, we have no empirical research to guide us on this question. Coalition theory would presumably suggest just that new governments, like old ones, should tend toward inclusion of the median legislator.

Of the thirty-five governments elected in our survey (see tables 9.1 and 9.2), twenty-eight retained their party makeup throughout the period between elections[14] and seven (those marked with asterisks in the tables) changed theirs. The seven show a wide variety of results for congruence to the citizen median. On balance, the changes are slightly helpful. In the Italy 1992 and Ireland 1992 elections the later governments are almost exactly at the same position as the previous ones, so there is no change in their relation to the citizens. In France 1981 and Norway 1981 changes in the makeup of the governments brought them closer to the median citizen. The French Socialists, who had a majority, paid rather limited attention to their Communist coalition partners, who eventually left the coalition in frustration, leaving the new, single-party majority closer to the median citizen (see table 9.1). The Norwegian Conservatives expanded their single-party minority government to include two additional center-right parties, creating a government majority somewhat closer to the median (average distance 1.8 instead of 2.3). In New Zealand defections from the National Party after the 1993 election, perhaps in part anticipating the new PR election rules to be in place in 1996, cost the single-party government its majority, but, as best we can tell, left the government's general policy position unchanged. Nine months before the 1996 election, however, the minority government changed to a majority by adding the new United Party, made up of defectors from both major parties. These additions certainly brought the new government closer to the median citizen. In Denmark, minority governments changed hands from Social Democrats to a rightist coalition partway through the 1981 legislative term, but moved in the other direction (to a majority of Social Democrats and three center parties) partway through the 1990 term. The 1993 change reduced the distance from the citizen median from 2.3 to .9, very helpful to congruence, but the 1981 change increased the distance from 1.1 to 1.5.

Having so few cases, we cannot securely draw inferences from these results. If we expand the analysis to include all the cases for which we have citizen data within two years of the election and party data within five years, we have 102 cases, of which 79 represent the governments formed immediately after the election and 23 represent new party governments formed later in the legislative term.[15] As those governments are concentrated in proportional design systems, it is easy to confuse government-specific and country-specific results. Table 9.3 shows all the distances between citizen median and government for the first and subsequent governments in the fifteen elections in ten countries with multiple governments between elections.

A look at the full set of multiple government cases for which we have data confirms the impression that changes in government tend to be in the direction of governments slightly closer to the median citizen. The last column in the table shows the average difference between the first government formed after the election and all the subsequent governments. We see that only one election (Denmark 1981) has a positive difference, showing movement away from the median; eight are essentially unchanged or slightly closer; six are .4 or more closer to the median citizen. Even at the level of the individual government, the 1981 Danish case turns out to be the only one of the 23 cases across ten countries in which a later government was more than .1 scale points further from the median citizen (measured at the time of the election) than was the original government. In 14 cases, the distance is essentially unchanged (difference of .2 or less). In some of these, for example, most of the Italian governments, the same basic coalition was reconstructed with changes in some small parties or the prime minister; in others, as in Germany 1983 and Norway

Table 9.3. Multiple Governments Between Elections and Distance from Median Citizen

Country	Average Distance All Gov1 from Median[2]	Election Year	Distance of Government from Median Citizen at Election[1]				Average Change from Gov1
			Gov1	Gov2	Gov3	Gov4	
Belgium	.8	1978	1.0	1.1	.7	1.1	−.0
Denmark	1.3	1977	.9	.3			−.6
		1981	1.1	1.5			+.4
		1990	2.3	.9			−1.4
Finland	1.2	1979	1.6	1.0			−.6
France	2.0	1981	1.6	1.4			−.2
Germany	1.4	1980	1.4	1.3			−.1
Ireland	.5	1992	.2	.2			0
Italy	1.1	1979	1.6	1.2	1.2	1.2	−.4
		1987	.6	.6	.6	.6	0
		1992	1.2	1.2			0
New Zealand	1.3	1993	1.7	1.7	1.7	− ?[3]	−.?
Norway	1.6	1981	2.3	1.8			−.5
		1989	1.6	1.4			−.2
Sweden	1.6	1979	1.7	.9			−.8

[1]Gov1 is the first government formed after the election; Gov2 is the second government, if the first did not continue until the next election. Brief, purely caretaker governments are not included.

[2]Average distance between first government and median citizen for all elections in that country in data set. Number of elections included in average is the following: 6, 8, 3, 5, 5, 7, 4, 2, 3, 4.

[3]In New Zealand we do not have an estimate of the left-right position of the new United Party that joined the government, but as it was made up of members of both major parties, it almost certainly was closer to the median than the National Party, thus reducing the distance of the government.

1990, the new government was about as far away from the electorate as its predecessor, although on the other side of the left-right scale.

In the remaining cases the new government is clearly closer to the median. Such changes could come about by dropping an extreme party from the government (Finland 1979, France 1981, and Sweden 1979), adding moderate parties to a government (Denmark 1977, Italy 1979, New Zealand 1993,

Norway 1981), or even expanding to a near grand coalition, as in Belgium 1978 (third government). In Denmark 1993 the supported Conservative/Liberal minority coalition formed after the 1990 election resigned after the release of an official report sharply criticizing its handling of refugee applications in apparent violation of the country's asylum laws.[16] It was replaced by a majority government in which the opposition Social Democrats were joined by the three centrist parties that had supported the previous government.

I do not want to make too much of a rather small number of cases. But it seems that lack of proximity between the election and the government does not harm the strong congruence between government, policymakers, and the median citizen characteristic of these systems. On the contrary, it seems to be very rare for government changes to move away from the median citizen and quite common for them to move toward the median. Further, government changes between the elections were at least as likely to create government majorities (and thus greater accountability) as destroy them. In every way, then, this analysis supports the proportional model of congruent representation against its majoritarian rival.

Constitutional Design and Representational Congruence

The analyses in chapters 8 and 9 convey a consistent message about representational congruence. The majoritarian vision works only fitfully. The simplifications and distortions necessary to create decisive elections frequently exact a heavy cost in distance between the citizen median and the position of the government. By conscious design and the imperative of electoral decisiveness, the opposition is given little opportunity to mitigate that distance in policy making. In contrast, the proportional influence vision generally works quite well. Despite the suspicions of majoritarians, postelection bargaining among representatives generally results in governments tied to the citizen and legislative medians. The greater influence given to the opposition almost always creates even greater congruence between citizens and influential policymakers. Changing of governments between elections usually reduces distances, rather than increasing them.

Neither the majoritarian nor the proportional pattern is completely determined. There are majoritarian governments close to the citizens (Canada 1980) and bargained proportional governments relatively further away (Norway 1993). The distortions in vote-seat representation can result even in a legislature and government closer to the citizens than purer reflection of the votes (France 1988). Substantial variance from country to country and even from election to election in the same country is particularly characteristic of

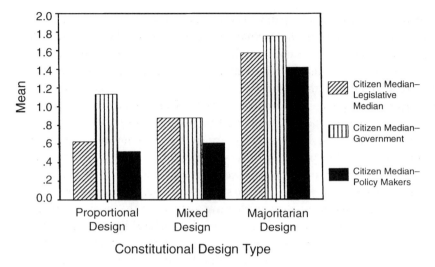

Figure 9.3. Left-Right Distances: Citizens, Legislatures, Governments and Policymakers by Constitutional Design Type

representation in the majoritarian designs. Formation of explicit preelection coalitions or even strong expectations of alternative governments can freeze the postelection bargaining process in proportional systems, making elections more decisive but their outcomes often less congruent. The balance of complexities strongly favors the proportional influence vision in representational congruence. Figure 9.3 summarizes the performance of the basic constitutional designs on congruence measures, as figures 4.1 and 5.1 did, respectively, for voter mandates and effective representation.

On the left are the elections in the predominantly proportional design systems and on the right, elections in the majoritarian design systems. The three bars show, respectively, the average distances from the median citizen of the median legislator, the government, and the policymakers. The average legislator in the proportional design systems is only .6 from the median citizen; the average legislator in the majoritarian systems is nearly three times that distance at 1.6. If ultimately it is the median legislator who determines policy, as some theorists expect, the proportional design models have a very large advantage.[17] The average government in the countries with proportional influence designs was 1.1 scale points from the citizen median; in the countries with majoritarian designs the distance was 1.8 scale points. The proportional design advantage here reflects that on average elite bargaining is more likely to produce median governments than are the "mechanical" interactions of election rules with party offerings and voter choices. This effect is much sharper if we consider the influential policymakers: .5 scale points from the median in the proportional design systems and 1.4 scale points in the majoritarian designs. Minority governments and strong committee systems are particularly helpful in reducing the distance between median citizen and policymakers in the proportional influence designs.[18]

In chapters 8 and 9 these relations were explicated by means of looking at the stages in the electoral and policymaker selection processes. Citizens vote to choose their legislative representatives. In the parliamentary systems (which include all these countries except the United States), the legislature then chooses the government. To make policy, the government parties then negotiate with opposition parties to various degrees, depending on the status of the government and the control of other key institutions. In the majoritarian vision these three stages are compressed into one, as the voter majority supposedly gives a legislative majority to its preferred party, which forms the government and controls policy making. In the proportional vision, the stages remain distinct; at each stage, representational influence is entertained for all significant policy positions, but a net final policymaker position should be centered around the median.

We can usefully summarize these stages in statistical terms by examining a system of multivariate regression equations (table 9.4). Although this presentation involves statistical oversimplification, it helps clarify the interaction of multiple factors and suggests how these fit together as one moves across the stages of the process.

The table provides a brief regression-based overview of each stage. The first set of (two) equations predicts the distance between the median citizen and the median legislator; the second set of (three) equations predicts the distance between the median citizen and the government; the third set of (four) equations predicts the distance between the median citizen and the policymaker position. The top half of the table shows the standardized coefficients, which facilitate comparison across variables and which are familiar to most readers. The bottom half shows the unstandardized coefficients and standard errors, which provide more (and more reliable) information about the strength of the relations.

Across the top of the table are the successive independent variables in the systems of equations, beginning on the left with the two main features of the constitutional arrangements, followed by a feature of the party system. In the middle are some critical and by now familiar linking processes indicated by the visions of democratic connection: the identifiability of future governments, the creation of government majorities, and the disproportionality of vote-seat representation in the legislature. At the right are the citizen-

Table 9.4. *Regression Overview of Relations in Chapters 7–9*

	Constitutional Arrangements		Party System	Identifiable Future	Government	Vote-Seat	Distance from Citizen Median		
	Electoral Rules Threshold	Government Committee Control	Distance: Citizen Median-Median Voted Party	Government	Majority	Disproportion			R(N)
	(.7–35)	(0–.5–.10)		(0–100)	(0–1)	(0–24)	Legislature	Government	

Standardized regression coefficients

Left-right distance between citizen median and legislative median

.41**	.13	.45**	—	—	—	—	—	—	.69 (78)
-.02	.21	.42**	.07	.06	.38**	—	—	—	.73 (78)

Left-right distance between citizen median and government postion

.41**	-.13	.21*	—	—	—	—	—	—	.37 (79)
-.20	.13	.20*	.31*	-.12	.34*	—	—	—	.51 (79)
-.18	-.01	-.09	.26*	-.15	.07	.69**	—	—	.70 (79)

Left-right distance between citizen median and policymaker position

.34*	.25	.14	—	—	—	—	—	—	.59 (79)
-.41	.40*	.12	.18	.22**	.60**	—	—	—	.73 (79)
-.40*	.28*	-.13	.13	.19**	.38**	.58**	—	—	.83 (79)
-.31*	.29**	-.08	-.01	.27**	.34**	.21*	.54**	—	.92 (79)

Unstandardized regression coefficients and standard errors

Left-right distance between citizen median and legislative median

.022(.008)	.21(.24)	.57(.11)	—	—	—		
−.001(.011)	.34(.26)	.54(.11)	.001(.002)	.09(.14)	.054(.020)		

Left-right distance between citizen median and government position

.021(.009)	−.20(.29)	.26(.13)	—	—	—	—	
−.010(.014)	.21(.31)	.25(.13)	.006(.002)	−.18(.17)	.047(.024)	—	
−.009(.012)	.02(.26)	−.11(.12)	.005(.002)	−.24(.13)	.010(.021)	.67(.11)	

Left-right distance between citizen median and policymaker position

.015(.007)	.33(.22)	.16(.10)	—	—	—	—	
−.018(.009)	.54(.21)	.12(.09)	.003(.002)	.30(.11)	.070(.016)	—	
−.018(.008)	.38(.18)	.13(.08)	.002(.001)	.25(.09)	.044(.014)	.48(.08)	
−.013(.006)	.39(.13)	−.09(.06)	−.000(.001)	.36(.07)	.040(.010)	.17(.07)	.46(.06)

*Significant at .05 level.
**Significant at .01 level.

legislature and citizen-government distances, which are bases on which relationships at the subsequent stages are built. The results parallel and summarize much of the previous discussion. High threshold election rules, especially single-member districts, are related to greater distances between the median citizen and the median legislator. The number of competing parties, which played such an important role in the process relationships themselves, turns out to have no direct relation to the distances, so is not shown in this table. Rather, we see a different feature of the party system, discussed briefly in chapter 8, the distance between the median citizen and the median voted party. If we line the parties up from left to right on the left-right scale and assign each party its percentage of the vote, we find the median voted party when we reach 50 percent reading across the party lineup. This corresponds to what the median legislator would be if there were perfect vote-seat representation. Its distance from the median citizen, however, is a product of the party configuration. Generally, the distance is small (about .5 across all of our cases) but is larger if there is a gap in the party system around the center (as there often is in Sweden or France) or if the whole party system seems somewhat displaced to one side of the citizen distribution (as in Italy). This variable is not in fact systematically related to the election rules or other party system features but is a valuable and significant control on the other distances in the equations.

As we see in line 1, both the election threshold and the party voted median are strongly significant predictors of the distance between median citizen and median legislator. The single-member district systems would be predicted to be about .7 of a point further from the median, even taking account of the median of the voted party system. This distance is not only statistically significant, but indicates substantively that the average legislative median produced by single-member district election rules is about twice as far from the median citizen as the average in the low threshold PR systems. We know from chapter 8 what cannot be seen here: this impact is itself highly variable, with some very close and other very distant legislative medians in the majoritarian type systems.

As line 2 shows quite nicely, the effect of the election rules is fully accounted for statistically (although not in each case, as we have seen) by the disproportionality of vote-seat relations, which is, of course, creating "artificial" single-party (or preelection coalition) legislative majorities in many high threshold (single-member district) legislatures. These majorities contain, by definition, the median legislator. The party system continues, however, to exert the same independent effect.

The next set of lines shows the equations predicting the distance between the citizen median and the position of the government party or coalition. The first equation shows the electoral threshold as being statistically significant and the party system median just at the conventional .05 level test (the unstandardized coefficient is barely twice the standard error). In the next line, we see again that the vote-seat disproportionality is a strong predictor of more distant governments, but so is the preelection identifiability of future governments. As discussed at length in chapter 8, such preelection identifiability usually inhibits formation of governments that cross the legislative median, which otherwise are a common feature of postelection bargaining. Adding these two features of disproportionality and identifiability greatly increases our ability to predict government formation (note the increase in the R-square) and reduces the electoral variable to less than 0 and to statistical insignificance. The party variable, again, is just at conventional .05 significance. The final equation in the government prediction shows that the disproportionality and party effects as well as constitutional ones are fully expressed through the legislative median distance itself, which has a large impact, understandably, on the government distance. But again, preelection identifiability of the government, which seems to freeze the bargaining process, continues to predict greater distance between citizen and government, even with all these other variables in the equation.

The last four equations predict the distance between median citizen and the policymakers, which is, of course, the final and most crucial distance of all. A notable feature of all four equations is the government control of the committee system, which consistently pulls the policymakers away from the median citizen. This variable is nearly significant in the first equation and definitely significant (at .05) in the next three, with a government-controlled committee system about .4 of a scale point further from the median citizen than its independent counterpart. This effect directly results from the way our measure of the policymaker position weights the position of the nongoverning parties, which are assigned less influence under government-controlled committee systems. The critical point for the empirical working of both visions is that such greater weight of the opposition brings the net policymaker position closer to the median citizen, which is what we might expect from the proportional vision but not from the majoritarian one. While the specific number of the coefficient will, of course, be shaped by our somewhat arbitrary influence weight, the direction is highly robust to whatever number we assign (assuming government parties still have the most influence). It is important to have this variable in the equations, moreover, as a control on other effects. As in the previous equations, the high threshold electoral rules are significantly related to greater citizen-policymaker distance in equation 1, and the subsequent equations show that this relation is mediated through the intervening political processes, as is the party system median, both becoming negative and insignificant in the last two equations.

All three of the connecting process measures (identifiability, majorities, and disproportionality) are associated with the majoritarian vision and linked empirically to greater distances between policymakers and citizens. Identifiability's effect is purely through the formation of more distant governments, as we can see from comparing the last two lines, the coefficient becoming slightly negative after government distance is in the equation. However, policymakers built on majority governments are consistently further from the citizen median than policymakers built on minority governments, even with all variables in the equation. As we saw in chapter 9, this effect, like that of the committee system, shows the advantage (for representational congruence) of giving the opposition greater weight in policy making, which is likely under minority governments (whatever exact weight one assigns). Disproportionality of vote-seat representation continues (significantly) to increase citizen-policymaker distance, largely because the oppositions are so badly underrepresented and thus less influential, even after the legislative and governmental medians are accounted for. However, the magnitude of the unstandardized coefficient is halved with the legislative median in the model.

The last two equations show the direct effect of the legislative median remaining significant, but most of the impact is coming through creation of such distant governments (as we see in the decline of the unstandardized legislative median distance coefficient from .48 to .17). Finally, it is notable that the explanatory power of each equation is greater than that of the previous one. The R-Square increases from .59 to .73 to .83 to .92, suggesting that each subsequent stage (election, government formation, policymaker negotiation) is contributing something independently to the explanation of citizen-policymaker distance.

There is no denying that this system of regression equations, with its high collinearity, is somewhat sensitive to the exact specification of variables, that there is some arbitrariness in some specific measures, and that the statistical significances are overstated. The elections in each country are not completely independent events. The basic relationships, however, are quite robust and consistently support the proportional vision advantage. (See also the comparison of correlations based on nineteen countries or seventy-eight elections in note 18.) Tracing these intervening connections, here through the regression equation system, in a way that corresponds to the case analysis in chapters 8 and 9 should give us further confidence that we are identifying the problems for majoritarianism associated with each stage. Changing the specific weights given to the opposition through the different committee systems and government status conditions would not, within a wide range of the plausible weights, alter the basic pattern. Even though correspondence between median citizen and policymaker should be a criterion of citizen influence especially valued in the majoritarian vision, it was the processes associated with proportionality that consistently created the best correspondence.

PART IV

Conclusion

10

Overview of Elections as Instruments of Democracy

This book explores the role that elections play in connecting the preferences of citizens and the selection of policymakers in twenty contemporary democracies. The exploration has been guided by the normative and empirical writings of scholars whose works articulate two great visions of elections as instruments of democracy. In the majoritarian vision citizens use elections to choose decisively between two competing teams of policymakers, providing the winner with the concentrated power to make public policy, allowing the loser only to continue to challenge in future elections. In the proportional influence vision citizens use elections to choose political agents to represent their diverse views continuously in postelection bargaining that will influence policy making. The predominant constitutional arrangements in these countries can be interpreted as designs intended to realize these visions.

The analyses in the preceding chapters have traced the electoral connections between citizens and policymakers. I developed measures of the concepts implied by each vision, describing their prevalence in elections in various countries and linking them to origins in constitutional design and to consequences for responsiveness and representative congruence. In this chapter I recapitulate my earlier findings and address some remaining issues. It is especially urgent to consider relations among various normatively desirable features of elections and to consider the general level of democratic performance on each.

System Trade-offs: Majoritarian or Proportional Processes

There are both theoretical and empirical constraints on the simultaneous realization of key features proposed by the two democratic visions. The primary theoretical constraint is the problem of the concentration of policy-making power. Concentrated power is valued by majoritarians for enabling elected governments to carry out their promises (mandates) and for giving voters clear information about responsibility for government actions (accountability). Unless public opinion is very homogeneous, however, concentrating power in the hands of the government will be detrimental to the normative principle of giving proportional influence to agents of all the electorate, which is the process most valued by the alternative vision.

The empirical constraint in using elections to connect citizens and policy-makers is the diversity of citizens' electoral support. The analyses in chapters 3 and 4 implied that a single cohesive party or at least an identifiable preelection coalition must gain unblocked control of the policy-making process to offer voters the forward-looking mandate conditions and retrospective accountability conditions necessary for the majoritarian vision. Unless such a party or coalition wins the support of most of the voters, the achievement of these majoritarian processes will limit the effective influence of many citizens in policy making. But it is empirically quite rare for a single party or preelection coalition to win even a bare majority of votes, let alone a large preponderance of them. Most of the majority party victories observed in these countries were founded on voter pluralities, converted into policy-making majorities through the electoral and policy-making rules. Under such conditions, high levels of achievement of the processes valued by majoritarians, measured in chapters 3 and 4, must constrain achievement of the effective authorized representation process measured in chapter 5.

Figure 10.1 shows the aggregate trade-off between desirable election conditions implied by the majoritarian vision and by the proportional vision. For the sake of simplicity, the conditions in each country are expressed as averages of all the elections in that country, so the country's electoral experience is reduced to a single point on the scattergram. A great deal of information is unaccounted for in this simplification. But the clear patterns can reassure us of the essentials of the findings as well as enable us to locate countries of special interest. The horizontal axis summarizes the conditions implied by the majoritarian vision and discussed in chapters 3 and 4, averaging net clarity of responsibility (see table 3.4) and mandate conditions (see table 4.3). New Zealand, at the far right, achieved perfect scores for the majoritarian processes in the elections from 1972 through 1993. Elections in Italy and Denmark, on the far

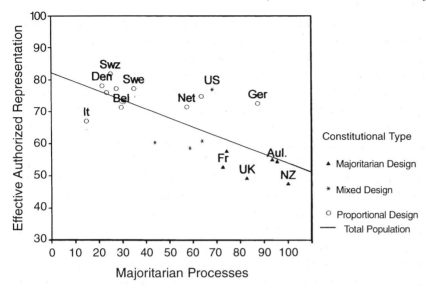

Figure 10.1. Majoritarian and Proportional Processes: Twenty Democracies

left of the graph, averaged under 30, with mandates and responsibility limited by various combinations of uncertain coalition prospects and minority governments. The vertical axis is the "standard" measure of effective authorized representation (see table 5.4 and table 5.A in the appendix to chapter 5). On this dimension the lowest scores are in New Zealand and the United Kingdom, whose governments were based on less than 45 percent of the voters and little influence for the (underrepresented) opposition parties. The high scores in Denmark and Sweden reflect both fairer representation and a great deal of bargaining influence for opposition parties. Switzerland, highest scorer of all, enjoyed its unique continuing grand coalition of the four largest parties in its government.

The most obvious feature of the figure is the downward sloping best-fit line, indicating the negative relationship between the majoritarian and proportional processes. The United States and Germany, to be sure, manage to achieve at least average majoritarian conditions (although well short of the best of the majoritarian systems) and still have good authorized representation. But most countries fit along the down-sloping line that trades off effective authorized representation for majoritarian identification and control. Given the benefits that each model confers, it would be desirable to succeed with both, rather than trading one off against the other. Mutual reinforcement would create an upward-sloping line. The negative slope, however, is expected from the theoretical and empirical constraints.

A second feature that can be observed in the figure is that the constitutional designs are generally performing as expected. Chapter 2 examined both election rules and legislative policy-making rules, the two key features of the constitutional arrangements that can be used to "limit" democratically or "extend indefinitely" the power of the people. That examination showed that we could classify most constitutional designs in the twenty democracies as predominately majoritarian or predominately proportional. The legend to the right of the figure indicates that the majoritarian design systems are marked by triangles, the mixed and proportional design systems by other symbols. The majoritarian constitutional designs predominate in the lower right-hand part of the figure, while the proportional ones are in the upper left. This pattern is just what we expect from the empirical theory covered in chapter 2 and the subsequent analysis in chapters 3–5. Despite some variation in particular elections and some independent effect of the national party systems, on average the elections in each country match our expectations rather well.

A third feature of figure 10.1 is the absolute distribution of countries in the graph. There are no countries in the lower half of the figure, where countries would be located if they provided effective representation for fewer than half of the citizens. Even in the United Kingdom and New Zealand, the democracies that performed worst on effective authorized representation, the scores seldom fell much below the 50 percent level. Figures in that range generally reflected domination by a government winning 40–45 percent of the vote, plus substantial legislative representation for the opposition, giving them at least a national forum for election campaigning. Obviously, this scenario differs very much from the situation in nondemocracies.[1] It speaks well to the general success of elections in conferring basic representation in democracies.

From the majoritarian perspective, we see some substantial failures of the democratic process. Countries in the upper left of the figure perform poorly in creating responsible governments and elections in which citizens could foresee and realize the consequences of their choices for government formation. But no countries appear in even the middle or lower left of the graph (Italy is the closest), so it is apparent that the countries that are least successful in providing accountability and mandates are quite high on effective representation, and the relatively poor representation systems are quite high on majoritarian linkages. Our knowledge of other countries tells us that dual failure is possible. Consider the first democratic elections in Russia and Poland, in which more than a third of the electorate supported small parties that failed to pass a 5 percent threshold for admission to the legislature—yet there were still no party majorities. But in the twenty established democracies, unhelpful processes on one dimension tend usually to be balanced by supportive processes on the other.

System Performance: Achieving Alternative Responsiveness Ideals

Chapter 6 treated the two visions as hypotheses about the performance of elections as instruments of democracy, rather than as promoting conditions valued in their own right. Its concept of performance used the voting choices of citizens as a baseline for assessing responsiveness in selecting policymakers. The analytic discussion suggested, however, that differences in the conceptualization of good electoral performance inherent in the visions themselves make it difficult to test their hypotheses against each other. Achieving concentrated power and achieving dispersed power imply somewhat different criteria of democratic responsiveness.

Generally, we would expect the designs to succeed on their own terms, but not on the terms of the alternative vision. Majoritarian designs should be much better at translating the voter majority into unchecked majority governments able to carry out their election promises and be held accountable for their performance. If that is what we mean by responsiveness, then majoritarian designs should show more responsive election outcomes. But they may do this at the price of excluding many citizens from having an influence on policy making, so their performance is poorer by proportional vision criteria. The proportional designs should be much better at generating policy-making coalitions that give influence to large proportions of the electorate. If that is what we mean by responsiveness, then proportional designs should show more responsive elections. Unless the vote is highly concentrated behind a single party or coalition, however, they have to do this at the price of blurring the voter-policymaker connection both prospectively and retrospectively. This conceptual disagreement suggested by the logic of the visions themselves is not entirely reconcilable.

One caveat must be emphasized as we move from the normative ideals to their empirical realization. Because voters seldom give clear majorities to a single party or preelection coalition in any country, the majoritarian vision is interpreted as a plurality vision in treating responsiveness. To the extent this is normatively doubtful, the majoritarian systems seldom fulfill their promises.

If we know nothing more about voters than their expressed choice in the election, and we accept the majoritarian vision as a plurality vision, the two visions press us toward measures of performance similar to the two types of conditions shown in figure 10.1. We expect a trade-off between them. Figure 6.7 demonstrated this outcome, in which most elections (except for a few unmitigated disasters that excluded the plurality vote winner from power) fell on a trade-off line between two types of responsiveness failure. The simple correlation between ideal responsiveness by the standards of the two visions is −.58 (123 elections, mixed designs excluded).

Rather than belaboring the trade-off, figure 10.2 reminds us above all of the generally good responsiveness to votes of each constitutional design type on its own terms. It again averages the electoral experience of each country. The horizontal dimension is the score on the majoritarian or proportional processes from figure 10.1, with each type of design assigned the type of linkage theoretically predicted from its constitutional rules. For example, the horizontal dimension places Britain by its average accountability plus mandate score, but Denmark by its effective authorized representation score. The vertical dimension is the achievement of the plurality and proportional ideals of democratic responsiveness to the vote outcomes in selecting policymakers, respectively for each design type (from table 6.2).[2] The four mixed designs are excluded here. Reference lines are drawn at the 50 percent (halfway to maximum) points.

The figure enables us to see three things. First, all these democratic systems fall in the upper-right-hand quadrant. All of them are providing the kinds of conditions we expect in their electoral and policymaker processes. All of them are relatively successful in approaching the kind of responsiveness ideal we expect from their design type, assuming we accept the plurality standard for the majoritarian designs. Despite various examples of failure in specific elections, the overall performance is quite good. Democracies generally, if imperfectly, deliver the goods they promise. They do so both in achieving the kinds of desired process conditions discussed in chapters 3–5 and summarized in figure 10.1 and in achieving the responsiveness standards discussed in chapter 6. This dual achievement is by far the most important point about figure 10.2.

A second point about the figure can be seen by distinguishing the majoritarian design types (triangles) and proportional design types (circles). Perhaps most striking here is that the majoritarian systems show more diversity across the systems. We saw in earlier chapters that the majoritarian systems exhibited quite a bit of diversity from election to election, with an occasional minority government in Canada and France or wrong winner in Australia and New Zealand marring otherwise consistent performance. Here we see also that the countries themselves vary a good deal in their averages. This is, I think, directly attributable to the conjunction of all-or-nothing processes posited by the vision itself and the peculiarities of the specific election rules (single-

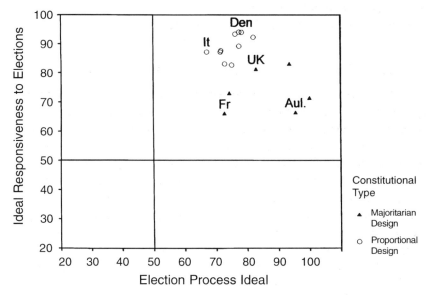

Figure 10.2. Ideal Electoral Process and Ideal Responsiveness to Elections

member districts) used in most of these countries to achieve majority legislative control. In a short run of only a quarter of a century and five to ten elections, we can see a lot of variance in the average cross-system outcomes. We cannot be sure whether these will converge on a score or whether some countries, such as Canada, have preference distributions that pose difficulties for the typical majoritarian design. By contrast, the proportional influence designs, despite the indirect nature of their government formation process, and even the fall of governments in some countries, end up more consistently in the same place.

As a whole the majoritarian systems are a bit better in approximating their process ideals than their responsiveness ideals. They tend to fall toward the lower right of the quadrant. Australia and New Zealand (the second triangle close to Australia) exemplify this most clearly. I do not want to make too much of this point because it is shaped in part by the specific measurement procedure. But the detailed analyses in chapter 6 imply that it is the occasional all-or-nothing failures that most seriously diminish ideal responsiveness in the majoritarian systems. Both Australia and New Zealand experienced more than one legislative majority government by a party that finished second in the election. The opposite seems to be true of the proportional systems, in which the tendency in almost all countries to rely on majority voting rules in legislative confidence and policy-making votes consistently depressed effective authorized representation and achievement of the proportional ideal.[3]

System Performance: Closeness to the Median Citizen

The left-right scale is a powerful comparative tool that allows one to go beyond simply assuming that nothing more about voters and their representatives can be known than vote choices. In each of the countries in this study the left-right scale seems to tap meaningfully into the national political discourse. A great advantage is that it enables us to disentangle citizens' preferences from their votes, which are limited by the party offerings. Of equal importance, it allows us to see where citizens stand in relation to all the parties, not just to their final choice. Its advantage over any particular policy measure is to provide a common metric across countries and across citizens and parties and to incorporate multiple issues in a single scale. The potential problems, of course, lie precisely in the assumption that the left-right scale's distances are equivalent for different citizens and parties in different settings.

The left-right scale for citizens was used here in a very simple and limited way to locate the median citizen as self-identified on the scale. Thus, the surveys use the whole sample and make quite minimal assumptions about the information available to citizens. There is room for a lot of error still to generate a good approximation of the true citizen median. Identifying the location of parties depends here on surveys of political experts in each country, using the average of several experts to rate each party. This procedure avoids creating artificial linkages between citizen preferences and party positions but assumes, of course, that the experts' substantive ideas about the meaning of the scale positions correspond roughly to the ideas of the citizens in that country. Our comparisons assume nothing about the substantive equivalence of scale positions across countries but assume some comparability of the differences between positions.

Two points about the relations between the visions of democracy and the left-right scale should be reiterated. First, the scale, at least as used here, is appropriate for the majoritarian vision but perhaps less so for the proportional vision. Majoritarian theory tends to assume a single dimension of political issues, on which a true majority position can be located. Such a true majority position makes it possible to talk meaningfully about mandates and the connection between what "the voters want" and which governments come to power. As formal theorists have so persuasively demonstrated, these matters become conceptually much more difficult in multidimensional situations, in which there simply may be no single dominant majority position. The proportional influence vision, on the other hand, permits, even encourages, different majorities to form on different issues and can thus, in principle, respond more flexibly to complex, multidimensional situations. (However, assessing what is a good response is not thereby made a trivial problem.) Relatedly, our choice of the citizen median, although relevant for both models, is especially appropriate for majoritarian theory. Governments located at this point can defeat in a majority vote any alternative policy proposed. For these methodological reasons, a failure of majoritarian designs to outperform their proportional counterparts on measures using the left-right scale is especially telling against them.

A second point concerns governments versus policymakers. As discussed in chapter 7, both majoritarian and proportional influence theory have models that connect the median citizen, the government, and the policymakers. Majoritarian theory stresses governments, which are assumed to have the concentrated power to carry out their promised policies and be held accountable for them. If the de facto policymaker coalition varies from the government, this will be troubling for majoritarians. Proportional influence theory, on the other hand, seems to predict that often governments will include the party at the median but may build from it, pulling the government position off the median. Providing some, but lesser, influence to the opposition parties will often pull the policymaker coalition back toward the median. (Granting some influence to representatives of all parties is also intrinsically desirable to proportional influence theorists, but here I am considering only the effect in relation to the citizen median, framing the issue, to some extent, in majoritarian terms.)

The problem of governments versus policymaker coalitions becomes especially acute when minority governments are formed. Such governments are, of course, contrary to the majoritarian model. But they may be quite compatible with the proportional influence point of view, as we explored first in chapter 5. A minority government is forced to give additional influence to parties outside the government. This may be a way of increasing authorized representation; it also can pull minority governments closer to the citizen median. Minority governments are more common in countries featuring proportional influence designs.[4]

For these reasons, we might have expected initially either that both designs would usually perform well, with different kinds of failures, or that there might be a trade-off between government congruence (by majority governments in majoritarian systems) and policymaker congruence (by minority governments in proportional systems.) From chapters 8 and 9, however, we know that this is largely not the case. As we see in figure 10.3, the primary result

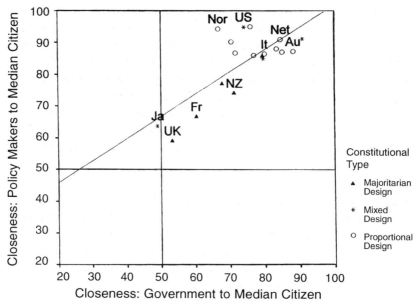

Figure 10.3. Average Closeness to the Median Citizen: Nineteen Democracies

from the left-right scale analysis is that majoritarian systems frequently perform poorly (on average) in creating either governments or policymaker coalitions close to the median voter.

In figure 10.3 I have reversed the direction on the distance measures from the previous chapters, so that the best performance area is again the upper right corner of the figure. The two dimensions are closeness of the government to the median citizen on the horizontal dimension and closeness of the policymakers to the median citizen on the vertical dimension. The transformation from distance to closeness was made by subtracting the distance between citizen median and the government (policymaker) from 5 scale points, which is about the maximum possible distance from these citizen medians on a 10-point scale, given the kind of distributions we saw in table 7.1, and expressing the result as a percentage of 5 scale points. Thus, a government exactly at the citizen median had a full 5 points and a 100 percent closeness score. A government 2½ points away got a score of 50 percent. A government 5 points away (as if the National Front had gained control in France in 1993 or PDS had gained control in Germany in 1994) would score close to 0 by this closeness measure. We see that the best-fit line slopes up and to the right, showing that government closeness to the median and policymaker closeness to the median are related to each other, not a trade-off as in describing the majoritarian and proportional conditions in figure 10.1.

We have no way of determining absolutely what poor performance here may be. The worst governments in these countries in this time period, in terms of closeness to the median voter, were about 2 ½ points away, which is half of the potential scale distance usually available. This was the situation of the Japanese LDP in 1990 and the Conservative Thatcher government in Britain in 1983. It is encouraging for democracy, of course, that we do not see extremist governments ruling centrist electorates or vice versa. Neither do we find very conservative governments ruling leftist electorates, which we might find in, say, an authoritarian dictatorship of the right (Spain probably looked like that in the last years of Francisco Franco); or very leftist governments dominating conservative electorates (as perhaps in Czechoslovakia after the Soviets reestablished Communist dictatorship in 1968). There is, then, a positive message here about democracy in the general placement of the countries. I have again shown the 50 percent reference lines, so we can see clearly that all the systems are in the upper-right-hand quadrant.

Nonetheless, the majoritarian designs perform on average notably less well than the proportional ones, even on the measure of closeness of governments to the median citizen (the horizontal scale). There is substantial variance in the majoritarian cases, which is a familiar story. In this time period, the United Kingdom and France perform worst, their governments averaging 2 or more points from the median on the 5-point scale (60 percent); Australia and New Zealand do better but are still 1 ½ points away, about the same as the governments in the worst-performing proportional systems (Norway and Sweden). Canada is on average the best-performing majoritarian system, rather similar to the average proportional system at a distance of 1 scale point. Most of the majoritarian systems had notable variance between their worst and best governments.[5]

The Scandinavian systems show the expected effects of minority governments on the government-policymaker difference. Sweden, Norway, and Denmark are all well above the best-fit line, as their combination of minority governments and shared committee systems, which help the opposition parties affect policy, pulled left and right governments closer to the median. The majoritarian systems are helped little by this effect (as we see in their location below the best-fit line). The United States, interestingly, is at the same position as Denmark, with moderately distant governments (about 1 ⅓ scale points, or 75 percent) pulled sharply closer to the median by the frequent experience of divided government (and lack of perfect party cohesion) helping the opposition party.

Again, on average the proportional systems are more successful in getting governments (and even more so the influential policymakers) close to the median citizen. This finding contrasts notably with the trade-off we saw in creating desirable conditions based on votes as the preference measure (in figure 10.1) and the generally good "own system ideal" approximations of electoral responsiveness (in figure 10.2).

Electoral Responsiveness and Left-Right Congruence

The left-right scale can be used to examine not only the success of the constitutional design types in creating similarity of views between citizens and policymakers, but also the relation between electoral responsiveness and representative congruence. In a democracy, citizens presumably expect that the formation of governments and policymaker coalitions will be responsive to the choices citizens express in elections. Yet obviously the majoritarian and proportional visions of democracy have somewhat differing ideas about ideal responsiveness when it comes to relating the vote distribution among parties to the formation of governments and policymakers. We can consider each of these in relation to the left-right scale.

Consistent with the conclusions drawn in chapters 8 and 9, the proportional approach to responsiveness is associated with greater congruence between the median citizen, the government, and the policymakers. The closer to the proportional responsiveness ideal (see table 6.2, last columns), the less distance between the median citizen and the government (r = −.40) and the policymakers (r = −.76). This relation is not only consistent with, but follows from the appropriate linking processes. Good vote-seat correspondence and all the measures of effective authorized representation from chapter 5 are significantly related to less distance between the median citizen and the legislature, government, and policymakers. Democratic representation, as Pitkin observes, involves not only a momentary agreement between ruled and rulers, but a process that forms and sustains congruence as policymakers are chosen and authorized.[6] Although there are important differences within and across the proportional influence design systems, the better the fit to the proportional ideals of both process and overall responsiveness, the better the congruence.

Recall further that one of the main concerns about proportional designs, their failure to create governments that endure between elections, does not prove to be a disadvantage in sustaining congruence of views. Government turnover tends to give weight to a wider diversity of views, as discussed in chapter 6. Moreover, the first government formed after the election is on average no closer to the citizen median than later governments. On the contrary, the detailed analysis in chapter 9 showed that when the first government does not endure until the next election, the later ones tend to be not further away from but closer to the median citizen. The difference is not so great that I wish to argue that government changes are beneficial to citizen-government congruence,[7] but generally they are not harmful. Thus, if the policy position of the government were considered the ultimate touchstone of responsiveness to the electorate, the advantage would go decidedly to the proportional influence systems.

On the other hand, the better the governments ($r = +.37$) and policymakers ($r = +.56$) approximate the majoritarian (plurality) responsiveness ideal, the further they are, on average, from the citizen median. Generally, this is so because of the processes of party competition and electoral victory (see chapter 8). Contrary to expectations from a Downsian image of two-party competition and majorities, competition even in majoritarian design systems is rarely confined to only two parties, seldom results in vote majorities for one of them, and infrequently finds both main contenders offering policy commitments close to the median voter. As soon as even fairly small third parties enter the picture, a variety of competitive configurations can plausibly arise. And they do. When one large party is far from the median, a common situation, it may nonetheless win because several other (closer) parties split the vote or, sometimes, the voters worry about incumbent performance in office or are distracted by secondary issues. In addition, in some elections both of the large parties (or preelection coalitions) are quite a distance from the median.

Examination of the governments that fail to include the plurality winner further illuminates the picture. As noted in chapter 6, when we count preelection coalitions as appropriate for plurality winning, the failure to include the plurality winner in the government is about equally prevalent in the two main types of systems. There is little difference in congruence with the citizen median between majoritarian governments that do and do not include the plurality winner. The few unmitigated failures in majoritarian process terms produce on average governments that are no further from the median voter than their counterpart elections in which the plurality winner became the government.[8]

Two New Zealand elections illustrate how majoritarian rules and party competition can create misleading outcomes if we assume simple relations between votes and preferences. In 1981 the wrong party, the plurality vote loser, won the legislative majority and took power, excluding the plurality winner: a process disaster. But in preference terms the two largest parties were about the same distance from the citizen median and fairly close to it — Labour about a point to the left and the National Party about a point to the right. In preference terms the outcome was not a disaster: either outcome was equally good, and both were, compared to averages in other countries, quite acceptable. In 1993, on the other hand, the elections generated the right majoritarian process winner, as the National Party won 35 percent of the vote, the plurality, and a slim legislative majority. But the National Party was much further from the voter median (1.5 points) than the Labour Party it defeated (.2 points) and substantially farther than the cross-national average. Two left parties split the left/center vote, leaving the National Party with enough to carry the legislature. In preference congruence terms it is 1993, not 1981, that shows a poor democratic outcome.

The main problem with congruence in the majoritarian systems is that the plurality winner is too far from the median — and is then given by the election rules a legislative majority that precludes the need to bargain with smaller parties at or across the median (see chapters 8, 9). The majoritarian congruence problems in these countries did not stem primarily from the 15 percent of cases in which the plurality winner was excluded from power. It arose at the previous stage, as party competition and voter choices awarded most votes to a party far from the median. In the proportional influence systems, by contrast, failure to include the plurality party was associated with less citizen-government congruence. An irony here is that such failures (as noted in chapter 8) tend to occur in the presence of high government identifiability, a majoritarian property that limits postelection bargaining. An open, unconstrained bargaining process in the proportional design systems tended to result in governments that included the median legislator, who was, in turn, close to the median voter.

Why We Are Not at the End of the History of Democracy

The idea that elections can act as instruments of democracy in alternative ways is familiar. Thus, it has been possible to be guided by the voluminous scholarly writing and research on majoritarian and proportional democracy. Yet there are few, if any, systematic efforts to describe and compare a large number of democratic elections across the full range of processes and criteria identified in these literatures. Because so many problems had to be solved, my findings inevitably have a somewhat provisional character.

There are several areas in which the analyses in this book make a contribution, but particularly invite further work to confirm or reconsider what has been concluded here. In each case the logic of what was needed to test or even explore the critical relations forced the analysis to go beyond current scholarly consensus about concepts and measures:

1. *Identifiability and majoritarianism.* Majoritarian theory assumes that the voters have before them alternative future governments, so that elections can play a decisive role in the selection process. But the empirical study of

this situation is underdeveloped. One area that cries out for more serious theoretical and empirical work is the appearance of announced preelection coalitions between political parties. We know too little about the origins of such coalitions and about the great variety of forms (shared manifestos, withdrawal of coalition partners, recommendations to voters) that they can take. But in a number of countries such coalitions unmistakably play a critical role at both electoral and legislative levels. They link vote outcomes more directly to government formation, but because they often constrain interparty bargaining they may actually weaken congruence with the median voter.

Less well defined, yet still seemingly important, is the emergence of assumptions about the postelection coalition formation pattern. In some cases, voters have good reason to expect that the working of the election rules will result in a legislative majority for one party or another (although we know rather little about how voters make this inference). But in others, the voters seem to take their cue from the interparty attitudes of the political leaders. Again, we know too little about the emergence of preelection identifiability to be confident in our understanding. We can see a strong fit among election rules, reported identifiability, and postelection party behavior, but we are only beginning to understand the nature of the connections.

2. *Governments and policymakers.* Most comparative studies of the impact of constitutional arrangements focus on the number of political parties and their legislative representation or on the formation and durability of governments. Only recently has empirical research begun to examine systematically and comparatively the policy-making processes inside the executive and legislative institutions. This has seemed less critical when comparativists focus on majoritarian systems like Britain or France (or even Ireland or Canada), in which governments maintain relatively unchecked control of policy making. But in the past fifteen years much excellent work has suggested how in political systems with more proportionally oriented designs the internal structure and processes give important policy-making roles to the opposition political parties (see chapter 2 and the references therein). Furthermore, where the government does not command majority control of the legislature (or power is disbursed through other institutional structures such as strong presidencies or legislative houses chosen by the provincial governments), it is an unacceptable simplification to assume that control of government is the end of the story. Such an assumption ignores influence connections that are an essential part of one of the great visions of democracy and thus inevitably underestimates the performance of proportional influence designs in terms of their own responsiveness ideal. As it

turns out, these power-sharing rules, contrary to assumptions of the majoritarian vision, usually improve the fit between the position of the median voter and that of the policymakers. I cannot claim to have made more than a crude beginning (in chapter 5) at estimating these processes, but analyses of elections as instruments of democracy must go beyond legislatures and governments to take policy-making processes into account.

Another way of thinking about this point is that much contemporary analysis has focused on election rules and proportionality of voter representation in legislatures and governments, traded off against the creation of "artificial" legislative (and government) majorities. We have seen that this fine empirical and theoretical tradition is relevant to electoral responsiveness and representative congruence, although those are far from identical. But these analyses have tended to neglect the earliest line of thought about democratic "limits" on the power of the people, the Madisonian version (itself with deeper historic roots) that stresses policy-making institutions requiring the sharing of power. The works of Lijphart (1984) and a few others have helped renew interest in power-sharing institutional arrangements. The very recent studies of committees and parliaments (for example, Doering et al. 1995) have begun to create an empirical basis for assessing their role within the legislative process. Despite the difficulties of measuring proportionality of influential resources in these processes, in addition to legislative elections, success is essential. The analyses in chapters 5 and 9, especially, indicate that this older tradition has a valuable part to play in our understanding the way democracies can use elections to provide all citizens with some policy-making influence.

3. *Votes, left-right positions, and substantive behavior.* In this study I have used the positions of citizens and political parties on the left-right scale, as estimated by expert country observers, to estimate and explore the connections between citizen preferences and policymaker commitments. Such commitments are assumed to shape policymaker behavior. As was demonstrated in chapters 8 and 9, these left-right scale analyses reveal a great deal about party competition and its consequences that cannot be inferred from voter and party distributions alone. Vote outcomes are quite inadequate, or at least insufficient, measures of the preferences of voters among parties. The left-right scale metric has enabled us to some extent to get behind the vote to consider underlying voter preferences in relation to all the parties.

Nonetheless, what has been revealed also implies how much more needs to be done. On the voter side, we need to understand much more about the relations among voters' preferences, their perceptions of party positions, and their choices under different party configurations. On the policymaker side, democratic theory ultimately directs our attention to what policy-makers do, not just to what they say. Matthew Gabel and John Huber (2000) have shown that expert placements are statistically related to party election promises (manifestos) and to the self-placements of party voters.[9] While the comparisons reassure us about the robustness of the placements, they do not allow us to see the extent to which parties try to carry out their promises and act consistently with their positions. Various studies have noticed that party manifestos are at least somewhat predictive of party behavior in office, but that many other factors also shape public policy.[10] There are many linkages that need closer investigation. Multidimensional preference distributions are one problem. The possibility of deadlock, rather than negotiated compromise, in coalition and minority governments is another that desperately needs further attention.[11] Above all, perhaps, we have not been able to test one of the critical assumptions of the majoritarian vision: that when the responsibility of parties for policy is clearer, the parties will be more likely to act as reliable agents for their voters. We need better empirical investigation and theoretical understanding of corrupt and electorally deviant behavior[12] as an obvious step beyond the current analysis.

Beyond these three areas of progress and possibility are some vital issues that could not be adequately studied in this analysis of twenty democracies over the past quarter century. Two of these are essential if we are to extend the study of elections as instruments of democracy to the many new democracies established in the "third wave" of democratization.[13] One is the early development of party competition. Most of the twenty democracies studied here had party systems developed long before our starting point in the early 1970s. The exceptions, Greece and Spain, showed some manifestations of party system instability that are far more common in new democracies. Much more pronounced examples of inadequate information on the part of voters and party leaders, limited organization and coordination, rapid consolidation or splintering of parties, limited parliamentary discipline, and so forth can be found in the newer democracies. These features affect the connections between votes and policymakers in many ways. Some literature—and hints in our current analysis—suggests that the patterns of organization and competition emergent in early elections may shape subsequent events.[14]

A second limitation of the set of democracies in this study is the relative simplicity and comparability of the constitutional designs. Most of the systems are parliamentary, with a chief executive chosen by the legislature and removable by the legislature. The United States and Switzerland are the major exceptions, with the French mixed presidential-parliamentary arrangement also receiving special attention. Substantial efforts were make to fit them into the analysis. The newer democracies in Latin America and Eastern Europe have more frequently chosen presidential and mixed designs in executive-legislature relations that will require (but also permit) more extensive work on the role these designs can play.

On the electoral side, there are, of course, many possible electoral rules that have been proposed or applied in a few countries or subnational elections, but which are too seldom used nationally for us to have developed adequate understanding of them. Preferential voting, for example, receives no special attention in my analysis but deserves much fuller consideration. So does the interplay between executive and legislative elections, which must be taken more fully into account as systems with strong and directly elected executives are considered.[15] The possibilities of alternative electoral systems are nearly limitless, in their own right and as interacted with various configurations of voter preferences, and will doubtless keep political scientists engaged for the indefinite future. But most obviously, high-threshold PR is nearly a missing category of election rules in our analysis. Only Greece is really a PR system that had, for the majority of its elections in our analysis, a moderately high effective threshold (17 percent).[16] Because the expert surveys failed to include Greece, we were not able to make adequate use even of that single high-threshold PR system. Because the high-threshold systems here are almost all single-member district systems, which have many special limitations[17], we may underestimate the possibilities in majoritarian design.

In this regard it is also worth keeping in mind that although the analysis in this book has concentrated on averages and general patterns, the majoritarian systems were especially notable for their high variance in many performance areas. The all-or-nothing nature of majoritarian designs and processes can make analysis based on a small sample of cases especially misleading. Similarly, while the interactions among social structure, political preferences, and institutions can always offer pitfalls to the unwary (or even wary) analyst, small effects are particularly likely to have large consequences in majoritarian systems.

Another empirical limitation of the present analysis is the relatively static nature of the constitutional designs and party systems in the present time frame. The availability of relatively good data on citizen preferences and party placements at points has enabled us to sample the performance of elections over a decade apart. But in most of these countries the basic constitutional designs and party systems were relatively unchanging through the period. The exceptions are extremely interesting, but too few to be the subject of statistical analysis. We did see that the temporary sharp reduction of the PR threshold for three elections in Greece greatly reduced vote-seat disproportionality, but also made it much more difficult to elect majority governments, as was also true of the 1986 election in France (fought under PR election rules, rather than single-member districts.)

Two countries attempted fairly major changes in constitutional design at the very end of our period of analysis, thus offering wonderful opportunities for future observation.[18] However, as is well known, the huge upheavals in Italy in 1993–94 involved many factors that changed the political party system as well as the election rules. It is difficult to disentangle citizen concern with low proximity and lack of clear responsibility from other sources of dissatisfaction with the Italian political system, consistently the worst-rated in Europe by its citizens.[19] As a cause of the systemic upheavals, general dissatisfaction obviously interacted with the impact of such short-term factors as the collapse of Communism and the "clean hands" criminal investigations that decimated the traditional party and governmental leadership.[20] It is also difficult to know, therefore, how much of the change to highly identifiable preelection coalitions, rather than postelection bargaining, is attributable to the change in election rules (from pure PR to 75 percent single-member districts with only partial compensation from the remaining PR districts).

At the very end of the period under consideration here, voters in New Zealand chose in a referendum in 1993 to change from single-member district majoritarianism to a German-style mixed SMD/PR, with compensation and only a 5 percent threshold. Voter dissatisfactions with various disproportionalities in representation were certainly a factor in this decision.[21] Anticipation of the new 1996 election rules seems to have been a factor in the breakdown in the party configuration in the legislature in 1993–96. The 1996 election itself immediately produced greatly improved vote-seat proportionality, but also created great difficulties in negotiating and sustaining a majority government. Thus, we see traces in each country of some of the consequences we might expect from changes in the constitutional designs, but it was too soon to be sure if new equilibria had really emerged.

What Has Been Done

This book has been driven, explicitly and, I hope, consistently, by a normative assumption and the desire to investigate an empirical claim. The normative assumption is that democratic policymakers should do what their citizens want them to do. The empirical claim is that competitive elections, the hallmark of contemporary democracies, play a critical part by linking the preferences of citizens to the behavior of their policymakers. This is the role of elections as instruments of democracy.

Most democrats probably assume, in their optimistic moments, that elections somehow play this role. Moreover, there is a great deal of research on what are obviously parts of this process, such as the effects of election rules, the logic of party competition, the formation of governing coalitions, and the legislative process. Yet, on closer examination, the empirical studies as well as the commonplace arguments seem to be embedded in quite different assumptions, values, and hypotheses about just what elections as instruments of democracy should do, can do, and usually do in fact.

I have tried in this book to explore two very large clusters of alternative images of citizens, elections, and policy making. I have identified these as majoritarian and proportional visions of democratic elections, hoping that the term *vision* captures the mix of conceptual, normative, and empirical elements that seems operative here. Historically, I began by invoking the early debates about the American constitution and Alexis de Tocqueville's "two opinions which are as old as the world . . . the one tending to limit, the other to extend indefinitely, the power of the people."[22] To "extend indefinitely" the power of the people has come to mean to give unconstrained policy-making authority to a coherent political party, whose candidates have been elected by the citizen majority in competitive elections. Whatever the historical emergence, for modern democrats, I have suggested, to "limit" the power of the people has come to mean to disperse political power among them, requiring minimal majorities to expand or to take account of minorities through discussion and negotiation. A great variety of institutional mechanisms, both in elections and in postelectoral policy making, have been introduced for this purpose. The main variants of constitutional designs in the stabilized democracies of the last quarter of the twentieth century can be understood as exemplifying particular expressions of these alternative visions.

In trying to understand the underlying premises of the visions as well as the working of their institutional designs, I have drawn heavily on both formal analyses and empirical studies. I have found the former invaluable for suggesting the assumptions and problems involved in collective choices. I have found the latter to contain rich theories and findings about specific connections in practice. However, in trying to see how elections can and do connect the preferences of citizens to the public commitments of policymakers in more than 150 elections in twenty democracies I have had to combine them in original ways. It is, I think, the effort to present a coherent analysis of the normative and conceptual underpinnings connected to the empirical relations — successes and failures — that is the most ambitious goal of this work.

Both the early conceptual discussion and the findings of the first half of the book intimated the unlikelihood of a single design that could optimize all values for democratic elections. My initial theoretical analysis argued that concentrated power approaches and dispersed power approaches each possess distinctive advantages as means for citizens to shape policies. But notable disadvantages adhere in each. The empirical analysis of the institutions and processes of citizen control and influence in chapters 3–6 strongly supported the idea that to some degree these must be traded off against each other, at least as long as there were substantial disagreements among citizens about desirable approaches to public policy (see also figure 10.1).

While different arrangements can be devised to create majorities, the embedding of these properties in the constitutional rules seems to require some kind of distortion in representation and the exaggeration of small shifts into large consequences. Leaving the creation of majorities to political elites often involves problems of multiple and minority government that undercut properties of responsibility and mandates that majoritarians value. Minority governments can usefully encourage bargaining with representatives of larger segments of the electorate, especially if helped by power-sharing legislative rules, but for that very reason can make it more difficult for voters to know whom they should punish if policies turn sour. In analyzing empirically the connections and ideals implied by each of the visions, each emerged as relatively successful by its own standards, if we take the vote outcomes as our baseline and with the critical provision that we accept plurality standards for the majoritarian ideal (see chapter 6 and figure 10.2). As shown by the quite different kinds and distributions of failures (some spectacular) in each approach, their performance is not a logical implication of the premises of the visions but is based on generally successful realization of the empirical hypotheses. This part of the book serves to support, as well as draw upon and connect, much of the superb previous scholarship on these issues.

Yet we can begin to go beyond this acceptance of each vision in its own terms. Chapters 7–9 show both the possibility and the urgency of making the attempt. Insofar as there was a single conceptual solvent to the tangled and contradictory clots of process values, the present analysis found it in the left-right congruence of voters and policymakers. As long as clarity of responsibility and the excitement of first past the post horse races remain attractive as processes, the majoritarian side will not remain unsupported. At least until it is demonstrated that such clarity is unhelpful in pressing policymakers to keep their promises, it is well that the debate continues. However, the persistent superiority of the proportional influence designs in linking the citizen median and the policymakers should give pause to those attracted by the idea of the decisive election as a direct tool for citizen control. The majoritarian vision assumes that identifiability, unchecked majorities, and clarity of responsibility will sustain governments expressing majority preferences not distant from them. The frequent appearance of the latter underlines the question, Mandates for what?

The generally good congruence between the citizen median and the governments and policymakers in the proportional design systems should be reassuring to those worried about dependence on elite coalition formation or the instability of postelection governments. With surprising consistency, each proved compatible with good citizen-policymaker congruence. In these countries at this time, the proportional vision and its designs enjoyed a clear advantage over their majoritarian counterparts in using elections as instruments of democracy. It remains to be seen if new democratic designs and new circumstances will challenge these findings.

Notes

Chapter 1. Elections as Instruments of Democracy

1. I owe this expression as well as much of my conceptualization of the relation between elections and democracy to Cohen 1971. See esp. 3–7. Similarly, Pitkin, "Our concern with elections and electoral machinery, and particularly with whether elections are free and genuine, results from our conviction that such machinery is necessary to ensure systematic responsiveness" (1967, 234).

2. A number of liberal democracies also make some occasional use of direct citizen involvement in policy making through the referendum, a popular vote on a proposed law. See Butler and Ranney 1978. But even in Switzerland, where the device is used more frequently than elsewhere, most legislation is made through the representative institutions. In this book I shall concentrate almost exclusively on elections that choose the policymakers.

3. By *competitive* I mean simply that the voters can choose among alternative candidates. In practice, at least two organized political parties that have some chance of winning seem to be needed to make choices in legislative elections meaningful. People must also be allowed basic freedoms to form and express preferences.

4. See, for example, the various requirements proposed by Dahl 1956, 63–81, and Dahl 1971, 3. Moreover, for sustaining democracy as a type of political system, the resources and problems inherent in the economic and social environment, the attitudes and values of the citizens, and the strategies of the leaders are probably more important than variations in the institutional arrangements. (These arrangements do affect what leaders must do to sustain democracy.) For empirical analysis of such factors, see Powell 1982 and the large literatures cited therein.

5. Pitkin puts this nicely: "We require functioning institutions that are designed to, and really do, secure a government responsive to public interest and opinion. . . . For this purpose, our basic prerequisites seem very few. We would be reluctant to consider any system a representative government unless it held regular elections, which were 'genuine' or 'free.' We would be reluctant, further, to consider a government representative unless it included some sort of collegiate representative body in more than an advisory capacity" (1967, 234–35). For variations in usage of the concept of democracy, see Collier and Mahon 1993. On the general empirical assumption that genuinely competitive elections identify contemporary democracies, see, for example, the discussions in Powell 1982, chap. 1, Diamond 1996, and the literatures cited in both works.

6. For a discussion distinguishing "majoritarian" or "populist democracy" approaches from their alternatives, see, e.g., Dahl 1956, esp. 36–37 n. 2. Dahl sees "Madisonian democracy" (and the American constitution and its tradition) as a compromise between "the power of majorities and the power of minorities" (4), although he does stress primarily the side emphasizing restraints on majorities, drawing heavily on the *Federalist Papers*. For contemporary works making a similar distinction but articulating more clearly proportionality, rather than simple restraint, as an alternative to majoritarianism, see, e.g., Steiner 1971, Lehmbruch 1974, and especially Lijphart 1984. As will become evident, I am especially indebted to Lijphart's formulation. The proportionality formulation establishes an explicit positive democratic ideal.

7. Dahl 1956 and Riker 1982a use the terms *populist democracy* and *populism* to characterize this ideal and its empirical analogues. However, I think both of these analyses accept rule by unchecked majorities (or their representatives), rather than minorities, as essential elements that make this vision democratic.

8. The classic statement articulating proportionality, rather than merely restraints on majorities, as a positive ideal, is perhaps John Stuart Mill. See Mill [1861] 1958, esp. chap. 7 (e.g., 103: "In a really equal democracy every or any section would be represented, not disproportionally, but proportionately").

9. A third argument in favor of proportionalism is that the policymakers should choose the policy desired by the citizen majority *on each issue*. Because many issues will be considered by the national government between every election and different sets of citizens will form the majority on different issues, it is important that the policy-making coalition not be locked into place by the immediate election outcome. This argument depends on the variety of issues and majorities potentially forming between each election. If there were the same majority on all issues, then concentrated power would be fine, as long as it reflected the citizen majority. But this identity of majorities may be rare in large, national systems. Although this is potentially an important argument for proportional approaches, it is not one that I am able to see how to explore empirically with available data. Therefore, I am setting it aside in this analysis.

10. Dahl 1989, 104: "If we accept the idea of Intrinsic Equality, then no process of lawmaking can be morally justified if it does not take equally into account the interests of every person subject to the laws."

11. Similarly, Dahl 1989: "The record of human experience provides convincing evidence that people who . . . are deprived of the opportunity to defend their own interests will almost certainly not have their interests adequately taken into account" (104). Also relevant is the strong evidence presented by Poe and Tate (1994) that democracies in

general are much less likely to abuse "personal integrity rights" than are nondemocracies. Poe and Tate use a variety of measures of democracy, trying to avoid defining such human integrity rights as part of their measure of democracy itself, with consistently robust results (table 1, 861). Also see Henderson 1991. These studies do not, however, examine the effect of different types of democratic designs.

12. In principle these assumptions themselves could be investigated empirically through an examination of the fate of minority preferences under majoritarian and proportional versions of democracy. I shall not explore these relations in this study but simply examine the degree of minority representation in the policy-making process. See chaps. 5, 6, 9 below.

13. In this book, I generally assume that the voters are themselves representatives of all citizens. We know that voter turnout varies across democratic systems (from around 50 percent in Swiss and American elections to around 90 percent in Australia). See, e.g., Powell 1986 and Franklin 1996. Voters may differ from the citizen average in various ways. See the review of a large number of studies summarized by Lijphart 1997, 2–5. I have not explored the implications of these differences in this book.

14. See the excellent discussion of these (and other) issues in Pitkin 1967, esp. chap. 7.

15. See esp. Fiorina 1981.

16. See Dahl 1956, Downs 1957, Eulau and Prewitt 1973, esp. chap. 22.

17. Burke [1774]; also see Pitkin 1967, esp. chap. 7.

18. As we shall see in considering governmental accountability in chap. 3, the problem of information and lack of clear responsibility in the face of dispersed power makes it difficult for citizens to exercise retrospective control over representative bargaining agents. Although American students of congressional elections have paid some attention to this problem, I have not yet found a useful way to study this role with the data available at the cross-national level. In majoritarian systems, where power is highly concentrated in the hands of disciplined party government, there seems to be little useful scope for it apart from government accountability. But it would be an appropriate counterpart to the analysis of the influence of representative delegates in chap. 5, below.

19. Lippmann 1925, 126; quoted by Pennock 1979.

20. Riker 1982a, 242. In a similar vein Schumpeter rejected the "classical" version of democracy because "there is, first, no such thing as a uniquely determined common good that all people could agree on or be made to agree on by the force of rational argument" (1942, 251). He replaced it with his famous argument that democracy should be conceptualized as a struggle by alternative leaders for the citizens' vote: "The principle of democracy then merely means that the reins of government should be handed to those who command more support than do any of the competing individuals or teams" (273). Schumpeter here emphasizes the prospective, rather than Riker's retrospective, formulation.

21. Riker makes somewhat uncomfortable company as a majoritarian. Most of the fire in *Liberalism Against Populism* (1982a) is directed, very powerfully, against the major alternative majoritarian formulation, the forward-looking "mandate" or "populist" view of citizen policy control. Riker's social choice–based analysis, emphasizing the (potential) substantive meaningless of collective citizen preferences as revealed through any voting mechanism, could even be offered as a defense of the proportional influence vision (as hinted above). Indeed, while he recommends the plurality method to elect legislators and

executives, as a means of sustaining a two-party system that can decisively reject incumbents (113), his suspicion of majorities also leads him, like Madison and others suspicious of populist majoritarianism, to favor additional institutions to restrain the party majorities (250–51). Many proponents of the proportional vision (see n. 6 above) would applaud. Riker rejects this view and remains a majoritarian because, it seems to me, he thinks that in the end, even after many stages, some choices must be made, and these can never be logically justified as the fair outcome of citizens' preferences under all possible configurations of preferences. He finds greater democratic justification in the possibility of a *decisive* rejection of incumbents, even if, in his words, "the kind of democracy that thus survives is not, however, popular rule, but rather an intermittent, sometimes random, even perverse popular veto" (244). Pushed to this conclusion, one is left with rather little of the fundamental idea that democracy should give citizens control over policymakers. While recognizing the power and importance of the insights from social choice analysis, I am more optimistic that very often it is possible to interpret sensibly the preferences, and distastes, of citizens as revealed in polls and even elections. In chaps. 7–9 I shall argue that the complexity of citizen preferences can often (to some degree) be meaningfully reduced to a unidimensional left-right scale against which the position of policymakers can be compared.

22. See Schlesinger 1966 and the discussion and analysis in Eulau and Prewitt 1973, chap. 22.

23. Closely associated is the large literature on "responsible party government." See American Political Science Association Committee on Political Parties 1950 and Ranney 1962. I use the mandate language here because the responsible party government literature often blends the idea of retrospective accountability and choice between future mandates, which for some purposes can be usefully distinguished variants within majoritarianism.

24. Quoted by Ranney 1962, 9. This view is, of course, much more optimistic than those of Riker and Schumpeter, as discussed in nn. 20 and 21 above.

25. See n. 14 above.

26. These policies, in turn, may help shape citizens' preferences in the future, but figure 1.2 sets aside this dynamic interaction.

27. The essential role of political parties in organizing and structuring elections to make them meaningful for citizens was pointed out by Bryce early in the twentieth century in one of the first comparative studies of democratic politics (Bryce 1921).

28. Nor do we know whether the citizens voted "sincerely," for the party they perceived as closest to their true preferences, or "strategically," taking account of the likelihood that the party could actually gain office. Nor do we know how well informed the citizens who voted for the party were about its position. See the discussion in chap. 7, below.

Chapter 2. Constitutional Designs

1. Substantial exceptions in France, Greece, Italy, and Norway during the time period examined here are explicitly discussed below. Other small changes are included in the average "effective thresholds" shown for the countries in table 2.1 but do not change the classifications.

2. Dennis Mueller offers a succinct expression of the difference in approaches: "Basically there are two alternatives: (1) the citizens can elect 'a government,' i.e. select that party whose policies they most prefer, that party they wish to see run the executive branch, or (2) the citizens can elect a truly representative body, i.e., a group of representatives that will vote as the citizens themselves would have voted had they taken part in a grand 'town meeting' of the entire electorate. To achieve each mode of representation a different electoral rule is required" (Mueller 1991, 334).

3. "Of all the hypotheses that have been defined in this book, this approaches the most nearly perhaps to a true sociological law" (Duverger 1954, 217). In subsequent pages, esp. 225–26, Duverger explains both the "psychological" and "mechanical" factors that promote two-candidate competition in district elections.

4. In 1942 E. E. Schattschneider anticipated Duverger's general arguments in proposing single-member district elections as the explanation of two-party politics in the United States, emphasizing their exaggeration of the representation of the winning party and tendency "to discriminate radically against lesser parties." He notes that this will encourage voters to vote for major party candidates, rather than minor party candidates, thus capturing Duverger's "psychological" as well as "mechanical" effects. He extended the argument to a discussion of the destruction of the Liberal Party in Britain (1942, 74–80) but does not directly consider other election rules or multiparty systems.

5. My theoretical formulation here is especially influenced by Cox 1997, who is not, of course, responsible for my errors of interpretation. See also his discussion of the separated empirical and formal-theoretical traditions (Cox 1997, 10–12). My empirical work is especially influenced by Rae 1967 and Lijphart 1994.

6. There is some ambiguity, however, about why reduction to two candidates in each district should mean reduction to only two parties nationally; another possibility is different patterns of two-party competition in different regions, as has tended to happen in Canada. Duverger worried about this originally, with no clear solution; Cox suggests the importance of controlling the chief executive in unifying party competition in different regions (Cox 1997, chap. 10).

7. See Lijphart 1994 on "malapportionment" in concept and practice.

8. Representation could be won with less, if many parties split the vote, so .75 percent is an upper threshold, not a lower threshold or minimum requirement. The lower and upper thresholds are averaged by Lijphart in his analysis. Representation will always depend on party competition; Lijphart's analysis assumes that the number of competing parties will be one greater than the district magnitude (Lijphart 1994). On the theoretical argument as to why this should be the maximum, see Cox 1997, and the discussion in chap. 9 below. Lijphart assigns an effective representation score of 35 to the single-member district systems.

9. In 1994 Italy made a major change in its election rules, moving in a more majoritarian direction, but not all the way to single-member districts or a high threshold. New Zealand adopted the German version of PR in 1996. These elections are not included in the present study because the absence of information about left-right positions taken by new political parties, needed for chaps. 8 and 9, precludes their analysis.

10. In the German system half of the seats in the Bundestag (lower house) are elected by single-member districts. But the other seats are distributed to compensate almost fully the

parties that fail to win single-member district seats; seats can even be added to the Bundestag for this purpose. All parties winning at least 5 percent of the vote or three individual districts are compensated in this way.

11. The formula for calculating the effective number of parties winning votes or seats is N = one divided by the sum of the vote or seat proportions squared.

12. See the discussion in Lijphart 1994; however, most of the vote-seat disproportionality measures yield similar results.

13. For more extensive discussion and references on party cohesion in parliamentary systems, see chap. 3 below, especially note 8.

14. Strom's specialization measure was not reported in the 1986 edition of *Parliaments of the World*, so is not included here. His measure of limitations on committee memberships of individuals, presumably encouraging their specialization, does not seem further to discriminate within these systems.

15. See Forell 1976, esp. 76; and Jaensch and Teichman 1979, 55–56.

16. Further support is offered in a report by Damgaard (1995, 316) of expert ratings of the relative influence of party members in the committees over the positions taken by the parties as a whole. Again, we would expect that weak committees with few independent powers would not have memberships that developed the expertise to shape party policy. The policy would be directed from the party leadership at the top, which in the case of the governing parties means also from the cabinet. Strong committees with independent powers would be more likely to be the centers of expertise that can shape party policy. If the opposition parties are given significant roles in these committees, there might even be an opportunity for indirect opposition influence on policy. These data are also consistent with the general classification. In the countries in our top group (see table 2.2) the committee members were estimated to have substantial (medium or high) influence on party policy positions in eight of the nine countries. (Spain, the only exception, is a country whose rules would seem consistent with substantial committee influence, but with experts reporting little influence of committee members on party policies.) Damgaard's experts also report high influence of the committee members in Italy and medium influence in Finland. On the other hand, the experts reported low influence by committee members over party policy in France, Greece, Ireland, and the United Kingdom — the countries at the bottom of the table.

17. There is some disagreement among scholars about the potential for independent influence of the French presidency when its incumbent's party (or coalition) does not control the assembly.

18. See the special issues of *West European Politics* (Volcansek 1992) and *Comparative Political Studies* (Shapiro and Stowe 1994).

19. For a discussion of the cultural and historical origins of constitutions, see Powell 1982, chap. 4.

20. For example, consider the committee analysis in Damgaard 1995 as well as the deliberate cross-district malapportionment (underrepresentation of urban districts) in legislative representation. More generally, see the discussion in Manuel Sanchez de Dios, 1999.

21. In 1996 New Zealand changed its election rules to PR, with the immediate loss of

parliamentary majorities, but this postdates our period of analysis. Like Greece in 1989–92, New Zealand retained other majoritarian features.

22. In addition to the two issues of *Parliamentary Government,* see *Committees of the House of Commons: A Practical Guide,* (Ottawa: Clerk of the House of Commons, 1994).

23. Changes in the committee system in Denmark in the early 1970s are taken into account in the analysis; there were changes also in the decision rules in Finland in the early 1990s. Neither of these fundamentally changed the type of system.

Chapter 3. Accountability

1. Not included here are elections in Norway 1973, Italy 1994, and Spain 1982, in which the configuration of parties had changed so much between elections that it was not possible to calculate gains or losses for the governing parties.

2. Representation on semiautonomous policy-making bodies, such as central banks, can also have this effect in some countries, as can representation on constitutional courts. Much will depend, then, on the way these institutions make their own internal decisions, but this is a topic beyond the scope of this book.

3. The class of preelection coalitions is both theoretically and empirically fascinating. It is, however, not always as clearly demarcated as the other categories. While the majority status is usually clear, the nature of the preelection agreements varies substantially. In France, for example, the presence of the agreements was usually clear by at least the second round of legislative voting, when party candidates systematically withdrew in favor of their coalition partner. But whether or not joint preelection policy proposals were announced in France varied from election to election, especially on the part of the left. In other countries I have relied on the accounts of the election in *Keesings Contemporary Archives,* supplemented by country studies, to decide whether or not the parties explicitly presented the voters with a preelection agreement to govern after the election. (Also see Mueller and Strom 1999.) While the situations are generally unambiguous, in some cases, as in Sweden in 1976 and 1979, there seems to have been a clear understanding that a set of parties would govern together, but not a specified agreement about policies or electoral cooperation. As the Swedish coalitions did not endure until the next election, they do not affect the current analysis. If we had enough cases, we could in fact create a continuum of closeness and components of the preelection agreements that would be quite interesting. See also the discussion of government identifiability in chap. 4 below.

4. The average government lost 3.2 percent in the 153 cases in which it was possible to compute government gains and losses. (In four cases the changing configuration of competing parties made such a comparison impossible.) The averages losses were 1.3 for pure minority governments; 1.1 for supported minority; 4.0 for postelection coalitions; 2.7 for preelection coalitions; 4.6 for single-party majority governments.

5. There is a very large literature on economic voting; a number of the best recent studies are beginning to take explicit account of political conditions, using more complex models than Guy Whitten and I were able to do. See esp. Stevenson 1997, 1998, and

Palmer and Whitten 1998. Stevenson finds various political conditions mediating economic impacts but does not identify clarity of responsibility as critical among these.

6. As stated in the table note, Finland (4.9), France (3.4), and the United States (6.1) are deleted from the table averages because the majority status of their governments is less comparable to the simpler parliamentary cases. In Finland the rules for policy making require two-thirds majorities to pass legislation requiring tax increases, so the incumbent government, although commanding a solid majority of parliamentary seats and secure against eviction, still had to bargain with the opposition on many occasions (Arter 1987, 49–50). In France the minority government had strong backing from the Socialist president; in the United States the postelection coalition was the familiar divided government situation in which one party (in 1989 the Republicans) controlled the presidency and the other controlled Congress.

7. For an interesting theoretical analysis that makes a similar argument, see Laver and Shepsle 1991 and Fiorina 1991.

8. The Rice cohesion index takes the percent of the party members who vote together and subtracts the percent who disagree. (It usually uses only bills on which there is some disagreement.) Thus an average cohesion of 90 is created by 95 percent voting together and 5 percent opposing. An average cohesion of 70, the upper range of American congressional legislative cohesion, is created by 85 percent voting together and 15 percent opposing (Schwartz and Shaw 1976). In Sweden in mid-1970s, a typical parliamentary government, the average of five parties was 91, ranging from People's at 88 to the governing Social Democrats at 95 (Clausen and Holmberg 1977). In France from 1967 to 1973, the ruling Gaullists and the Independent Republican allies each had average cohesion indices of about 92, 96 percent voting with the party and 4 percent opposing (Converse and Pierce 1986, 557). For additional discussions of party cohesion in a variety of parliamentary systems, see Epstein 1967; Ozbudun 1970; Berglund and Lindstroem 1978; Loewenberg and Patterson 1979; Mezey 1979; Von Beyme 1985, 224 ff; Bowler, Farrell and Katz 1999.

9. According to the *Statistisches Jahrbuch fur die Bundesrepublik Deutschland.*

10. See, for example, the account of the revisions of the government bill on the regulation of new chemical products in Bulmer and Patterson 1987.

11. Moreover, there is the troubling problem of classifying government status in Finland and the United States. If we classify them as having minority governments, a regression analysis predicting the Laver-Hunt influence score with majority status (.2, .4, .6, .8, 1.0) opposition committee power (0, .5, 1.0) and dummy variables for party incohesion and opposition control of the upper house in 1989 yields regression coefficients of -4.5, .17, 1.6, and 1.1 for the four variables (standardized betas of $-.78$, .05, .38, .21). With the nineteen cases, majority status and party incohesion are significant at .05; the other two are not. If we use just a dummy variable for all minority governments, instead of the full majority status score, then the committee variable becomes significant. Also see chap. 5, n. 26.

12. See the influence regression reported in note 11. In the vote regressions, the dummy party cohesion variable is worth about 3 percent of the vote, which is about the same as the full distinction between majority and minority government. See Powell and Whitten 1993.

Chapter 4. Conditions for Mandates

1. See Birch 1971, 97–101; Ranney 1962; Ware 1987, 56–59.

2. E. E. Schattschneider puts this clearly: "Moreover, party government is good democratic doctrine because the parties are the special form of political organization adapted to the mobilization of majorities. How else can the majority get organized? If democracy means anything at all it means that the majority has the right to organize for the purpose of taking over the government. Party government is strong because it has behind it the great moral authority of the majority and the force of strong traditional belief in majority rule" (1942, 208).

3. See Schattschneider 1942 and esp. American Political Science Association 1950. The APSA committee drafting the latter document was chaired by Schattschneider.

4. On the British nationalization(s) of the steel industry as an example of the problem of party mandates in practice, see Pennock 1979, esp. 284. Data on British public opinion on the issue are presented in Butler and Stokes 1969, 177–80, 190–94, 212.

5. We could, of course, further extend this line of argument into consideration of the formation of preferences themselves. Electoral activity as a means of educating the citizens has long been stressed by proponents of democracy as one of its desirable features. However, majoritarians and their opponents tend to draw different conclusions about how and what sort of shaping or development of preferences is desirable. See Ware 1988, 58–59, 79–85. The account in this book deliberately sets aside these arguments and does not attempt to investigate the (potentially important) impact of electoral processes on the formation of voter preferences and expectations.

6. Knowing how the parties will behave in office is obviously difficult. Voters may legitimately use a variety of clues. These may include the explicit party platforms or manifestos that set forth commitments to the voters. Parties in most contemporary democracies do make such promises; there is some evidence that they tend to keep their word on most of them (Klingemann, Hofferbert, and Budge 1994; Rose 1984, 65). (But see Stokes 1997 on the Latin American experience.) The voters may also rely on more general ideological or group-sympathetic party images (conservative party or a workers' party), or on past experience with the party in office (Fiorina 1981).

7. The working of election laws to create majorities through distortion in representation was discussed in chap. 2. Also see chaps. 5 and 8 below.

8. See also the discussion of preelection coalitions in chap. 3 above.

9. This analysis builds initially from the concept in Strom 1984. With the help of graduate students, I coded each election, using primarily *Keesings Contemporary Archives* accounts of the elections, supplemented by other sources. In some countries, especially France, Norway, and Sweden, there were marked differences between the identifiability on the left and the right. In these cases, the left and right were coded separately and the scores were averaged to arrive at the country score.

The coding in its current use was based on the following:

0 = Low = Election account shows no expectation of postelection majority government committed to policies; after the election there is frequently protracted negotiation to form a government.

50 = Medium = Substantial, but not certain, expectation of majority control of the legislature by a party or party coalition, or continuation of current government.

100 = High = Explicit preelection agreement or strong expectation of postelection majority.

In case of preelection agreements, the following supplemental coding was used:

100 = explicit agreement to form a government;

90 = explicit agreement to cooperate in elections but no joint policy statement;

75 = joint policy statements but no explicit agreement to form a government;

50 = general perception of cooperative behavior but no explicit agreement.

10. A more complicated situation appeared in Austria in 1994, where all the parties seemed to agree that a radical right shift in the leadership and policies of the third largest party, the FPOE, made it an unlikely coalition partner for either larger party. Moreover, it was generally assumed that whichever of these won the plurality would hold the chancellorship in a new grand coalition. Under these circumstances the voters had a clear idea of how their vote would shape the future government, and the role of the vote was fairly significant.

11. See the summary by Gallagher, Laver, and Mair 1995, 32–33, and the discussion and analysis by Stevenson 1997.

12. It turns out in fact that in the proportional design systems the average incoming government was composed of parties that had collectively *lost* .75 percent of the vote in this election compared to the previous one. In the majoritarian designs the average incoming government had gained 1 percent. Intuitively, the difference in relative losses and gains seems to speak to greater responsiveness to elections in the majoritarian design systems. But on close analysis, this apparent advantage of the majoritarian designs seems to be a mechanical consequence of the ways vote losses of plurality parties can be distributed in two-party versus multiparty systems, rather than a perverse rejection of the will of the voters in the latter. In two-party systems, when a governing plurality party loses votes (which most do), all those lost votes go to the opposition party. If the incumbent loses very many votes, there will be a new plurality party, which usually becomes the government — showing up as a vote gain for the new government. (See also the extended discussion in chap. 6, n. 15 below.) However, in multiparty systems, vote losses of plurality parties in government can go to all kinds of parties, not necessarily or primarily to the largest opposition. This lack of constraint means less frequent change of plurality party when that party loses votes and, hence, more frequent formation of governments made up of vote losers as much as winners. We must be very careful, therefore, in characterizing the differing patterns of postelection connection between votes and government formation. Moreover, as I demonstrate in chap. 6, there are alternative ideals of responsiveness against which the outcomes can be compared.

13. See the literature on the differences between preferences of voters and nonvoters in chap. 1, n. 13.

14. Note that the classification in table 4.2 assumes that the elections in the middle category from table 4.1, with implicit preelection coalitions, do meet the requisite condition of identifiability.

15. These seven were Australia 1990; France 1993; New Zealand 1978, 1981, and 1993; Spain 1989; Britain, Oct. 1974.

16. The elections in which the second-place vote winner gained an absolute legislative majority are Australia 1969, 1987, and 1990; France 1967 and 1973; New Zealand 1978 and 1981. Four of these are single party and three are preelection coalitions. There were also wrong party winners before our time period in Australia 1954 and 1961, Britain 1951, and Canada 1957. Elections in which the party finishing second in the vote won a legislative plurality and was allowed to form a minority government occurred in Canada in 1979 and in Britain in February 1974. See also the discussion in chap. 6 below.

17. A rare exception was Germany in 1982, when the FDP broke up its coalition with the SPD, which had been presented to the voters as a preelection coalition in 1980. But political elites recognized the legitimacy problem created by breaking up an explicitly announced preelection coalition and called a new election so that the voters could choose on the basis of the new coalition alignment.

18. Comments about statistical significance here are based on 156 cases and assume independence of the cases.

19. See Powell 1982, chap. 5; Ordeshook and Shvetsova 1994; and Cox 1997, chap. 11, for empirical analyses of the interaction of election rules and social conditions in shaping the number of political parties. Each contribution also contains substantial citations to the larger literatures discussing these issues.

20. The unstandardized coefficients in the regression equations predicting past government status and future government identifiability from the election threshold are reduced only about 20–25 percent when the effective party vote variable is added to the regression equation, and remain statistically significant at the .01 level of significance. (These equations do not include the committee variables, as multicollinearity begins to become a serious problem when both constitutional variables and the effective number of parties are all in the equation.).

Chapter 5. A Vision of Dispersed Political Power

1. For the purposes of this account, I simply accept this critical assumption of modern democratic thought, usually a part of both majoritarian and proportional visions. For a more elaborate treatment of the meaning of intrinsic equality, its origins and implications, see Dahl 1989, 84–88, and chap. 7.

2. Dahl 1989, chap. 4.

3. See the valuable discussion of the origin and implications of dual legislative houses in Tsebelis and Money 1997, esp. chaps. 1 and 2.

4. For example, Madison's justification of the Senate, "No law or resolution can now be passed without the concurrence first, of a majority of the people, and then of a majority of the states" (*Federalist Papers* [1787–88] 1961, 402). More generally see Dahl 1956, chap. 1 ("Madisonian Democracy,") and the essays in Grofman and Whittman 1989.

5. This point is developed in Dahl 1989, chap. 11, drawing on the empirical work in Lijphart 1984. In his second edition, Lijphart adds independent central banks to the list of institutions constraining simple majority rule (Lijphart 1999).

6. Some important exceptions, especially the strong and federally linked upper legislative houses in Australia, Germany, and the United States, are discussed in chaps. 2 and 3 above.

7. This image of representation took various forms, however, and also ran into conflict with other, even older, concepts of representation, especially the distinction between the preferences and the true interests of those being represented. See the fascinating and complex analysis in Pitkin 1967.

8. See, for example, the excellent brief discussion by Rokkan 1968, 6–21.

9. Mill himself seems to have assumed simple majority voting would prevail inside the legislature (Mill [1861] 1958, 103).

10. Compare Lijphart 1984, which develops what is here called the proportional influence vision, (called there consensus democracy,) with his analysis of the "consociational" approach, which implies a full minority veto, in Lijphart 1977. Lijphart's extremely valuable analysis does not, however, try to trace the path from elections to policy making.

11. On the advantage to the status quo created by supermajority requirements, see Dahl 1989, 140–41, 153–54, 155–56; and Rae 1969.

12. While this may be true under some circumstances, it seems hard work to sustain it as a general proposition. But as far as I know, we have little empirical research on this problem.

13. It is in part for this reason that I prefer to use proportional vision rather than consensus democracy, which is Lijphart's term (1984) for this ideal. Even in his analysis of consociational systems Lijphart emphasizes proportionality in outcomes as the general operating practice for making rights of minority veto work in a democratic context — rights that may be necessary to keep a deeply divided society from tearing itself apart. However, on the theoretical virtues of unanimity as a decision rule, see, e.g, Buchanan and Tullock 1962, esp. chaps. 7 and 10, and p. 145.

14. As Laver and Schofield point out (1990, 171–81,) this is often contrary to what formal bargaining theory would predict. They suggest that it reflects an important norm emergent in parliamentary systems with relatively stable governments. See also Browne and Franklin 1973, Browne and Frendreis 1980, Schofield and Laver 1985, and the discussion in chap. 7 below.

15. See the studies of cabinet policy making in Laver and Schofield 1994 and Martin's innovative comparative work on influences of cabinet minister, prime minister, and opposition parties on the timing of government introduction of legislation under various conditions (Martin 1999).

16. Note that I do not assume that the opposition influence should exceed its relative size, as a pure veto model would imply. Proportionality is not the same as consensus.

17. Very great disproportionality in the first elections in Poland and Russia remind us that without some coordination in the offerings of party leaders to restrain the number of parties even PR rules with fairly low thresholds do not automatically create accurate vote-seat correspondence. More generally, see Cox 1997 and Powell and Vanberg forthcoming.

18. The potential varying influence of different parties in the government, and even factions within those parties, is an area for future research on these issues. There is certainly good reason to think that the party of the prime minister will have the most influence in governing coalitions, although the role of the PM, too, varies somewhat from country to country. See Laver and Shepsle 1994, Martin 1999.

19. See the excellent paper by Gabel and Huber 2000, showing the relations between the self-placement of voters for a party on the left-right scale, the placement of that same party by a set of country experts, and the content of the party's manifesto.

20. See Baumgartner 1987, 1989, for an excellent study of policy making in France that demonstrates the rare, but not unsuccessful, efforts of opposition to mobilize public opinion against government policy.

21. The German opposition parties after 1983 (the Greens and the Social Democrats) had quite a bit of influence through the committee system, which usually modifies most legislation; the majority government, however, gets the essentials of its policies eventually. But the Social Democrats, in particular, benefited from their control of the Bundesrat (upper house of the legislature), which enhanced notably their ability to negotiate with the CDU/CSU-FDP majority government (total bargaining weight = .45). Upper house control also helped the opposition in Australia. Both countries are assigned a political bargaining weight of .20, even though facing majority governments. Similarly, in Finland the requirement that two-thirds votes be used to raise taxes helped opposition parties against an ostensibly majority government.

22. In addition to table 2.2 and the text discussion, see the evidence reported by Damgaard (1995, 316) summarized in note 16 of chap. 2.

23. Such devices as parliamentary debate and the opportunity to question government ministers, including the prime minister, at a weekly "Question Time" give the opposition a chance to make their case publicly and to remind the government that new elections are not far away. These are especially important in highly majoritarian systems in which a cohesive governing party can impose its unchecked will in policy making during the period between elections. See also Baumgartner 1987, 1989.

24. It is possible that the anticipated electoral costs of sharing executive power may discourage influential opposition parties from joining a government (see Strom 1990).

25. I published a version of this effort to assess the effective authorized influence of all voters, based on the majority status of the government and the structure of the committee system, in 1989 (Powell 1989, 127–29). It differs only in minor details from the present approach. The Laver-Hunt expert survey went into the field early that same year with quite different objectives but containing the question included in the text. We can be, I think, quite confident that the respondents were uninfluenced by my (relatively obscure) article in estimating the impact of the opposition parties in their country.

26. I don't want to claim perfect correspondence between these approaches. It is interesting and revealing to transform the Laver-Hunt scale so it is conceptually as similar as possible to my probability weights (subtracting 1 and dividing by 8) and use the bargaining and structural weights to predict it (either excluding the Italian outlier or retaining it with a dummy variable). The unstandardized regression coefficients are .075 for the bargaining variable and .061 for the committee variable, plus an intercept of about .10. (Eighteen cases without Italy and Switzerland.) This suggests that if the Laver-Hunt scores were true measures of influence, and if we had the right time frame matchups, we should reweight our opposition probabilities from 10, 20, and 50 to something like 18, 25, and 48 for the government situations of majority, supported minority (outside institution control), and minority government, respectively. The committee influence impacts would be reweighted from 0, 12.5, 25 to about 0, 7.5, 15. This implies, in turn, that I am underestimating opposition influence facing majorities a bit and somewhat overestimating the boost from the opposition from the committee system. However, their relative roles are about right, both are important, and we are not outrageously out of line. In view of the relatively few cases, some special peculiarities of the late 1980s sample (e.g., despite

their general relation, government majorities and committee control are actually uncorrelated across this small subset of elections), and uncertainty about the exact time frame used by the Laver-Hunt respondents, I am reluctant to rework my original estimates on this basis alone. Moreover, some of the country results (e.g., the similar opposition "impact" in Germany and New Zealand, in the face of the country literatures) make one a little doubtful that all the respondents are using identical concepts and ranges of impact, in this single, relatively untried survey question. Most important, the outcome of such reweighting would not greatly alter the outcome of the analysis. (See below for a recomputation of the overall measure using Laver-Hunt scores as the probability estimates, showing the general robustness of the results.)

27. We cannot use the Laver-Hunt estimates for our entire sample because they asked the question only at one time point; conditions in some of these countries changed. However, we can use our regression analysis to construct an estimated Laver-Hunt influence variable from our bargaining, committee, and party discipline variables. The estimated Laver-Hunt opposition influence variable is the political bargaining variable multiplied by .0075, plus the committee variable multiplied by .0061, plus the dummy Italian variable multiplied by .52, plus the constant term of .10. This then becomes the new influence multiplier for the opposition in calculating the effective representation score. The new authorized effective representation score is calculated just as in table 5.4, except we use the estimated Laver-Hunt influence variable for the probability figure in column 6.

28. I do not mean to imply that all the possible problems have been solved and all avenues of influence considered. There is a rich agenda for future research on the connections between voters and policy making. In part this is an agenda of legislative influence studies to get a better understanding of the conditions under which elected representatives (both inside and outside of governing coalitions) help shape policy. In part it is an agenda to take into account connections through geographic constituencies, which are ignored here and which obviously become especially important if party cohesion is weak. American congressional studies have obviously made much interesting progress along these lines. There are various interactions among party cohesion, committee system strength, and various constituency connections that need comparative exploration. The current analysis merely sketches, I hope, the most important electoral linkages in most of the democratic systems here analyzed.

Chapter 6. Testing the Visions

1. Sometimes the term is equated simply with correspondence between actions of government and the preferences of citizens, or even with *democracy* itself (e.g., Lijphart 1984, 1; also see Pennock 1979, 260–63). For usage more comparable to mine, see Strom 1990, 73, and his general discussion and analysis of "decisiveness" (72–78).

2. On one side, the concept assumes that voters' choices do reflect their preferences in a meaningful way, avoiding various problems of information and, perhaps more important, the substantive alternatives presented to them by political parties. (I shall touch somewhat on this in later chapters.) On the other side, I shall not be exploring what parties actually do in office once they achieve influence in policy making, or the important role of elections, at least under some circumstances, in holding them to their commitments. (On this theme, see Powell 1989 and chap. 3 above).

3. Of course, as discussed in chap. 4 there are many difficulties with such claims, both because of the lack of information on the part of voters and the problems of multidimensionality of issue preferences. See Riker 1982a on "populism."

4. In his defense of "Westminster" systems and critique of the PR alternative, Michael Pinto-Duschinsky in his *Times Literary Supplement* essay of September 17, 1998, alleges such a lack of connection in the PR systems.

5. With a few exceptions, such as Canada in 1993, in most of the majoritarian countries the bulk of the votes are accounted for by considering the two largest vote winners. The implications of adding more parties to the graph are considered below.

6. Pinto-Duschinsky (1998) quotes approvingly a passage from Joseph Schumpeter that illustrates this slippage.

7. Another way of thinking about the seriousness of the problem is that it depends on how voters not supporting either of the two larger parties would have split their vote if forced to make a dichotomous choice.

8. Australia uses the alternative vote system, in conjunction with single-member districts, rather than first past the post plurality. The usual convention in vote-seat analysis of alternative vote systems is to refer only to the first-preference votes. I have followed that convention here. For further discussion of vote-seat connections in Australia, see Cox 1997, 92–95, and Wright 1983.

9. It is interesting to discover that the "15 percent failure rate" proportion roughly holds up in a longer time perspective. Looking back to the end of World War II, we find no other wrong party winners in New Zealand, but Britain 1951, Canada 1957, and Australia 1954, 1961, and 1969 all provide further examples of this kind of distortion.

10. Just as majoritarians typically compromise with their fundamental normative democratic principle by relying on voting pluralities, so proportional influence theorists typically accept that grand coalition may be impractical as a model of government formation. Only the Swiss have routinely built governments that include virtually all the larger parties, although examples of such governments are scattered through the proportional systems. We can, of course, construct versions of figure 6.1 that sketch various compromises with pure proportionality, e.g., excluding parties winning only a few percent of the vote or granting unshared majority power to parties winning over 50 percent.

11. The very close fit between votes and seats in the proportional design systems of these established democracies should not mislead us into thinking these relations are automatic or inevitable. They depend on party leaders anticipating the constraints imposed on the number of parties even by generous PR election rules, as the highly nonproportional results from the first free elections in Russia and Poland in the early 1990s remind us. For more detailed discussion see Cox 1997 and Powell and Vanberg 2000.

12. As mentioned in chap. 4, the preelection coalitions vary greatly in their formality and in the subjects covered in their arguments. (See especially chap. 4, n. 9.) I have tried in this analysis of responsiveness to count as "parties" only explicitly announced preelection coalitions, creating conditions in which it should have been quite clear to the electorate that the parties would govern together if they won enough support. Expectations of tacit support are not sufficient. In most cases the coalition is unambiguous, but in a few (as in the Austrian 1994 election discussed in chap. 4, n. 10) there is room for doubt, both in my coding and in the minds of the voters. The following brief summary sketches the outline of the 1969–94 preelection coalition situation affecting responsiveness: (1) countries in

which there were no identified preelection coalitions: Canada, Greece, New Zealand, United Kingdom; (2) countries in which such coalitions were unusual: Austria (1990, 1994 only), Belgium (1985 only), Finland, Italy (1994 only); (3) countries which usually had such coalitions: Australia, Denmark after 1977, France, Germany, Sweden after 1970; (4) countries with substantial variation across elections: Netherlands, Norway.

13. As we shall see in chaps. 8 and 9, there is some justification for this practice when we take account of the left-right preferences of the voters. One of the limitations of considering only vote choices is the inability to distinguish between party inclusion or exclusion on grounds other than size.

14. But see below, esp. table 6.2.

15. As suggested by the discussion at the end of chap. 3, and especially by table 3.5 and figure 3.1, it is possible to analyze electoral responsiveness by looking at the vote changes from one election to the next and their connection to government and policymaker change. As images of responsiveness often imply change connections, a few comments about this perspective may be appropriate. The most important point is that the results presented thus far hold up equally well from a change perspective. Each of the two visions of democracy presents its own set of expectations about the relation between change in support for a party and its fate as a policymaker. We could develop these in detail in a counterpart to figure 6.1 and explore their realization in practice. However, despite the apparent attractiveness of the language, the connections turn out to be somewhat more complicated to present and not worth replaying the previous analysis from this point of view. The reason for the awkwardness is that the change analysis begins with the fate of the incumbents. The majoritarian ideal assumes the incumbents were elected with a majority (plurality) of the vote and should be evicted from office only if they lose that majority (plurality). The opposition is in the opposite situation. But as we already know, incumbents in any system were seldom elected with a vote majority, and in a small, but notable set of cases did not have even a plurality. The situations are also complicated in the case of minority governments, which may gain votes but still not attain plurality status (e.g., Denmark 1975).

Nevertheless, a few overview comments will indicate the general patterning in the majoritarian systems. In elections in these systems the key normative expectation is that changes in which party wins the plurality of the vote — and only these changes — should lead to change in government (and policymakers). In fact the majoritarian design systems perform very well by this criterion. Of the twenty-three elections in which the plurality vote winner did not change, the incumbents stayed in power twenty times. Of the eighteen elections in which the plurality vote winner did change, the incumbents were evicted fifteen times. The exceptions are related to the familiar problem of vote-seat distortion in some single-member district elections. (E.g., in Britain in October 1974 there was a shift in the plurality vote winner from Conservatives to Labour, but Labour had already taken office as a minority government after the vote-seat distortions in February had given it a wrong party legislative plurality. Therefore, in October there was no correspondence between plurality change and government change.) Overall, in about 85 percent of the cases, the relation between incumbent vote change and government party change was accounted for by the process in which vote change sustained or replaced the plurality party's position as voter favorite; that vote position resulted in sustaining or replacing the party's plurality (usually majority) position in the legislature; and the plurality party in the legislature formed a government. The majoritarian vision to this extent works empirically in these countries and (with the substitution of plurality for majority) corresponds to the normative expectations. (Also see Powell 1999.)

16. See references in Powell 1982, chap. 7; Warwick 1992; Martin and Stevenson 1995.

Chapter 7. Citizen Preferences and Party Positions

1. Pitkin's comments on the " 'economic' theories of democracy," especially Schumpeter's formulation, are further revealing of her conclusions: "What constitutes representation is the very responsiveness on issues which these models relegate to a secondary position. Mere selection of one man for a job by others need not make him their representative." Pitkin 1967, 291–92, n. 35. This note also makes it clear that by political representation Pitkin is talking about essential features of democracy. Also see Dahl 1989, 95.

2. See chap. 1, nn. 20, 21 above, discussing the approaches of Schumpeter (1942) and Riker (1982).

3. My analysis assumes, however, that citizens do have "authentic" preferences of their own, at least about the general directions of public policies, if not about the details. I shall not consider manipulations of preferences or other topics in preference formation, including the relation between preferences and interests.

4. Some voting schemes do allow voters to rank their preferences and take account of these in redistributing votes for eliminated candidates (as in the alternative vote system used in Australia) or even also redistributing unneeded votes for winners (as in the single transferable vote system used in Ireland). These ordinal systems allow the vote to convey more information about voter preferences than simple categorical systems. The relations between votes and preferences still depend on the choices offered by the parties, however.

5. See, e.g., Pitkin 1967, 234.

6. See, e.g., the discussion in Cohen 1971, 3–7.

7. See, e.g., Inglehart 1984.

8. See esp. Inglehart and Klingemann 1976. Also see Barnes 1977, Castles and Mair 1984, Converse and Pierce 1986, Dalton 1985, Dalton, Flanagan, and Beck 1984, Huber 1989, Inglehart 1990. One must be cautious about using this tool in new democracies in which the left-right (or other) language of discourse may not have had time to settle on common meanings. Survey and anecdotal evidence suggests that in Russia in the early and mid-1990s, for example, there was considerable disagreement about the meaning of *left* and *right* as descriptions of positions on the critical issue of transforming the old command control economy. See the discussion and analysis of the substance of left and right positions in different countries in Huber and Inglehart 1995.

9. See esp. Inglehart and Klingemann, 1976.

10. Poole and Rosenthal 1985, Poole and Rosenthal 1991.

11. See, eg., the contributions in Budge, Robertson, and Hearl 1987.

12. Note that we are comparing only differences in general orientation; we are definitely not looking at specific policies or at implementation of policy positions.

13. I want to acknowledge at this point my debt to John Huber, who convinced me of the critical theoretical significance of the position of the median citizen in a long series of discussions as we worked on the analysis published in our 1994 article in *World Politics*. He is not, of course, responsible for my treatment here. But it will be clear that my analysis in this chapter and the next owes much to that joint work. See Huber and Powell 1994.

14. As mentioned in chap. 1, n. 13, I was not able to determine whether differences between the median positions of citizens and their subset of voters might account for divergence of government and policymakers from the citizen median in some elections. It remains an important topic for analysis.

15. Riker puts this very firmly: "The populist interpretation of voting (i.e., that what the people, as a corporate entity, want ought to be public policy) cannot stand because it is inconsistent with social choice theory. If the outcomes of voting are, or may be, inaccurate or meaningless amalgamations, what the people want cannot be known. Hence the populist goal is unattainable" (Riker 1982a, xviii). If what the people want can be reasonably summarized in a single left-right dimension, then majoritarians overcome this problem. Of course, not all multidimensional situations are equally problematic.

16. Lijphart 1977.

17. It proves to be quite difficult to construct measures that fully match the citizen preference distribution to that of the legislature, government, or policymakers. It seems that no single statistical measure will do. In a two-party system, for example, the party distribution in the legislature that puts one or (especially) both at the citizen median may not be the distribution that best approximates the citizen standard deviation (or other measures of spread). Even beginning with the policy preference groups creates complex problems, as the group will not be indifferent to which groups are in the government even if they are excluded. In general we can see that having only a few parties is going to make it hard to reflect the full citizen distribution in the policymakers, especially as the citizen variance increases. I leave it to others to consider how a full evaluation of the approximation of the proportional influence ideal might be developed.

18. See, initially, the landmark study of Miller and Stokes 1963. See also Achen 1977, Achen 1978, Barnes 1977, Converse and Pierce 1986, Dalton 1985, Miller 1964, Manion 1996, L. W. Powell 1982.

19. See Dahl 1956, chap. 4.

20. See Gable and Huber 1998, showing the general comparability between expert placements of parties on the left-right scale (as used in these chapters), self-placement of party voters on the same scale, and party positions derived from published party election manifestos.

21. Huber 1989.

22. As we have only the two elite studies and a variety of citizen surveys (but not one for each country at each election), it is necessary to make a somewhat arbitrary decision about how far away from the exact date of an election it is permissible to use a citizen survey to estimate the position of the median voter and an expert survey to estimate the positions of the parties. In general the median positions of the citizens and the parties are fairly consistent over time, but (as we shall see in more detail in chap. 8), there are some changes between the early 1980s and the early 1990s. In general I have used the following

convention: I estimate the position of the median voter from the closest election survey, but not from a survey more than twenty-four months from the election. Citizen positions were estimated primarily from *Eurobarometer* studies and from the two *World Values Studies* of spring 1981 and 1988–93 (depending on the country). New Zealand and Australia estimates used national election studies in both countries, with special thanks to Jack Vowles of the University of Aukland for making available the New Zealand studies of the 1990s. Spain 1979 was estimated from a figure in Gunther, Sani, and Shabad 1988, 263. Norway 1977 was estimated from Valen 1979. If there was no survey within twenty-four months, the election was dropped from the study. Examining the results of surveys within the twenty-four-month period for countries for which we have multiple surveys seems to show no major differences in estimating the median voter position. No Austrian surveys using the 10-point left-right self-placement question for citizens were found in the 1977–87 period, so Austria is not included in that time period. Most of the citizen surveys use 10-point scales. However, in the case of New Zealand, the surveys used a 5-point scale in 1981, 7-point scales in 1990 and 1993, and an 11-point scale in 1996. Those medians were translated to 10-point scales.

In the case of the parties, I estimate the party position from the closer elite survey, but not for elections more than five years from the elite study. This convention implies that the Castles and Mair survey of party experts in 1982 covers elections from 1977 through 1987 (Castles and Mair 1984.) As Castles and Mair did not cover Greece, Japan, and Switzerland, elections in these countries before 1988 are not covered with this convention. I have made an exception, however, to include the 1987 election in Switzerland, the only one for which we have proximate citizen data. Castles and Mair use 11-point scales (0–10); their medians were converted to 10-point scales, to be consistent with the citizen data and the later expert survey. This was done by taking the absolute difference between the score and 5.0 (the 11-point median), multiplying by .9 (to make the scale distance equivalent to the 10-point scale), and adding or subtracting, as appropriate, from 5.5 (the 10-point median). The Huber and Inglehart survey of experts in 1993 covers elections from 1988 through 1998 (Huber and Inglehart 1995). They also failed to include Greece, so despite the excellent citizen data from Greece, I do not include any of the Greek elections in the congruence analysis.

Combining the available citizen and party expert surveys by means of these conventions (with the Swiss exception noted) implied for our nineteen remaining countries the following elections included in the congruence analysis in the subsequent chapters: Australia = 6, Austria = 2, Belgium = 6, Canada = 3, Denmark = 8, Finland = 3, France = 5, Germany = 5, Ireland = 7, Italy = 4, Japan = 1, Netherlands = 6, New Zealand = 3, Norway = 4, Spain = 5, Sweden = 4, Switzerland = 1, United Kingdom = 4, United States = 2.

23. Also see Powell and Vanberg forthcoming.

24. E.g. Laver and Schofield: "The party controlling the median legislator . . . is effectively a dictator on policy" (1990, 111). They also report empirically that in 196 situations in which a single party did not control a majority, the governments that formed "either contained the median party on the left-right scale or were supported by it" in over 80 percent of the cases (113).

25. Yet another possibility would be a "veto players" model of the parties in the

government. For a discussion of several alternative models of government spending, including a veto players model, applied to predictions about German budgetary spending, see Bawn 1999.

26. Browne and Franklin 1973 provided the original analysis, verified in many subsequent studies. See esp. Browne and Frendreis 1980. Laver and Schofield present an empirical and theoretical review (1990, 167–81). In summary they observe that "the very close relationship between a party's legislative weight and the number of portfolios it received from its coalition partners . . . remains one of the most striking non-trivial empirical relationships in political science" (193).

Chapter 8. The Majoritarian Policy Vision

1. The relation between the median voter and the policymakers is discussed in the next chapter. The majoritarian vision generally assumes that majority governments completely control policy making, facilitating accountability as well as the implementation of mandates.

2. Downs 1957.

3. Downs's theory was stimulated originally by the behavior of the two main parties in the majoritarian British system in the 1950s. The British experience of the past twenty years seems to show both the limitations and strengths of Downs's theoretical idea. It shows, for example, that parties may prefer something other than winning. Leaders may prefer to pacify activists, for example, or be chosen by the activists without regard for general election results. The activists may prefer to stand for programs or hope to educate the electorate and change the voters' preferences. In 1983 the left won control of the British Labour Party, disavowed the party's previous practices while in office ("Winning isn't everything"), and adopted a range of policies sharply left of center. In a long and painful period of opposition, the Labour Party gradually concluded that in the British system "losing isn't anything" and adopted many of their opponent's policies in what was clearly and explicitly a "move to the (local) center." By 1997, when Labour eventually regained power, the two parties seemed very close in policy positions, although we do not have an expert evaluation at the time of that election. Of course, there were also many complications of additional dimensions, incumbency behavior, the rightist lurch of the Conservatives under Thatcher, a centrist third party (discussed below as a general problem with applying Downs's theory), and so forth. On applications of Downs's theory to empirical studies of American party competition, see the review and analysis in Groffman 1993.

4. See Kollman, Mill, and Page 1992; McKelvy and Ordeshook 1985.

5. For theoretical results, see, e.g., Alesina 1988; and the references in Huber and Powell 1994, n. 21.

6. For the moment I shall ignore cases in which the initial government did not endure throughout the election period and a second government was formed. As we shall see in the next chapter, the results hold when we take account of these.

7. The Social Democrats won 45.6 percent of the vote; the three parties in the conservative coalition won 45 percent. Christian Democratic and the Ecology parties, however,

failed to make the 4 percent national threshold. The resulting seat distributions gave the Social Democrats 47.6 percent of the seats and the three conservative parties 46.6 percent, making the Social Democrats the (bare) plurality winner and leaving the Communists (5.6 percent of the votes and 5.7 percent of the seats) with the balance of the legislature.

8. This comment assumes some comparability of the absolute meaning of the scale positions in each country at the two time points. While I think few would disagree with the statement, based on our general knowledge of world and country-specific events, I should emphasize again that the analyses of distance from the median that are at the heart of this chapter and the next do not depend on such comparability.

9. The increased ideological divergence between U.S. Democratic and Republican parties in the Congress in the 1980s is well known to students of American politics.

10. I have used the 1988 Canadian case because the World Values survey in Canada was carried out in May-June 1990, so is much closer to this election than to the 1993 election.

11. Only the United States has truly two-party electoral competition, so in a strict sense the others are not really a failure of the Downsian model.

12. Comparing the averages of groups of elections can generate misleading results, especially when there is some arbitrariness to the groupings. Correlation coefficients offer some reassurance about the results in the tables and figures and support the inferences in the text. Majoritarian rules and desired conditions are relatively less successful in creating representative congruence. High threshold election rules are a problem for the distance between citizen and legislative medians. Government identifiability is particularly a problem in government formation. The following correlations are based on seventy-nine elections in nineteen countries for which all data are available. Asterisks indicate significance at .05; double asterisks indicate significance at .01, assuming independence of cases. Positive correlations, we need to recall, mean more distance and thus less congruence. The effective electoral threshold (discussed in chap. 2) has a correlation of .51** with the distance between citizen median and legislative median, a correlation of .31** between citizen median and government. Government identifiability (coded 0, 50, 100) has a correlation of .23* with the citizen median-legislature distance, .41** with the citizen median-government distance. Mandate conditions (identifiability plus majorities, as in table 4.2 and figure 4.1) are .36** with the citizen-legislature distance; .31** with the citizen-government distance. The simultaneous relations between constitutional rules, identifiability, majorities, proportionality of vote representation and left-right distances from the median citizen are explored further in the regression analysis in chap. 9.

13. A more extended discussion of these issues can be found in Powell and Vanberg forthcoming.

14. Powell and Vanberg show that alternative measures of the positions of the parties also find medians in legislatures elected from single-member districts are significantly further from the median voter than those elected from low or median threshold proportional representation. They use the placements of the Laver-Hunt experts on the single issue of "public ownership of business and industry" and even a transformed scale based on proportions of left and right issue mentions in the party election manifestos, as well as

the placement on the general left-right scale by the two surveys of experts used here (Powell and Vanberg, forthcoming, table 3).

15. With 156 elections in twenty countries. the correlation between the effective threshold and effective number of parties receiving votes was −.43; between effective threshold and effective number of parties winning legislative seats the correlation is −.57 (both significant at .01). Lijphart 1994 similarly reports standardized regression coefficients between effective threshold and effective number of parties getting votes of −.34, effective number of parties winning seats of −.55, in equations including log of assembly size (108). The correlations with a dichotomous variable for single-member districts are −.37 and −.48. Using the subset of 79 elections in nineteen countries for which we have government distance data, the effective threshold correlations with effective party votes and seats are quite similar: −.45 and −.62, respectively; the corresponding SMD correlations are −.37 and −.53.

16. A special problem is created by the relation between individual district outcomes and aggregate votes and aggregate seats, especially in single-member district systems. There can only be one winner in a district in an SMD system. Votes for the loser are therefore always unrepresented. For the aggregate vote and seat outcomes to come out proportionally, the individual district outcomes must balance winners and losers to approximate the aggregate distributions. Such an outcome will depend greatly on the geographic concentration of party competition and voter support. See the more extensive discussion in Powell and Vanberg forthcoming.

17. See, for example, Kitschelt's excellent work on internal party processes and traditions of socialist parties in Western Europe (Kitschelt 1994, esp. chaps. 5, 6) and the general literature cited therein. He cites the Austrian, Swedish, German, and British social democrat or labor parties in the 1980s as too constrained by "the nature of membership recruitment and level of organizational entrenchment" to respond strategically to new electoral situations (253).

Chapter 9. The Proportional Influence Vision

1. One problem is that the assumption of a single dimension on which citizens' preferences can be interpreted already weakens one of the ideas on which proportional influence is justified — its ability to facilitate the formation of different majorities on different issues. A second problem is that the normatively privileged position of the median voter depends on that position minimizing the number of voters opposed to the given position. But some theorists, concerned about majority threats to minorities, may prefer to minimize the number of voters opposed to any *changes* in policy — thus privileging the status quo. The extension of this idea, of course, is the requirement of consensus, at least of all substantial groups. (See Lijphart 1977 on "consociational" systems.) While many believe consensus an unworkable requirement, various supermajorities are proposed by some theorists (see Dahl 1989, chap. 11). It is not clear what single position might be acceptable to such theorists. It is important to keep in mind, however, that supermajority requirements should further strengthen the relative advantage of the proportional designs over the majoritarian ones. Insofar as we find advantages for propor-

tional designs in distance from the simple citizen median, these loom even larger given the somewhat majoritarian-favorable assumptions. Yet a third problem is the measurement and substantive meaningfulness of the left-right scale itself in the discourse of each political system, as discussed in chap. 7.

2. Cox notes, however, that the M + 1 rule implies only an upper bound. We would expect such factors as the homogeneity of the society to shape whether it approaches that bound. Even in quite heterogenous societies we might expect problems of information and the like to impose practical limits well below the upper bound of a high district magnitude (low threshold) PR system (see Cox 1997, chaps. 5, 7, 11). For empirical analyses incorporating both election rules and social heterogeneity to explain the effective number of parties, see Powell 1982, chap. 5; Ordeshook and Shvetsova 1994; Cox 1997, chap. 11.

3. Cox 1997, 228–30.

4. This outcome assumes that there are not too many parties relative to the "carrying capacity" of the system, which in Cox's analysis is M + 1, where M is the number of representatives per district (district magnitude). Empirically, this seems to be a good assumption in the political systems in our sample, which have all had substantial experience with electoral competition. For new democracies this assumption is more problematic, as suggested by the Polish and Russian experiences in the early 1990s.

5. See the discussion in chap. 7 above, esp. nn. 24–26.

6. If the median legislative party does dominate policy making, contrary to the treatment above, the proportional influence systems will fare even better in producing policies at the citizen median than appears in the subsequent analysis. (See figs. 8.2 and 9.3 below and Powell and Vanberg forthcoming.)

7. In general the problem seems to lie in the spacing prediction. In some multiparty PR systems the parties do not seem to place themselves along the left-right continuum such that roughly the same numbers of voters lie between each position. Rather, both party size and spacing are "lumpy" and uneven. In a country such as Sweden there is quite a gap between left and right parties, which are collectively quite evenly balanced. When the citizen median is in this gap, the median legislator must be a fair distance from it. However, voter choices do not always correspond cleanly to left-right choices either.

8. This statement treats the United States as having a single-party majority. If we consider the situations in which one party controls Congress and the other party the presidency, we have postelection negotiation which, when it does not result in sheer deadlock, straddles the median nicely. This result underlines, in fact, both the majoritarian problem and the proportional advantage, assuming that negotiation can succeed.

9. It is especially interesting that the cases of changes between the two time periods—in Ireland, the Netherlands, and Norway—all involved the breakup of preelection coalitions and the negotiation of governments *closer* to the median. The differences are not too great, so we do not want to make too much of this. But see also the discussion below on government changes between elections.

10. See the discussion in Laver and Schofield 1990, 80–81.

11. The selection of cutting points for the groupings of elections by their level of effective representation is arbitrary. The levels and patterns shown in figure 9.1 are somewhat

sensitive to the specific cutting points chosen. Moreover, it makes some slight difference if we choose one of the different measures of effective authorized representation that were presented in chap. 5. However, the general pattern is very robust. The correlation coefficients between government-citizen difference and each of the three measures of effective authorized representation from chap. 5, were are −.26, −.32 and −.35 for the standard, the Laver-Hunt based, and the bargaining with adjacent parties measures (seventy-two elections; significant at least at .05, assuming independence of cases). The correlations with policymaker-citizen differences are much stronger: − .65, −.50, −.61. These numbers further demonstrate the success of the effective representation processes in creating governments and, especially, policymaker coalitions closer to the median citizen.

12. The influential policymakers are closer to the citizen median than the government in eighty-seven of the ninety-six cases. In only three cases is the policymaker mean more than .2 scale points further away from the citizens than is the government mean. In Spain in 1989 (supported minority) and in 1982 (majority) the Socialist government is virtually right at the citizen median; giving even a small amount of influence to the main opposition, the PP, which is quite far to the right of the citizens, pulls the government about half a scale point from the citizen median. In Austria in 1994, the large SPOe/OeVP coalition straddles the median and its mean is very close to the citizen median. Again, even a small amount of influence to the far right FPOe, which held 23 percent of the legislative seats, pulled the policymaker mean about .3 further from the citizens. We see in these cases that majoritarian concerns about giving influence to oppositions, especially extremist oppositions, can be well founded. But it turns out to be far more often helpful than harmful.

13. Consider the discussion of economic crises and government instability by Warwick 1992.

14. In two of these twenty-eight cases there were significant changes in the status of the government owing to changes in the party balance of executive and legislature (United States after 1992 and France after 1993). But the party composition of the government, and thus its ideological distance from the voters, remained unchanged.

15. For these purposes I did not count as new governments the situations in France 1993, United States 1992, and Spain 1979, where changes in government/legislative balance did not reflect changes in party composition of the cabinet. However, I did count as new two Italian governments in the late 1980s in which new prime ministers headed the "same" multiparty coalition in reconstructed governments.

16. See the account in *Keesing's Contemporary Archives*.

17. To this extent, using vote-seat correspondence to measure representation is not misleading, although in specific elections we may have vote-seat misrepresentation with good congruence, as in Canada in 1980 and Australia in 1990, for example, or even vice versa, as in Sweden in 1982.

18. These relations can, of course, be expressed in the familiar correlation coefficient form, as in note 11 above, although the classification of constitutional designs does not, as was argued in chap. 2, represent arbitrary cutting points on a continuous scale. The correlations also show the strong statistical significance of the relation between majoritarian design and greater distance of legislature, government, and policymakers from the citizen median:

Performance Measure	Correlation with Majoritarian Design	
	78 Elections	19 Countries
Legislature Distance from Median Citizen	.53**	.62**
Government Distance from Median Citizen	.28*	.46*
Policymaker Distance from Median Citizen	.59**	.66**

Note: Constitutional designs are coded as follows: proportional = 0, mixed = 1, majoritarian = 2. Asterisks represent significance at .05; double asterisks at .01, assuming independence of cases.

Chapter 10. Overview of Elections as Instruments of Democracy

1. Among these countries, the worst single score on effective representation after an election was recorded for New Zealand in 1993, where the governing party won an absolute legislative majority with only 35 percent of the vote. The opposition parties were severely underrepresented, getting only 40 percent of the seats from 65 percent of the vote, and had minimal influence on policy making (until breakup of the government party later in the term), yielding an effective authorized representation score under 40 immediately after the election. Yet, few would argue, I think, that this poor representation performance after an election is comparable to the suppression of citizens' rights and preferences in nondemocracies.

2. Precisely speaking, the positions in the graph are 100 minus the distance from the ideals discussed in chap. 6 and shown in table 6.2 and figures 6.6 and 6.7. For the majoritarian designs, the ideal was unchecked domination of authorized effective representation in policy making by the party winning the most votes in the election. For proportional designs the ideal implied that each party shared proportionally in authorized effective representation.

3. One response to this tendency to use simple majority rules in legislative votes, even in proportional design countries, might be to redefine the ideal. Just as we redefined majority vote standards to accept plurality winners as sufficient, we might redefine the proportional ideal as having some upper and lower bounds. We might argue, for example, that parties with less than 5 percent of the vote should not be counted against a proportional ideal, or that a party with 66 percent of the vote or legislative seats should be given 100 percent of policy-making control. In both cases the justification might be the real difficulties of achieving the ideal in practice. It seems difficult, though, to defend a particular compromise of proportionality as more than very ad hoc.

4. We recall, however, that some proportional design countries, such as Belgium and the Netherlands, virtually never settle for minority governments, while the latter are common in Denmark, Sweden, and Norway. On the other side, majoritarian design Canada experienced several minority governments.

5. Britain is the exception here, but addition of the 1997 election, with its victory for a

rather centrist Labour Party, would make it more similar to the general majoritarian pattern.

6. "An absolute monarch or dictator who chooses, for a reason of his own, to take public opinion polls and do whatever the people seem to want is not yet a representative government. We require functioning institutions that are designed to and really do, secure a government responsive to public interest and opinion" (Pitkin 1967, 234).

7. The relation between change of government and closer distance to the median citizen is not statistically significant, even at .10 level, let alone the .05 used routinely in this study.

8. We do not have enough cases of wrong winners in the left-right preference data to be sure whether it is typically the case that the plurality party loses only when the preference differences between the parties are not very great. In Canada 1979 the nonplurality government is 1.2 from the citizen median, while the plurality vote winner is much closer at .3. But in Australia 1990 the nonplurality government is actually closer (1.0) to the citizen median than the plurality loser (1.6).

9. Also see the comparison of expert party placements on the left-right scale with placements by another set of experts on several specific issues and with rescaled party manifesto positions in predicting the distance between the citizen median and the legislative median in Powell and Vanberg, forthcoming.

10. See, for example, Rose 1984; Budge and Hofferbert 1990; Klingemann, Hofferbert, and Budge 1993. But these studies (and methodological critiques of them like King et al. 1993) demonstrate the complexity of the relations. Public policies are shaped by contexts, resources, needs, and institutionalized commitments as well as by the preferences and electoral commitments of incumbent policymakers, making it difficult to disentangle the independent influence of the latter.

11. This is a deep, important problem in part because the implications of deadlock vary depending on what the status quo is. Little hard research shows that power sharing or even instability in, say, cabinet portfolio incumbency blocks policy change. The analysis in Huber 1998 suggests that cabinet portfolio instability inhibited health care cost containment in his set of countries, but only in the short run. If proportional influence approaches do in fact make policy deadlock or immobilism more likely — which is far from proven and likely to depend on many contingencies — then assessment of them will be shaped by whether one finds the current situation acceptable or intolerable. Consider the suspicion of proportional representation electoral rules among many nineteenth-century democrats, who considered them means of perpetuating the exclusion of the majority that prevailed under limited electoral franchise. (Yet in the twentieth century the most extensive welfare states have emerged in the proportional design countries; see, e.g., Lijphart 1999). Consider on the other hand the special defense of minority veto offered by Lijphart (1977) in "plural societies," where the alternative to compromise may be violence in defense of minority ethnic groups. Proportionality of policy distributions, as well as office holding, buttressed by ultimate minority vetoes, may be a practical way to avoid both deadlock and unacceptable majority exploitation. But one must still determine how to attain and sustain agreement on such proportionality in the first place.

12. Consider Stokes's analysis of spectacular Latin American examples in which new

governments reversed electoral promises about economic policy, a phenomenon with important implications (Stokes 1997).

13. The phrase, of course, is Samuel Huntington's. See Huntington 1991.

14. See, e.g., Lipset and Rokkan 1968, chap. 1.

15. See Shugart and Carey 1992, chap. 12, and Shugart 1995.

16. The other non-SMD systems with high effective thresholds did not fit this category. Ireland has candidate-oriented preferential voting; Japan used the single nontransferable vote in its multimember districts; Spain's moderately high threshold comes in large measure from inequality of district representation.

17. See the discussion of the "canceling problem" in Powell and Vanberg, forthcoming. Moreover, the present analysis suggests that in these well-established democracies, which have had time to develop good equilibria of information and expectation between parties and voters, only the single-member district systems routinely feature too many parties for the theoretical carrying capacity of the election rules. We do not have much empirical experience with what would happen in PR systems with high thresholds.

18. I cannot, however, presently analyze left-right congruence relations between the median voter and the policymakers in these systems because we do not have available expert ratings of important new parties in each.

19. See Keuchler 1991.

20. See, for example, the account in Gilbert 1995.

21. See Vowles et al., 1995.

22. Tocqueville [1935] 1945, 182–83.

References

Achen, Christopher. 1977. "Measuring Representation: Perils of the Correlation Coefficient." *American Journal of Political Science.* 21:805–18.

——. 1978. "Measuring Representation." *American Journal of Political Science* 22: 477–510.

Aldrich, John. 1995. *Why Parties?* Chicago: University of Chicago Press.

Alesina, Alberto. 1988. "Credibility and Policy Convergence in a Two-Party System with Rational Voters." *American Economic Review* 78:796–805.

American Political Science Association Committee on Political Parties. 1950. "Toward a More Responsible Two-Party System." *American Political Science Review* 44:(3, Supplement), 1–99.

Anderson, Christopher J., and Christine A. Guillory. 1997. "Political Institutions and Satisfaction with Democracy: A Cross-National Analysis of Consensus and Majoritarian Systems." *American Political Science Review* 91:66–81.

Arter, David. 1987. *Politics and Policy-Making in Finland.* New York: St. Martin's.

Austen-Smith, David, and Jeffrey Banks. 1988. "Elections, Coalitions and Legislative Outcomes." *American Political Science Review* 82:405–22.

——. 1990. "Stable Governments and the Allocation of Portfolios." *American Political Science Review* 84:891–906.

Barnes, Samuel H. 1977. *Representation in Italy: Institutionalized Tradition and Electoral Choice.* Chicago: University of Chicago Press.

Bartolini, Stefano, and Peter Mair. 1990. *Identity, Competition and Electoral Availability: The Stabilization of European Electorates 1885–1985.* New York: Cambridge.

Baumgartner, Frank. 1989. *Conflict and Rhetoric in French Policymaking*. Pittsburgh: University of Pittsburgh Press.

———. 1987. "Parliament's Capacity to Expand Political Controversy in France." *Legislative Studies Quarterly*. 12:33–54.

Bawn, Kathleen. 1999. "Money and Majorities in the Federal Republic of Germany: Evidence for a Veto Players Model of Government Spending." *American Journal of Political Science*. 43:707–36.

Berglund, Sten, and Ulf Lindstroem. 1978. *The Scandinavian Party System(s)*. Lund: Studentlitteratur.

Bean, Clive, Robert Chapman, Jack Vowles, Nigel Roberts, Theodore Anagnoson, and Antony Wood. 1981. *New Zealand Voting Survey, Post-Election 1981*. Canberra: Social Science Data Archives, The Australian National University.

Birch, Anthony. 1972. *Representation*. London: Macmillan.

Black, Duncan. 1948. "On the Rationale of Group Decision Making." *Journal of Political Economy* 56:23–34.

Black, Jerome. 1978. "The Multicandidate Calculus of Voting: Application to Canadian Federal Elections." *American Journal of Political Science*. 22:609–39.

Bowler, Shaun, David M. Farrell, and Richard S. Katz. 1999. *Party Cohesion, Party Discipline and the Organization of Parliaments*. Columbia: Ohio State University Press.

Browne, Eric, and Mark Franklin. 1973. "Aspects of Coalition Payoffs in European Parliamentary Governments." *American Political Science Review* 67:453–69.

Browne, Eric, and John Frendreis. 1980. "Allocating Coalition Payoffs by Conventional Norm: An Assessment of the Evidence for Cabinet Coalition Situations." *American Journal of Political Science* 24:753–68.

Bryce, J. 1921. *Modern Democracies*. 2 vols. New York: Macmillan.

Buchanan, James M., and Gordon Tullock. 1962. *The Calculus of Consent: Logical Foundations of Constitutional Democracy*. Ann Arbor: University of Michigan Press.

Budge, Ian, and Richard I. Hofferbert. 1990. "Mandates and Policy Outputs: U.S. Party Platforms and Federal Expenditures." *American Political Science Review* 84:111–32.

Budge, Ian, and Hans Keman. 1990. *Parties and Democracy: Coalition Formation and Government Functioning in Twenty States*. New York: Oxford University Press.

Budge, Ian, David Robertson, and Derek Hearl, eds. 1987. *Ideology, Strategy and Party Change: Spatial Analyses of Post-war Election Programmes in Nineteen Democracies*. Cambridge: Cambridge University Press.

Bulmer, Simon, and William Patterson. 1987. *The Federal Republic of Germany and the European Community*. London: Allen and Unwin.

Burke, Edmund. [1774] 1949. *Burke's Politics*. Edited by Ross J. S. Hoffman and Paul Levack. New York: Alfred A. Knopf.

Butler, David, and Austin Ranney. 1978. *Referendums: A Comparative Study*. Washington, D.C.: American Enterprise Institute.

Butler, David, and Donald Stokes. 1969. *Political Change in Britain*. New York: St. Martin's.

Cain, Bruce E. 1978. "Strategic Voting in Britain." *American Journal of Political Science* 22:639–55.

Castles, Francis, ed. 1982. *The Impact of Parties*. London: Sage.

Castles, Francis, and Peter Mair. 1984. "Left-Right Political Scales: Some Expert Judgments." *European Journal of Political Research* 12:73–88.

Clausen, A. R., and S. Holmberg. 1977. "Legislative Voting Analysis in Disciplined Multiparty Systems: The Swedish Case." In William Aydelotte, ed., *The History of Parliamentary Behavior,* 1959–85. Princeton: Princeton University Press.

Cohen, Carl. 1971. *Democracy*. New York: Free Press.

Committees of the House of Commons: A Practical Guide. 1994. Ottawa: Clerk of the House of Commons.

Converse, Philip E., and Roy Pierce. 1986. *Political Representation in France*. Cambridge: Harvard University Press.

Cox, Gary W. 1990. "Centripetal and Centrifugal Incentives under Alternative Voting Institutions." *American Journal of Political Science* 34:903–35.

———. 1987. *The Efficient Secret: The Cabinet and the Development of Political Parties in Victorian England*. Cambridge: Cambridge University Press.

———. 1997. *Making Votes Count: Strategic Coordination in the World's Electoral Systems*. Cambridge: Cambridge University Press.

Dahl, Robert. A. 1989. *Democracy and Its Critics*. New Haven: Yale University Press.

———. 1971. *Polyarchy: Participation and Opposition*. New Haven: Yale University Press.

———. 1956. *Preface to Democratic Theory*. Chicago: University of Chicago Press.

Dalton, Russell. 1985. "Political Parties and Political Representation: Party Supporters and Party Elites in Nine Nations." *Comparative Political Studies* 18:267–99.

Dalton, Russell, Scott C. Flanagan, and Paul Allen Beck. 1984., eds. *Electoral Change in Advanced Industrial Societies: Realignment or Dealignment?* Princeton: Princeton University Press.

Damgaard, Eric. 1995. "How Parties Control Committee Members." In Herbert Doering, ed., *Parliaments and Majority Rule in Western Europe,* 308–25. New York: St. Martin's.

Denardo, James. 1985. *Power in Numbers: The Political Strategy of Protest and Rebellion*. Princeton: Princeton University Press.

De Swaan, Abram D. 1973. *Coalition Theory and Cabinet Government*. Amsterdam: Elsevier.

De Tocqueville, Alexis. [1835] 1945. *Democracy in America*. Translation by Henry Reeve, Francis Bowen, and Phillips Bradley. New York: Random House.

Doering, Herbert, ed. 1995. *Parliaments and Majority Rule in Western Europe*. New York: St. Martin's.

———. 1995. "Time as a Scarce Resource: Government Control of the Agenda." In Herbert Doering, ed., *Parliaments and Majority Rule in Western Europe,* 223–46. New York: St. Martin's.

Downs, Anthony. 1957. *An Economic Theory of Democracy*. New York: Harper and Row.

Duverger, Maurice. 1954. *Political Parties: Their Organization and Activity in the Modern State*. B. North and R. North, trans. New York: John Wiley.

Epstein, Leon. 1967. *Political Parties in Western Democracies*. New York: Praeger.

Eulau, Heinz, and Kenneth Prewitt. 1973. *Labyrinths of Democracy*. Indianapolis: Bobbs-Merrill.

Fiorina, Morris P. 1991. "Coalition Governments, Divided Government and Electoral Theory." *Governance* 4:236–49.

———. 1981. *Retrospective Voting in American National Elections*. New Haven: Yale University Press.

Forell, C. R. 1976. *How We Are Governed*. 7th ed. Melbourne: Cheshire.

Franklin, Mark N. 1996. "Electoral Participation." In Lawrence LeDuc, Richard G. Niemi, and Pippa Norris, eds., *Comparing Democracies: Elections and Voting in Global Perspective*, 216–35. Thousand Oaks, Calif.: Sage Publications.

Franks, C. E. S. 1993. "Comments on the Report of the Liaison Committee." *Parliamentary Government* 44:5–7.

Gabel, Matthew J., and John D. Huber. 2000. "Putting Parties in Their Place: Inferring Party Left-Right Ideological Positions from Manifestos Data." *American Journal of Political Science* 44:94–103.

Gallagher, Michael. 1991. "Proportionality, Disproportionality, and Electoral Systems." *Electoral Studies* 10:33–51.

Gallagher, Michael, Michael Laver, and Peter Mair. 1995. *Representative Government in Modern Europe*. New York: McGraw-Hill.

Gelman, Andrew, and Gary King. 1994. "Enhancing Democracy through Legislative Redistricting." *American Political Science Review* 88:541–59.

Gilbert, Mark. 1995. *The Italian Revolution*. Boulder: Westview.

Grofman, Bernard. 1993. "Toward an Institution-Rich Theory of Political Competition with a Supply Side Component." In Bernard Grofman, ed., *Information, Participation and Choice: An Economic Theory of Democracy in Perspective*, 179–93. Ann Arbor: University of Michigan Press.

Grofman, Bernard, and Arend Lijphart, eds. 1986. *Election Laws and Their Political Consequences*. New York: Agathon Press.

Gunther, Richard. 1989. "Electoral Law, Party Systems and Elites: The Case of Spain." *American Political Science Review* 83:835–58.

Gunther, Richard, Giacomo Sani, and Goldie Shabad. 1988. *Spain after Franco: The Making of a Competitive Party System*. Berkeley: University of California Press.

Harmel, Robert, and John D. Robertson. 1986. "Government Stability and Regime Support." *Journal of Politics* 48:1029–40.

Henderson, Conway. 1991. "Conditions Affecting the Use of Political Repression." *Journal of Conflict Resolution* 35:120–42.

Hermans, F. A. 1969. "The Dynamics of Proportional Representation." In Andrew J. Milnor, ed., *Comparative Political Parties*, 219–24. New York: Thomas Y. Crowell.

Huber, John D. 1996. "The Vote of Confidence in Parliamentary Democracies." *American Political Science Review* 90:269–82.

———. 1998. "How Does Cabinet Instability Affect Political Performance? Portfolio Volatility and Health Care Cost Containment in Parliamentary Democracies." *American Political Science Review* 92:577–91.

———. 1996. *Rationalizing Parliament: Legislative Institutions and Party Politics in France*. Cambridge: Cambridge University Press.

——. 1989. "Values and Partisanship in Left-Right Orientations: Measuring Ideology." *European Journal of Political Research* 17:599–621.

Huber, John D., and Ronald Inglehart. 1995. "Expert Interpretations of Party Space and Party Locations in 42 Societies." *Party Politics* 1:73–111.

Huber, John D., and G. Bingham Powell, Jr. 1994. "Congruence between Citizens and Policymakers in Two Visions of Liberal Democracy." *World Politics* 46:291–326.

Huntington, Samuel P. 1991. *The Third Wave: Democratization in the Late Twentieth Century*. Norman: University of Oklahoma Press.

Inglehart, Ronald. 1984. "The Changing Structure of Political Cleavages in Western Society." In Russell Dalton et al., eds., *Electoral Change in Advanced Industrial Societies*, 25–69, Princeton: Princeton University Press.

——. 1990. *Culture Shift in Advanced Industrial Society*. Princeton: Princeton University Press.

——. 1997. *Modernization and Postmodernization: Cultural, Economic and Political Change in 43 Societies*. Princeton: Princeton University Press.

Inglehart, Ronald, and Hans-Dieter Klingemann. 1976. "Party Identification, Ideological Preference and the Left-right Dimension among Western Mass Publics." In Ian Budge et al., eds., *Party Identification and Beyond*, 243–73. London: John Wiley.

Inter-Parliamentary Union. 1976, 1986. *Parliaments of the World: A Comparative Reference*. New York: Facts on File Publications.

Jaensch, Dean, and Max Teichmann. 1979. *The Macmillan Dictionary of Australian Politics*. Melbourne: Macmillan.

Katz, Richard. 1980. *A Theory of Parties and Electoral Systems*. Baltimore: Johns Hopkins University Press.

Katz, Richard, and Peter Mair, eds. 1994. *How Parties Organize: Change and Adaptation in Party Organizations in Western Democracies*. Thousand Oaks, Calif.: Sage.

Keesings Contemporary Archives.

Keuchler, Manfred. 1991. "The Dynamics of Mass Political Support in Western Europe." In Karlheinz Reif and Ronald Inglehart, eds., *Eurobarometer: The Dynamics of European Public Opinion*, 275–94. New York: St. Martin's.

King, Anthony. 1981. "What Do Elections Decide?" In David Butler, Howard Penniman, and Austin Ranney, eds., *Democracy at the Polls*, 293–324. Washington: American Enterprise Institute.

King, Gary, Michael Laver, Richard I. Hofferbert, Ian Budge, and Michael McDonald. 1993. "Party Platforms and Government Spending: A Controversy." *American Political Science Review* 87:744–50.

Kitschelt, Herbert. 1994. *The Transformation of European Social Democracy*. New York: Cambridge University Press.

Klingemann, Hans-Dieter, Richard I. Hofferbert, and Ian Budge. 1993. *Parties, Policies and Democracy*. Boulder: Westview.

Kollman, Kenneth, John H. Miller, and Scott E. Page. 1992. "Adaptive Parties in Spatial Elections." *American Political Science Review* 86:929–37.

Laasko, Markku, and Rein Taagepera. 1979. "Effective Number of Parties: A Measure with Applications to Western Europe." *Comparative Political Studies* 12:3–27.

Lanfranchi, Prisca, and Ruth Leuthi. 1999. "Cohesion of Party Groups and Interparty Conflict in the Swiss Parliament: Roll-Call Voting in the National Council." In Bowler, Farrell, and Katz, eds., *Party Cohesion, Party Discipline and the Organization of Parliaments,* 99–120. Columbia: Ohio State University Press.

Laver, Michael, and W. Ben Hunt. 1992. *Policy and Party Competition.* New York: Routledge.

Laver, Michael, and Norman Schofield. 1990. *Multiparty Government: The Politics of Coalition in Europe.* New York: Oxford University Press.

Laver, Michael, and Kenneth Shepsle. 1991. " 'Divided Government:' America Is Not Exceptional." *Governance* 4:250–69.

——, eds. 1994. *Cabinet Ministers and Parliamentary Government.* New York: Cambridge University Press.

Lehmbruch, Gerhard. 1974. "A Non-Competitive Pattern of Conflict Management in Liberal Democracies." In Kenneth McRae, ed., *Consociational Democracy,* 90–97. Toronto: McClelland and Stewart.

Lewis-Beck, Michael. 1988. *Economics and Elections: The Major Western Democracies.* Ann Arbor: University of Michigan Press.

Lijphart, Arend. 1993. "Constitutional Choices for New Democracies." In Larry Diamond and Plattner, eds., *The Global Resurgence of Democracy,* 146–58. Baltimore: Johns Hopkins University Press.

——. 1984. *Democracies: Patterns of Majoritarian and Consensus Government.* New Haven: Yale University Press.

——. 1977. *Democracy in Plural Societies.* New Haven: Yale University Press.

——. 1997. "The Difficult Science of Electoral Systems: A Commentary on the Critique by Alberto Penades." *Electoral Studies* 16:71–77.

——. 1994. *Electoral Systems and Party Systems: A Study of Twenty-Seven Democracies, 1945–1990.* New York: Oxford University Press.

——. 1994. "Unequal Participation: Democracy's Unresolved Dilemma." *American Political Science Review* 91:1–14.

Lippmann, Walter. 1925. *The Phantom Public.* New York: Harcourt, Brace.

Lipset, Seymour Martin, and Stein Rokkan, eds. 1967. *Party Systems and Voter Alignments.* New York: Free Press.

Loewenberg, Gerhard, and Samuel Patterson. 1979. *Comparing Legislatures.* Boston: Little, Brown.

Loosemore, John, and Victor J. Hanby. 1971. "The Theoretical Limits of Maximum Distortion." *British Journal of Political Science* 1:467–77.

Mackie, Thomas T., and Richard Rose. 1991. *The International Almanac of Electoral History.* 3d ed. Washington: Congressional Quarterly Inc.

McAllister, Ian, and John Warhurst. 1988. *Australia Votes: The 1987 Federal Election.* Melbourne: Longman Cheshire.

McGillivray, Fiona. 1994. "Comparative Institutions and Policy Outcomes." Ph.D. diss., University of Rochester.

——. 1997. "Party Discipline as a Determinant of the Endogenous Formation of Tariffs." *American Journal of Political Science* 41:584–607

McKelvy, Richard D. 1976. "Intransitivities in Multidimensional Voting Models." *Journal of Economic Theory* 12:472–82.

———. 1979. "General Conditions for Global Intransitivities in Formal Voting Models." *Econometrica* 47:1085–1111.

McKelvy, Richard D., and Peter C. Ordeshook. 1985a. "Elections with Limited Information: A Fulfilled Expectations Model Using Contemporaneous Poll and Endorsement Data as Sources." *Journal of Economic Theory* 36:55–85.

———. 1985b. "Sequential Elections with Limited Information." *American Journal of Political Science* 29:480–512.

Manion, Melanie. 1996. "The Electoral Connection in the Chinese Countryside." *American Political Science Review* 90:736–48.

Martin, Lanny. 1999. "Coalition Politics and Parliamentary Government: Essays on Government Formation, Government Survival, and the Legislative Agenda." University of Rochester, MS.

Martin, Lanny, and Randolph T. Stevenson. 1995. "A Unified Model of Government Formation and Survival." University of Rochester, MS.

Mattson, Ingvar, and Kaare Strom. 1995. "Parliamentary Committees." In Herbert Doering, ed., *Parliaments and Majority Rule in Western Europe*, 249–308. New York: St. Martin's.

Mezey, Michael. 1980. *Comparative Legislatures*. Durham: Duke University Press.

Mill, John Stuart. [1861] 1958. *Considerations on Representative Government*. Edited by C. V. Shields. Indianapolis: Bobbs-Merrill.

Miller, Kenneth E. 1991. *Denmark: A Troubled Welfare State*. Boulder: Westview.

Miller, Warren E. 1970. "Majority Rule and the Representative System of Government." In Erik Allardt and Stein Rokkan, eds., *Mass Politics: Studies in Political Sociology*, 284–311. New York: Free Press.

Miller, Warren E., and Donald Stokes. 1963. "Constituency Influence in Congress." *American Political Science Review* 57:165–77.

Mueller, Dennis. 1991. "Choosing a Constitution in East Europe: Lessons from Public Choice." *Journal of Comparative Economics* 15:325–48.

———. 1979. *Public Choice*. New York: Cambridge University Press.

Mueller, Wolfgang C., and Kaare Strom. 1999. *Coalition Governments in Western Europe*. Ann Arbor: University of Michigan Press.

Norton, Phillip. 1975. *Dissension in the House of Commons: Intra-party Dissent in the House of Commons Division Lobbies 1945–1974*. London: Macmillan.

———. 1980. *Dissension in the House of Commons 1974–79*. Oxford: Clarendon.

Ordeshook, Peter, and Olga Shvetsova. 1994. "Ethnic Heterogeneity, District Magnitude and the Number of Parties." *American Journal of Political Science* 38:100–23.

Ozbudun, Ergun. 1970. *Party Cohesion in Western Democracies*. Beverly Hills: Sage.

Paldam, Martin. 1991. "How Robust Is the Vote Function? A Study of Seventeen Nations Over Two Decades." In Helmut Norpoth, Michael Lewis-Beck, and Jean-Dominique Lafay, eds., *Economics and Politics: The Calculus of Support*, 9–32. Ann Arbor: University of Michigan Press.

Palmer, Harvey, and Guy D. Whitten. 1998. "The Electoral Performance of Unexpected

Inflation and Growth." Paper presented at the 1998 Annual Meetings of the American Political Science Association. Boston.

Penades, Alberto. "A Critique of Lijphart's Electoral Systems and Party Systems." *Electoral Studies* 16:59–71.

Pennock, J. Roland. 1979. *Democratic Political Theory.* Princeton: Princeton University Press.

Pinto-Duschinsky, Michael. 1998. "Send the rascals packing: Defects of proportional representation and the virtues of the Westminster Model." *Times Literary Supplement,* September 25, 1998, 10–12.

Pitkin, Hanna F. 1967. *The Concept of Representation.* Berkeley: University of California Press.

Poe, Steven C., and C. Neal Tate. 1994. "Repression of Human Rights to Personal Integrity in the 1980s: A Global Analysis." *American Political Science Review* 88:853–72.

Poole, Keith, and Howard Rosenthal. 1985. "A Spatial Model for Legislative Role Call Analysis." *American Journal of Political Science* 29:357–84.

———. 1991. "Patterns of Congressional Voting." *American Journal of Political Science* 35:228–78.

Powell, G. Bingham, Jr. 1986. "American Voter Turnout in Comparative Perspective." *American Political Science Review* 80:17–44.

———. 1987. "The Competitive Consequences of Polarized Pluralism." In Manfred Holler, ed., *The Logic of Multiparty Systems,* 173–90. Dordrecht, The Netherlands: Martinus Nijhoff.

———. 1989. "Constitutional Design and Citizen Electoral Control." *Journal of Theoretical Politics* 1:107–30.

———. 1982. *Contemporary Democracies: Participation, Stability and Violence.* Cambridge: Harvard University Press.

———. 1986. "Extremist Parties and Political Turmoil: Two Puzzles." *American Journal of Political Science* 30:357–78.

Powell, G. Bingham, Jr., with Lynda W. Powell. 1978. "The Analysis of Citizen-Elite Linkages: Representation by Austrian Local Elites." In Sidney Verba and Lucian W. Pye, eds., *The Citizen and Politics: A Comparative Perspective,* 197–218. Stamford, Conn: Greylock Publishers.

Powell, G. Bingham, Jr., and Georg Vanberg. Forthcoming. "Election Laws, Disproportionality and the Left-Right Dimension." *British Journal of Political Science.*

Powell, G. Bingham, Jr., and Guy D. Whitten. 1993. "A Cross-National Analysis of Economic Voting: Taking Account of Political Context." *American Journal of Political Science* 37:391–414.

Powell, Lynda W. 1982. "Issue Representative in Congress." *Journal of Politics* 44:658–78.

Rae, Douglas. 1969. "Decision-Rules and Individual Values in Constitutional Choice." *American Political Science Review* 63:40–65.

———. 1967. *The Political Consequences of Electoral Laws.* New Haven: Yale University Press.

Ranney, Austin. 1962. *The Doctrine of Responsible Party Government.* Urbana: University of Illinois Press.

Riker, William H. 1980. "Implications from the Disequilibrium of Majority Rule for the Study of Institutions." *American Political Science Review* 74:432–46.

——. 1982a. *Liberalism Against Populism.* San Francisco: W. H. Freeman.

——. 1982b. "The Two-party System and Duverger's Law: An Essay on the History of Political Science." *American Political Science Review* 76: 753–66.

Robertson, David. 1976. *A Theory of Party Competition.* London: Wiley.

Rokkan, Stein. 1968. "Electoral Systems." In David Sills, ed., *International Encyclopedia of the Social Sciences* 5:6–21.

Rose, Richard. 1984. *Do Parties Make a Difference?* 2d ed. Chatham, N.J.: Chatham House.

Rose, Richard, and Thomas Mackie. 1983. "Incumbency in Government: Asset or Liability?" In Hans Daalder and Peter Mair, eds., *Western Party Systems: Continuity and Change,* 115–38. Beverly Hills: Sage Publications.

Sanchez de Dios, Manuel. 1999. "Parliamentary Party Discipline in Spain." In Shaun Bowler, David M. Farrell and Richard S. Katz, eds., *Party Cohesion, Party Discipline and the Organization of Parliaments,* 141–62. Columbia: Ohio State University Press.

Sartori, Giovianni. 1976. *Parties and Party Systems.* New York: Cambridge University Press.

Schlesinger, Joseph. 1966. *Ambition and Politics: Political Careers in the United States.* Chicago: Rand McNally.

Schofield, Norman, and Michael Laver. 1985. "Bargaining Theory and Portfolio Payoffs in European Coalition Government, 1945–1983." *British Journal of Political Science.* 15:143–65.

Schumpeter, Joseph. 1942. *Capitalism, Socialism and Democracy.* New York: Harper and Row.

Schattschneider, E. E. 1940. *Party Government.* New York: Holt, Rinehart and Winston.

Schwartz, John E., and L. Earl Shaw. 1976. *The United States Congress in Comparative Perspective.* Hinsdale: Dryden Press.

Shapiro, Martin, and Alec Stone. 1994. "The New Constitutional Politics of Europe." *Comparative Political Studies* 4: Special Issue.

Shugart, Matthew S. 1995. "The Electoral Cycle and Institutional Sources of Divided Presidential Government." *American Political Science Review* 89:327–43.

Shugart, Matthew S., and John M. Carey. 1992. *Presidents and Assemblies: Constitutional Dynamics and Electoral Design.* New York: Cambridge University Press.

Stevenson, Randolph T. 1997. "How Parties Compete: Electoral Performance and Government Participation in Parliamentary Democracies." Ph.D. diss., University of Rochester.

——. 1998. "The Electoral Effects of Incumbency: Cabinet Decision-Making and Electoral Performance in Parliamentary Democracies." Paper presented at the 1998 Annual Meetings of the American Political Science Association. Boston.

Steiner, Juerg. 1971. "The Principles of Majority and Proportionality." *British Journal of Political Science* 1:63–70.

———. 1974. *Amicable Agreement versus Majority Rule: Conflict Resolution in Switzerland*. Chapel Hill: University of North Carolina Press.

Stokes, Susan C. 1997. "Constituency Influence and Representation." Paper presented at the Annual Meetings of the American Political Science Association. Washington, D.C.

Strom, Kaare. 1984. "Minority Governments in Parliamentary Democracies." *Comparative Political Studies* 17:199–227.

———. 1990. *Minority Government and Majority Rule*. New York: Cambridge University Press.

———. 1995. "Parliamentary Government and Legislative Organization." In Herbert Doering, ed., *Parliaments and Majority Rule in Western Europe*, 51–82. New York: St. Martin's.

Taagepera, Rein, and Matthew S. Shugart. 1989. *Seats and Votes: The Effects and Determinants of Electoral Systems*. New Haven: Yale University Press.

Tsebelis, George, and Jeannette Money. 1997. *Bicameralism*. New York: Cambridge University Press.

Valen, Henry. 1979. "Structural Cleavages and Ideology in a Multiparty System: Norway." Paper presented at the 1979 International Political Science Association Meetings, Moscow.

Verba, Sidney, Norman H. Nie, and Jae-on Kim. 1978. *Participation and Political Equality*. Cambridge: Cambridge University Press.

Volcansek, Mary L., ed. 1992. "Judicial Politics and Policymaking in Western Europe." *West European Politics* 15: Special Issue.

Von Beyme, Klaus. 1985. *Political Parties in Western Democracies*. New York: St. Martin's.

Vowles, Jack, Peter Aimr, Helen Catt, Jim Lamare, and Raymond Miller. 1995. *Towards Consensus? The 1993 Election in New Zealand and the Transition to Proportional Representation*. Auckland, N.Z.: University of Auckland Press.

Ware, Allen. 1987. *Citizens, Parties and the State: A Reappraisal*. Princeton: Princeton University Press.

Warwick, Paul. 1992. "Economic Trends and Government Survival in West European Parliamentary Democracies." *American Political Science Review* 86:875–87.

Wonnacott, Thomas H., and Ronald J. Wonnacott. 1984. *Introductory Statistics for Business and Economics*. New York: John Wiley.

Wright, J. F. H. 1984. "An Electoral Basis for Responsible Government: The Australian Experience." In Arend Lijphart and Bernard Grofman, eds., *Choosing an Electoral System: Issues and Alternatives*, 127–35. New York: Praeger.

Subject Index

accountability: and clarity of responsibility, 50–51; conditions for, 11–12; and constitutional design, 86–87; and majoritarian vision, 12; as model of democracy, 10–11

Australia, 82

Austria: election of *1990*, 186; election of *1994*, 72*n*10, 216*n*12

authorized representation: coding of effective representation, 109; coding of representation score, 94–95; and congruence, 214; and constitutional design, 112–13; defined, 13; and dispersed power, 13; and effective representation, 109–12; and election laws, 95; and minority government, 115–20; and opposition influence, 97, 103; preconditions for, 94; and responsiveness, 130–31, 135; and support parties, 101–02; voters who receive, 98–99

Belgium, election of *1985*, 73

bicameralism: and dispersed power, 37; and clarity of responsibility, 62

cabinet portfolios, proportional distribution of, 92

Canada, election of *1988*, 186, 195

citizen control, preconditions for, 5

citizen preferences: connection to voting, 16, 160–61; and left-right dimension, 162; measuring, 162

clarity of responsibility: and accountability, 50–51; and bicameralism, 62; and committee system, 63; and concentrated power, 5; and decision rules, 62; defined, 11; factors determining, 51; and federalism, 62; and government majority status, 52–53; and government stability, 61; and party cohesion, 60

committee system: and clarity of respon-

Author Index